Praise for Hannah Howard

"From places as far-flung as Norway and as near as New Jersey, Hannah Howard celebrates romance, family, good work and good food, growing up, and making a home in a voice that is hopeful and generous and true. *Plenty* is a book for lovers and friends, husbands and wives, mothers and fathers, daughters and sons. It will fill you up and give you reason to carry on."

—Dinah Lenney, author of *The Object Parade*

"What's clear in *Plenty* is Hannah's love of all things food, not only gigantic alpine wheels and the sizzle of a knob of butter in a hot pan, but her passion for storytelling around food and her respect for the many women warriors pioneering in what has long been a male-dominated industry. *Plenty* is an important book—a long-overdue tribute to the inspiring tribes of women in the food world. It's also a deeply personal book. For Hannah, food is not only an obsession but a darker compulsion. As she says herself, her love for food is profound and profoundly complicated. In *Plenty*, Hannah writes with vulnerability, generosity, and unhindered emotion as readers bear witness to the ups and downs of her journey toward motherhood—from recovering from an eating disorder to the anticipation of finding a partner in New York, from the harrowing experience of miscarriage to the birth of her daughter in the middle of a global pandemic. This memoir made my heart swell."

—Natasha Scripture, author of *Man Fast: A Memoir*

"Hannah Howard writes with exceptional candor, insight, and intelligence."

—Rosie Schaap, author of *Drinking with Men*

"Hannah Howard brilliantly captures the complicated relationships so many of us have with food, love, sex, and ourselves in lyrical prose that will make you hungry for more."

—Kimberly Rae Miller, author of *Beautiful Bodies*

PLENTY

ALSO BY HANNAH HOWARD

Feast: True Love in and out of the Kitchen

PLENTY

A Memoir
of food
& family

Hannah
Howard

Little
a

Published by Little A, New York

www.apub.com

Amazon, the Amazon logo, and Little A are trademarks of Amazon.com, Inc., or its
affiliates.

ISBN-13: 9781542022736 (hardcover)
ISBN-10: 1542022738 (hardcover)

ISBN-13: 9781542022750 (paperback)
ISBN-10: 1542022754 (paperback)

Cover design and illustration by Holly Ovenden

"The Choice" written by Sarah Wise/Sarah Wise Music (BMI) and Ann Klein/Red
Charvel Music (BMI), 2016.

Printed in the United States of America

First edition

In loving memory of Garima Kothari, and the food women we lost during the COVID-19 pandemic.

In another kind of birth
I returned you to the earth
Signed my name and set you free
You didn't belong to me.

—"The Choice," Sarah Wise and Ann Klein

Love is no assignment for cowards.

—Ovid

Contents

Heroes

Finding my people has always felt crucial. Maybe it's because I'm an only child. Or because I was the only Jewish girl in my class at school. I've always had the sense of being a bit weird, a bit of an outsider—a feeling that slowly lessens, of course, the further I get from middle school.

In high school, my family moved from Baltimore to New Jersey. Everything was different—we traded a row house in the city, a place incessantly loud with traffic and shouting teenagers and mean old-lady neighbors, for an eerily quiet suburban house in Princeton, complete with a fenced-in yard. On the weekends, my parents would let me take NJ Transit, the commuter train, into Manhattan with my friends Jose, Rinku, and Cindy, a little band of misfits. When the conductor wasn't looking, we'd put our feet up on the blue vinyl of the seats in front of us, watching the bucolic green out the window morph into trash-strewn marshes and container-truck parking lots, and finally the black of the tunnel that meant we were entering the city. Emerging from Penn Station, hit by the smell of stale piss and those teeth-achingly sweet candied nuts for sale on every Midtown corner, the hard shine of skyscrapers bouncing sunlight above us, we felt miraculously grown up. In NYC, we weren't even a little bit weird.

One Sunday, we found ourselves paying the five-dollar entrance fee to an off-off-Broadway matinee. The show involved audience participation. "Raise your hand if you were cool in high school," one actor asked the crowd, his hair in the tallest Mohawk I had seen in real life. He was painted in glitter, and his chest sparkled in the spotlight. Nobody raised their hand. My friends and I exchanged conspiratorial glances. I took it as a sign from the universe: maybe I was going to be okay.

◆ ◆ ◆

I've worked in food and hospitality since my first summer job, scooping gelato in Hoboken. When it was slow, I read Anthony Bourdain's *Kitchen Confidential* under the gelato cart's awning. I loved food entirely. But I also fell hard for that Bourdainian swagger—that machismo, the wild intensity that seemed intrinsic to the restaurant experience. Part of me saw the aggressive culture as a challenge. I was tough, too.

In real life, the adrenaline rush of a busy night of restaurant service was even better than I had read about; I started hostessing for a Michelin-starred French restaurant on the Upper West Side, and then took a job as a server in a cheese and wine bar. My new world was rough around the edges but sophisticated, the work hard in a physical and mental way I hadn't yet experienced. People talked a big game and expected a lot—no slouching over the host stand even eight hours into a shift, knowing which tables to joke with and which to leave in peace, understanding the difference between the Aligoté and the Albariño. The restaurants were run according to a strict hierarchy, a tradition dating back to Auguste Escoffier's military-inspired brigade system and stubbornly integrated into the restaurant world's psyche to this day. Through college, I felt as if I was living two lives: student and restaurant person.

I loved that second identity. I loved the people; they were brilliant, challenging, and totally different from me. I loved the physicality of a shift on my feet and how tired I felt by the end of it, how sore and how satisfied. How the work took me out of my own insufferable thoughts. I loved leaving a shift with a fat wad of cash in my pocket. I loved the cute bartenders who made me esoteric drinks after closing and told me outrageous stories. I loved being a part of something.

It's been seven years since I left my last restaurant manager job. I didn't leave the world of food entirely, just the working-in-a-restaurant-every-day-and-every-night life, which I found ultimately too exhausting and too brutal to sustain. What I had hoped would be creatively juicy instead felt like a grind, the same thing night after night after night. I've chosen to write about food instead. I draft press releases when an olive oil wins a prestigious award. I compose descriptions for wheels of Gouda that will be printed out and laminated, then hung on tiny hooks behind the cheese counter in various grocery stores. And I wrote a book about working my way through restaurants, falling in love with food and (the wrong) men, and recovering from a brutal eating disorder.

Plenty is about food people. Not just about any food people but *my* food people. And not just my food people but my food women.

Foodland is notoriously male-dominated, in contrast with the domestic realm of cooking, which so often falls in the hands of women. Men run the restaurant world for many reasons: boys' club networks, male-centric kitchens where women are made to feel totally out of place, and male investors' preference for spending their money on other men who remind them of themselves—or who they want to be. But at the core of all the reasons men dominate our professional food landscape is the stubborn idea that important cooking and culinary innovation is the dominion of men.

It's not true, of course.

It's profoundly not true.

My own wonderful, complicated food mentors were men. There was Max McCalman, the first *maître fromager* in the US. I worked with Max at the now defunct Picholine on the Upper West Side, where he taught me all about Alpine cheeses made from the milk of cows that grazed in high mountain pastures. Max helped me land an internship at the Artisanal Premium Cheese Center, where I sprayed wheels of stinky Époisses de Bourgogne with brandy in the cheese caves until my fingers numbed from the cold and smelled of fermenting socks.

Max was followed by Steven Jenkins, who hired me to work with him at Fairway Market and rescued me from a sort of quarter-life crisis after I had quit my restaurant management job. He took me under his wing. We spent afternoons swigging extra-virgin olive oil straight from the bottle and reading from Madeleine Kamman's *When French Women Cook.* I busied myself writing endless descriptions for slightly different kinds of smoked salmon while Steve screamed at customs agents for detaining shipments of balsamic. When I had a question about our new jars of briny Basque *boquerones* that made me pucker in delight, he'd pull some book from his shelf for me to read. "If you lose it, I'll murder you," he'd say. "I'm not joking."

Where were my women mentors? I've worked side by side with some truly badass women, but they have been vastly outnumbered by men. These women have had biting senses of humor and serious talent; they have inspired, amazed, and surprised me. Some have gone on to become my friends. Why not my mentors? This is something I've thought about a lot. Most were my peers rather than authority figures, and the few who have risen to positions of power seemed to be more focused on safeguarding their own careers in a misogynistic system than in taking a young and (over)eager woman under their wing.

When I first started thinking about writing this book and identifying my women food heroes, I conjured up a list of chefs and entrepreneurs who'd hosted TV shows, appeared on magazine covers, and given keynotes at flashy events. I started researching and interviewing, but something left me cold.

I kept coming back to my friends—and to the people I wanted as friends. When it came to what I admired, it wasn't fame or money or any of the outward markers of success. Not that there is anything wrong with fame, money, and success. (I've spent a good portion of my life chasing these things!) But I realized that really delving into the story of women in the industry was a much more personal story for me. Food is so many things beyond awards and notoriety; it is a point of passion and connection, a way that we show our love and commitment to one another. It's a powerful way to cultivate community and family. The many people who make me believe in what we—all of us food women—are creating and preserving are so often in the trenches, working their asses off, living the food life, succeeding and failing and continuing to show up. They are peeling parsnips, driving tractors, fighting with spreadsheets, kneading dough, teaching other women how to chiffonade, and dreaming up change as I write these words. They are out there living full, complicated, and delicious lives of plenty that aren't being documented.

This book is about them. And for them. For you.

The Redwoods

Anyone who has been lucky enough to stand in a redwood forest and look up—as I have—knows it's hard not to be overcome by awe. The trees grow up to 350 feet tall, the height of a thirty-five-story building. Sometimes they are so huge that it's impossible to see all the way up to their tops. Standing on the ground, they make any human feel miniature.

Among the oldest living organisms in the world, they can grow for more than two thousand years. On the California coast, a single tree lived during the rise and fall of the Roman Empire. That tree still stands today.

But it doesn't stand alone. There is no "single" tree in a redwood forest. Instead, the towering trees have comparatively shallow root systems: their roots only reach down six or ten feet into the soil. But what they lack in depth, they have in breadth. What gives the trees their enormous strength is the span of their roots, which spread as far out as a hundred feet. Their roots interlock with other redwood trees, creating a vast and powerful network. That's one of the reasons redwoods thrive in forests, and it's the collective root system that supports the statuesque trees through storms and floods. Alone, the giant trees would topple every time a strong wind blew by. Entwined together, they keep growing strong. There is no such thing as a solitary redwood.

◆ ◆ ◆

The cheese was perfect. It oozed out of its snow-white skin, leaving a puddle on the cutting board. It tasted of sweet milk and buttered mushrooms and joy.

It was 2006, the summer after my freshman year of college. I had a new internship at the Artisanal Premium Cheese Center, which was a total dream job. I spent my mornings in the cheese caves—glorified refrigerators with fancy technology to control humidity. Each cave was packed with rows and rows of wooden shelves filled with blues, bloomies, and washed rinds, which I spritzed with a spray bottle of cider or wine. I wore two sweaters in July. I turned and flipped the wheels for hours, rubbed their ruddy bellies with a damp rag. After the work, I washed my hands twice, scrubbing carefully. Still, they smelled ripe.

In the afternoons, I helped organize the wine and cheese—or whiskey and cheese, or craft beer and cheese—for the classes that were hosted at the center's sleek new teaching kitchen. The Artisanal Premium Cheese Center was a straight shot west from Penn Station in an inconspicuous office building by the West Side Highway. I'd confirm the lineup of cheeses with the instructors and nestle the white wines into a bucket of ice. I'd edit, or sometimes write, the notes I planned to hand out and place next to the half glasses of wine I'd pour and the one-ounce slivers of cheese I'd arrange like clock hands on white plates.

A cater waiter would arrive around four o'clock to slice baguettes and tie white napkins around water pitchers. I'd help out and make sure everything was in order. I wasn't required to stay for the classes, but usually I did—access to those tastings was one of the best job perks for a budding food geek like me. I'd sit in the back and scribble notes in my journal. Even though I'd attended "Cheese 101" a handful of times by the end of the summer, I'd always leave with a new nugget of knowledge about Brie (the creamy, luscious cheeses actually have less fat than their hard counterparts because they have more water weight!)

or a new cheese discovery (soft-ripened Stracchino-style water buffalo's milk cheese is ridiculous, and even more so with a glass of something bone dry and bubbly).

I waxed poetic about real-deal cave-aged Gruyère and Stichelton—a raw milk take on the iconic English Stilton—but I also spent no small amount of time writing obsessive logs of what I had eaten that day in calories and points. Someone had forwarded me an article about the dangers of carbs, so I added those to the ever-growing list of foods I monitored and feared. I eyed the baskets of fresh baguettes with longing and suspicion.

I hadn't yet received my anorexia diagnosis—that would come a few short months later—but I did try to save whatever sad allotment of calories I allowed myself for cheese. That afternoon, I stared at the plate in front of me. I knew we were supposed to cut and serve the cheeses in one-ounce portions, but didn't that piece of Camembert look a little big?

I was falling in love with the little buttons of fresh chèvre, the craggy-rinded tommes, the gigantic Alpine wheels that we took cylindrical tastes from with a sonde—a cheese plug—to gauge their ripeness and deliciousness. Officially, I was working toward a degree in anthropology and creative writing, but the cheese world was another kind of school. Every day, I learned something new.

I was a young woman starting to forge a career in food—though I didn't know it yet. I was just following my passions, seeking acceptance and soaking up knowledge in a world where producers spent decades perfecting their craft, where chefs worked night after night on improving a dish, on creating culinary excitement. I had always loved food. At home, the kitchen seemed to be the heart of our family. Out in the world, sharing food meant connection. It is an integral part of our lives that offers sustenance and is often an elemental part of our identity—culture, history, comfort, joy, pride, fear, anxiety, love. For me, it was a beautiful obsession, complicated by a darker compulsion. I wanted to taste everything and learn everything about what I was tasting, the person who made that cheese, their traditions, their dreams. I was also afraid of my own appetites and learned to loathe my body in a world that taught me that there was only one punishingly narrow way for a young woman to look. My love for food was profound and profoundly complicated.

One late morning, my boss summoned me out of the caves and into the office. A French cheesemaker with a tiny goatee was visiting from Alsace. He unpacked a lineup of cheeses from a rolling suitcase, poured bubbly into plastic cups, and cut hunks from his beauties. My coworkers gathered around to try his wares. Half my brain was trying to follow his heavily accented lecture on cow breeds and importing regulations. The other half—later I would recognize this as my eating-disordered brain, cruel, small-minded, tiresome, and relentless—said, *If you eat this cheese, you cannot eat dinner.* It said, *If you eat this cheese and dinner, you pig, you cannot eat anything tomorrow.*

I ate the cheese.

Later, the cheesemaker left his perfect wares in our little office kitchen. Everyone went back to work. I put my second sweater back on to counteract the cold that permeated the caves and tied my apron around my waist. But my stomach was grumbling, and I couldn't stop thinking about that double crème with the subtle earthy funk. I took off my apron. I didn't wash my hands. I snuck back to the little kitchen and sliced off a sliver. Just a sliver. It tasted obscenely good. My body vibrated with wanting. Another sliver. And another. Soon the whole wheel was gone, and then the next one, leaving only a gloppy smudge on the cutting board and a sinking feeling in my stomach: dairy and shame.

◆ ◆ ◆

I used to think my fucked-up-ness around food—the love, the fear, the compulsion—was somehow unique. It's not. *What a relief that it's not!* When I could escape my self-obsession long enough to observe those around me in my burgeoning food career, I noticed that my cheese mentor at the trendy restaurant where I worked after Artisanal was on a perpetual diet. She eschewed nightshades and carbs and downed shots of apple cider vinegar, and then switched between fasting days and days spent mainlining mac and cheese straight from quart containers that were lined up in the kitchen. At my next restaurant job, my manager took the whole nine-hour shift to eat one plastic cup of Greek yogurt, licking a scant spoonful in quiet moments, a faraway look in her eyes. It was at that same restaurant that I caught the hostess throwing up in the bathroom in the thick of a busy service.

Nobody ever talked about any of this, least of all me.

My anorexia diagnosis morphed into the frustratingly vague EDNOS, eating disorder not otherwise specified (thanks, *DSM*). Without a clear, official title, it became just an undiagnosed, embarrassing secret. I did weird things with food—restricting, bingeing, and other permutations of misery centered on using food as a drug and hating my body. It was a war I fought 24/7. I lost every battle.

Things started to change for me almost nine years ago now, when I got sick and tired of being sick and tired, as they say. After one last epic binge—an all-night affair with a giant plate of cookies and every last morsel in my kitchen, down to the bottom of a jar of almond butter—I mustered the courage to go to a recovery meeting in a dingy room atop a bodega by Union Square. There, I listened as people shared about doing what I did with food, feeling what I felt.

"I used to throw away brownies and then pour coffee grounds on top so I wouldn't eat them. Then I'd fish them out and wipe off the coffee and eat them anyway."

"I used to wake up in the morning and think, *What did I eat yesterday?* My worth was based on the answer to the question."

"I used to think my purpose in life was to lose weight."

I heard: "I don't have to bear this horrible thing alone. So much can change." I knew I had found my people.

My image of a person with an eating disorder was an emaciated blonde girl from a cheesy after-school special. According to the National Eating Disorders Association, *Eating disorders have historically been associated with straight, young, white females, but in reality, they affect people from all demographics.* I met plenty of young white women of privilege in the recovery meetings I started attending more and more often, but I also met old women and women of color as well as men. I met people of all shapes and sizes and backgrounds and attitudes, amazing people who shattered my idea of what people with eating disorders looked like.

I also met chefs, food writers, mixologists, and restaurant managers. Some of them told me that their recovery made them better at what they did. Others said it wasn't quite so simple.

Years ago, I cringed as I hit "send" on the first essay I wrote and published about my eating disorder. What would my coworkers—cheesemongers and specialty food buyers and restaurant editors—think? Would I diminish my legitimacy as a food writer? As a feminist? I was terrified to share about what had been, for as long as I could remember, my deepest darkest secret.

By then I had heard plenty of people talk about their own food demons, and heard others talk about the frenzied and sometimes dysfunctional culture found behind the scenes at restaurants (and cheese counters, markets, cooking shows, and food blogs), but I had never heard much about the two combined. It made perfect sense to me—just as alcoholics may gravitate to jobs behind the bar, so many of us professional food people struggle with eating and body issues. We're drawn in. What better way to channel an unhealthy obsession with food than to turn food into our careers?

I needn't have worried about my essay. The response was a chorus of "me too." The essay spawned another. And that second essay led to my first book, *Feast: True Love in and out of the Kitchen*.

People who I'd never suspected had struggled began confessing their own stories—my friend the Instagram-famous baker who had starved herself until she landed in the hospital, the "wellness" blogger who couldn't stop getting up in the middle of the night to binge on gluten-free goodies, the binge-eating server. My email in-box was full of people thanking me for sharing my story and telling me theirs. At first it was reassuring—again, that reminder that I am not some kind of freak, that we are in this together. But then it became depressing. It seemed like everyone I spoke to had experience struggling with food behavior or body image—usually both. Is nobody spared?

Writing and sharing and speaking and commiserating wasn't a magic pill that erased my shame. Very, very slowly, it dissolved.

Body positivity is a matter of social justice. We live in an extremely fat-phobic culture that stigmatizes people in larger bodies and puts pressure on all people to shrink our bodies. Eating disorders are a symptom of a patriarchal, misogynistic culture—the idea that women's bodies exist to please, to be judged. But those of us who suffer from them are not necessarily bad feminists. We are humans. We are doing the best we can. This culture is not optional; it is the air we breathe. When we reach out to each other, we can do a whole lot better. Understanding this is not a cure, but it is a start for food people and for all people.

One of my friends in recovery, a stylist and recipe developer who works with all the most prestigious food mags, told me this: "It's a constant struggle—but that doesn't mean that I'm miserable. It's a challenge that I'm open to. I love my work and I love food—and I love finding a way to make it all work." Hearing stories like hers gave me the confidence that I, too, could figure out a way to make it all work.

But it wasn't always easy. As I got ready to launch my book with readings and panels and events, I was genuinely proud and excited. But then an old friend came knocking at my door, that eating disorder voice that still seems to live in the crevices of my mind, no matter how many meetings I attend, how much therapy I go to, how much I journal or meditate. That voice is simple and relentless and mean. It's also a little dumb, but that doesn't make it less convincing. *You're too fat to publish a book,* it would say.

What does that even mean? That is definitely not a thing.

Especially a book about eating disorders. Everyone is going to be looking at you with disgust and judging you. They will see a failure. Who do you think you're kidding?

But all those meetings and therapy sessions and minutes spent watching my thoughts pass like clouds in the sky were not for naught. By that time, I had recovery friends to call. I knew what to do. They listened, they commiserated, and immediately I felt just the smallest bit better. The thing about the eating disorder voice is that, left to marinate in the confines of my brain, it grows in ferocity and power. But when I share it, it loses its teeth. The words sound less scary and more absurd as they leave my mouth.

The worst part about my eating disorder—when it was at its height—was not that my brand-new jeans wouldn't zip, or the way I'd wake up thinking about food, or even the stomach-turning self-loathing that would threaten to drown me nearly every time I passed a mirror. It was the loneliness. Having and keeping such a big secret kept me apart from even the people I loved the most. It separated me from the world. It was as if in the heat of summer, I wouldn't take off my hoodie, my hat, my scarf. I was sweltering and terrified of being seen. And yet, it was what I wanted most. It was what I needed.

It's been such a relief to shed those unnecessary layers. Painful, at times. Scary most of the time. Sometimes I still reach for them at the back of my closet, where they wait for me, trusty and suffocating.

It turns out I was never hungry for the seventeenth cookie. *If the sixteenth cookie hadn't done the trick, how would number seventeen?* I was hungry for connection. Hungry for so much more.

I am a redwood. Aren't we all? I really thought I was supposed to do it all alone. That I needed to hunker down and tend to my own roots. In recovery, I learned to call someone else and ask about their day. I learned that my own experience, even or especially if it was painful or cringe-worthy, could help someone else. Working with other people in recovery made me feel like all that time I'd spent in the dark hole of my eating disorder wasn't totally wasted. I let my roots spread and snarl and catch. I asked for help. I listened. I looked out, not just down.

What comes next? After we stop bingeing and starving ourselves and counting our days in calories, life stretches out before us, glittering and terrifying.

"After I stopped bingeing, I felt better," one of my recovery mentors said. "I felt sadness better, and fear better, and anger better."

That was true for me, too. My eating disorder was an excellent distraction for pretty much everything. If my whole sense of worth wasn't going to be wrapped up in the number on a scale, where was it going to come from? What was I going to do with the endless stretch of lonely nights that had been so neatly filled up by planning a binge, curling up with bags and pints and TV, then hiding all the evidence and vowing to diet harder, better, stronger in the morning?

These days, I sometimes teach cheese classes and tastings. I remain in love with stinky cheese, and crumbly cheese, and pretty much all cheese. I know more than I used to, but I still have plenty to learn. Sometimes I still eat too much, or not enough, but I try my best to cultivate self-compassion and kindness. I haven't binged in more than eight years. Every single day, I am grateful.

Today, the staff of a specialty food store—one of my clients—is trying a lineup of new sheep's milk beauties. One is coated with herbs and another is washed with cardoon thistle—meaty and full of funk. We open a Belgian beer and whittle off slices of cheese and discuss. Someone has crafted these wheels with their hands; someone else has carefully aged them on wooden boards in a cold, damp room. Now they're here, and we appreciate them, savor them. Later tonight, I will eat dinner with my husband. My puppy will look at us with his puppy-dog eyes, and I will give him a piece of shrimp. For now I sit at my desk, and I write. I know that my value has zero to do with what I've eaten for lunch or the softness of my belly. I know I have people to call when I temporarily forget this. I used to think the obsession about food and my body was my fate forever, just something I was stuck with. Today I experience something new: freedom. And peace.

Jenise

Jenise packed a picnic for us to take to the airport: nutty Swiss cheese, almonds she had roasted with rosemary, bread that was dense with nuts and seeds. There was also a mason jar full of pesto, which looked like baby food made from fresh-cut grass. But I knew it was going to be delicious.

We were on our way to an island off the coast of Washington State to see Justin, who had been her boyfriend, sort of, but now was just a friend. Jenise said things were 100 percent cool between them, not weird at all, which I decided to take her word for. After all, we were going to stay at Justin's place. We were going to meet his new girlfriend, too. The girlfriend was a cook.

The island is one of the San Juan Islands and is shaped like a horseshoe. I had only seen it in pictures, thick fir trees atop an endless expanse of the cobalt sea. Immediately, I wanted to go.

Jenise and I worked together at The Lula, a cheese and wine bar, where she was the chef and I was a server. A gorgeous Black woman, with braids almost to her butt, Jenise had a hippie-chic sense of style I envied. She spent her long days in the tiny basement kitchen, prepping little crocks with caramelized onions and lardons for mac and cheese and roasting trays of macadamia nuts for endive salad.

I had met Justin only once, a few months before our trip when I'd accompanied Jenise to his going-away party. We left for Justin's shindig after work and it was way past midnight by the time we arrived all the way downtown, where the Lower East Side and Chinatown start to meld into each other. I wasn't yet twenty-one, but I was close enough. The bar was too loud for talking, so I sipped my whiskey sour, which was what Jenise was drinking, relieved to follow her lead. Justin was a white boy with Bambi eyes and long brown hair that needed washing. When he gave Jenise a hug, I noticed the way their bodies melted into each other.

Everything I knew about Justin came from Jenise. The two had become friends at a fine-dining restaurant in Midtown, where Jenise cooked on the line and Justin was a fish cook. Apparently, he could fillet a fish faster and with more precision than anyone else on staff. He biked everywhere because the subway made him skittish—he was from rural Illinois and he hated being underground.

Justin had been having a tough time before he'd decided to leave. The work he had once loved had suddenly felt soul-crushing. He'd been getting drunk every night. One evening he'd blacked out and woken up bike-less, with a black eye. He'd had a panic attack riding the subway to work the next day and decided that was the last straw, he was out. When a friend called to say there was a job taking charge of a kitchen on a remote island clear across the country, the timing was perfect. All the ingredients were grown in the restaurant's garden, and the garden sat right on the ocean. The cooks went swimming at night. Justin said yes without asking too many questions.

To get to the island, Jenise and I would fly from New York to Seattle, then take a three-hour bus ride to the Anacortes Ferry Terminal, then hop on a boat. Justin would pick us up on the island side and take us to the restaurant. It was going to be a long journey. We were going to need our provisions.

But the TSA agent didn't like Jenise's pesto—she extracted the jar from her carry-on at security.

"No liquids," the agent said, moving to toss the basil-y goodness into the garbage without fanfare.

"It's not really a liquid," Jenise insisted, to which the stern TSA woman only shook her head. "It's pesto. I guess pesto *could be* liquidy, but mine is more of a paste. There's only enough olive oil to hold everything together. If you shake it, you can see." She held up her creation.

"Pesto?" Our adversary suddenly seemed interested.

"I used walnuts, because I didn't have any pine nuts. But it came out really good. Would you like to try some? Or is that weird?"

"I know all about pesto," Ms. TSA said. "I'm Italian."

"Oh good," I chimed in. "Jenise makes the best."

"No way. My grandmother definitely makes the best." She let us keep it. She never broke a smile.

Up in the air, we laid out our picnic on the little fold-down plane tables. We dipped our bread and cheese in the pesto and ate until we were satisfied. Jenise fell asleep with her head on my shoulder. Her scarf tickled my chin. In my earphones, Neutral Milk Hotel sang: "And one day we will die and our ashes will fly from the aeroplane over the sea, but for now we are young, let us lay in the sun . . ."

Jenise's breath rose and fell in time with the bass. We were on our way. We were going to see Justin; we were going to scope out another kind of life.

◆ ◆ ◆

The day Jenise became my friend was the first day The Lula opened for brunch. We'd both worked there since opening day, several weeks before, and every single night had been line-out-the-door, can't-catch-your-breath busy. We'd exchange smiles and sighs during our shifts; that was all we had time for. But something surprising happened during that first brunch service: nobody showed up.

Jenise was working alone in the tiny kitchen in the basement, and I was on the floor upstairs. I had done all my side-work and then some—stacked all the napkins I'd folded in a precarious tower and polished every wineglass to a shine. I kept fiddling with my iPod, looking for a song to distract me. When Jenise came upstairs to check the stock in the lowboy fridge, we got to talking. The conversation was about a guy, I'm pretty sure. And about how much work Jenise had to do. She untied and retied her apron. She had been there since dawn and hadn't had a day off that she could remember. There were purplish circles under her eyes.

"I bet I can help," I said, gesturing to the empty dining room.

It was July, the height of cherry season, and Jenise had several boxes of them to carry up the half flight of stairs. The way the restaurant was set up, you had to go outside to 52nd Street to move between the kitchen in the basement and the dining room at street level. The cherries were shaped like hearts, lipstick red and candy sweet. Outside the window the sun blazed, and sirens wailed.

"We're going to make clafoutis," Jenise told me. She had to explain to me what clafoutis are—a pan full of cherries covered in a buttery batter and sprinkled with powdered sugar. "Want to pit cherries with me?"

"Sure," I said. "Let's do it up here in case anyone comes in. We can listen to whatever you want. Do you have an iPod?" It was circa 2007, the pre-smartphone and pre-streaming era, and I was bored with my own music. I helped her carry the boxes of cherries upstairs. We stacked them behind the bar.

Jenise plugged in her playlist. The youngest members of the staff, Jenise and I were natural allies. I was a college junior at Columbia and Jenise was only a few years older. She had grown up in Brooklyn and landed a Bobby Flay Scholarship to the French Culinary Institute in SoHo. Life could be chaotic, but the kitchen had always been a refuge for her, a place for creativity and quiet possibility. Food was a morsel of joy during days that could feel long and dark. She was the first person in her family to go to college, and she said that her family was equal parts mystified and proud.

Her internship at Geoffrey Zakarian's Town restaurant (RIP) had turned into a full-time line cook job after culinary school. Her mentor was tapped as the consulting chef for the opening of The Lula, and when it came time for the owners to hire a full-time chef to run the kitchen, that mentor had recommended the young, brilliant Jenise.

We kept talking long after the cherries were pitted.

"I also have basil to pick," Jenise suggested.

My shift was almost over. Only one table had come in, a couple who shared a mac and cheese and a piece of chocolate cake. I stayed late to pluck the green basil leaves from their stems. We sang along to Jenise's music and laughed until my cheeks started to ache. After that, we started comparing our schedules to find time for a latte before work, a glass of wine after. When Jenise was having a tough time with her family, she spent Christmas with mine, joining us for our tradition of Chinese food and a movie. Afterward, she came back with me to the house on 114th Street I shared with twenty college kids. It was pretty much empty for the holiday. We watched Christmas movies, baked chocolate-chip cookies, and talked, staying up until I heard her soft snores, her cheek fall onto the beat-up couch in the big, empty living room.

We had something in common, this search for the pleasure, release, and connection that we found in working with food. This longing and ambition. This willingness to throw ourselves so totally into something. I felt lucky to have her friendship.

◆　◆　◆

By the time we boarded the ferry to the island, our snacks were long gone.

I watched Jenise's face fall as she opened her flip phone.

"What's wrong?"

"Justin can't make it to pick us up after all."

"Okay. But we're going to see him soon—we're staying at his place, right?"

"It's just such typical Justin," Jenise told me. "He says things are different here. I guess we'll see for ourselves."

The wind threw our hair into our faces as the ferry neared our destination. I was prone to seasickness—all kinds of motion sickness—but I felt great. It was high summer, achingly bright even through our sunglasses. The air tasted of salt and strawberries. Besides a row of mountains that rose above us, their tips still whitened by snow, everything was blue blue blue, sea and sky. It felt like we were worlds away from New York City.

Justin's girlfriend, Sophie, was waiting for us as the ferry pulled into the dock, leaning against her old green sedan. None of us had met before, but she gave Jenise and me long, meaningful hugs. She wore flip-flops and no makeup. Her hair was dark and wild, and she was stunning.

"I'm so happy you're here," she said. "It's going to be a squeeze in the car. It's zucchini season, and ours are the size of babies. It's been the best year for zucchini. We're taking them with us tonight to the party at the other side of the island."

Sophie wasn't kidding. The vegetables filled up the trunk and the back seat; they had been wedged into the footwells. We fit the summer squashes around our suitcases and sat with them at our feet and on our thighs. Their bulbous flesh was dimpled and cool. The car was dusty inside, but fresh air blew through the open windows.

"What's tonight?" Jenise asked.

"Justin didn't tell you about the bash?"

◆ ◆ ◆

Justin had to work, so Sophie brought us and her carful of squashes up Deer Harbor Road, which wound its way along the ocean to a big gap in the dense evergreen trees. We parked in a vast field scattered with a few other cars and walked up a hill until we heard the din of laughter and ukuleles. Carrying the squashes in wooden crates, we were just a little out of breath. Jenise and I were worn out from our long trip but giddy at the prospect of our adventure finally starting to unfold. We were struck a little dumb by the sheer beauty of the island.

"The bash" was the right phrase for it. A group sat in a circle, banging on drums and singing. A makeshift kitchen was set up on a picnic table full of bags of onions, cutting boards covered with hunks of cheese being sliced, and a big soapy bin for washing up. We placed our squash among casseroles and bowls of half-eaten chips. Partygoers tossed a salad, sliced and arranged the zucchini bounty onto pizza dough. Another group gathered around a fire, where they lowered a pan of free-form pizza into the flames. Sophie introduced us around. Someone handed me a shockingly cold beer.

"Where's Justin?" asked a boy who looked younger than us. He was barefoot and his eyes were smudgy with eyeliner.

"He's at work," Sophie explained.

"Of course, he's always at work," said the eyeliner boy. I worried for Jenise. We had come all this way to see Justin. Jenise had taken her first time off since The Lula opened in spring. It didn't look like he had done the same.

A wooden swing hung high from a tree branch, and Jenise and I took turns flying above the party. At the top of the arc, we could see where the island lowered itself into the Salish Sea. We ate pizza laden with melty cheese and blistered squash. We talked to a man with a tambourine and a goatee and a young woman planning a bachelorette party. To me, she seemed too young to be getting married, but we brainstormed destinations—Napa? New Orleans?—and went back for seconds, then thirds of pizza. Later, the eyeliner boy started to dance, and we joined him. Jenise borrowed the tambourine and shook it over her head. The sun sank in slow motion. The night sky was the color of the ocean, except for a blanket of stars. We lay on the grass and looked up at them until Sophie said we should head back to the Coop.

The Coop was what everyone called the house where Justin lived with another cook, a performance artist, a woodworker, and an unemployed lapsed Mormon. The woodworker had been recruited to turn what was once a gigantic chicken coop into a home for humans. The guys lived for free in exchange for their labor. There were also actual chickens outside, which they looked after, and a trampoline.

When we arrived, there was another party going on, but Justin wasn't there yet. The living room was full of people and thick with smoke from weed and cigarettes, which a woman with a backward baseball cap sat rolling, looking very serious. Everyone gave us full-contact hugs like we were long-lost friends even though we were strangers.

Sophie showed us to our room, which was where the chickens used to live. There was one big bed and roosters carved into the walls. The bathroom was in an outhouse, where a spider was at work spinning a miraculous web in one corner.

By the time Justin got home from work, we were dizzy with exhaustion from the long day traveling, the beer, and the joint we'd shared with the Coop friends. He wriggled in between Sophie and Jenise on the sunken-in couch. We passed around another joint. For the first time that day, Jenise looked truly content.

"Where did you take the girls?" he asked Sophie, and we told him about the bash and how breathtaking this place was, how far away from Midtown Manhattan in every single sense.

"Did you make it to Doe Bay?"

"Not yet," Sophie said, "but it's the first day. They just arrived!"

Justin's eyes woke up. "We have to go to Doe Bay!"

"Now?" Jenise asked. It was after one, and I was struggling to stay awake.

"I haven't been swimming yet today," said Justin. "And it's the perfect time for swimming."

"Really? One thirty AM is the perfect time?" Sophie seemed to read my mind. My eyes were starting to feel heavy.

"It will be the perfect first island night." He tilted his head back to drink the last from his beer can, slammed it on the table, and sprang from the couch. "I can drive your car, Sophie."

"I'll drive," she said. We invited the friends sprawled on the Coop couch, but they declined. Sophie drove Justin, Jenise, and me for what could have been ten minutes or an hour, I was too high and exhausted to keep track. We rolled down the windows and the cool air on my face felt unfathomably good.

Outside was loud with the hum of crickets. It occurred to me as we walked down to the water, arms around each other's shoulders, that we didn't have bathing suits.

"We have nature's bathing suits!" said Justin. His voice seemed to ricochet off the cricket sounds.

It was moonless—the blackest black—and so I could not see much as he threw his clothes onto a rock and made a great splash into the sea.

I was in the thick of my eating disorder, caught in an endless restrict-and-binge cycle. I had plenty of sizes of clothes in my closet, and I hated the way I looked in and out of everything. Getting naked in front of friends or strangers was unthinkable.

I hesitated. But if it was too dark to see Justin, it would be too dark for anyone to see me. And more importantly, too dark for me to see myself.

"Are you going in?" I asked Jenise. She had already stepped out of her flowy skirt.

"Fuck yes."

I was the last one in the water. I didn't jump from the outcropping of rocks like the others had. I hated the way my thighs rubbed together without my pants on. Suddenly, I worried I didn't belong with these beautiful people, in this beautiful place. Listening to the twinkle of their laughter, I felt somehow lonely. I slithered into the bay slowly, self-conscious and drained.

The sea was ice water, but I didn't mind. It shocked me awake. It held me entirely. I felt changed, suddenly invigorated and optimistic. I couldn't see my body, but I could feel it floating, the blood in my veins awake and powerful.

I found Jenise and held on to her shoulders. They were slick and soft and strong. The four of us shrieked with joy. I let myself be part of their reverie.

"I'm so happy we're here," I told her.

"This could be our life," she said. "Can you imagine?"

The island was already becoming home, full of friends and bashes and a night that never ended. "I can."

◆ ◆ ◆

Time unfolded differently on the island. Sure, we were on vacation, but the hours felt elongated. They liquefied into each other. Sophie left to cater a wedding on a nearby island before we woke up the next morning. Jenise jumped on the trampoline and I wrote in my journal. We walked barefoot on the wet grass until our calves ached. We didn't wear shoes until it was time for dinner at the restaurant where Justin was cooking two nights later. It was the island's fanciest restaurant, right on the water, and still pretty laid back. The vibe is rural, miles and miles of evergreen forests, with a cute little downtown called Eastsound, where couples dine at picnic tables and shop for craft beer. The restaurant was perched on a bluff looking south over Ship Bay, near downtown.

Jenise and I gazed on to the bay as an endless progression of courses arrived in front of us: pork belly with tiny strawberries, chèvre ravioli in a lemony broth, scallops that were nearly translucent. She lifted each plate up to her face and inhaled, and so I did the same. We drank a fizzy rosé, and with all the ocean air, the wine, the bright flavors, I felt fizzy, too.

"I'm worried about Justin," Jenise said, a fact that had been obvious to me. Since we had arrived three days ago, he had been either working or drunk.

"Is it the booze?" In those three days, the empty beer can pile outside the Coop had grown into a mountain. We were contributing, too, but none of us kept up with Justin.

"It's everything—he seems just as depressed as he was in New York. How can anyone be depressed here?" She emptied her flute and a waiter whisked over to refill it. The bubbles rushed to the top of the glass. "Can I tell you something I never tell anyone?"

"Always," I said, and meant it.

"My family is religious. Really religious. They're Seventh-day Adventist." I knew Jenise had a tense relationship with her parents and her brother—that she was the proverbial black sheep—but that was about all she'd disclosed. I thought of our Christmas together. I knew next to nothing about Seventh-day Adventists, so I asked. Jenise told me about her experience: her family didn't eat meat, or drink alcohol, or coffee, or soda. As a kid, she was not allowed to play on Saturdays, their Sabbath. It was quiet time reserved for family, reflection, and God. Her mom spent most of her days proselytizing and praying.

I grew up Jewish, which, for me, meant on the Sabbath we occasionally went to synagogue, where the lesbian former-opera-singer rabbi was a friend of my parents. Religion meant singing the Hebrew alphabet song and matzo ball soup on Passover, a point of culture and connection. We sang Bob Dylan tunes at my bat mitzvah before the klezmer band played, then went to an Indian restaurant for dinner. What Jenise was describing seemed like an entirely different universe.

"I didn't have my first coffee until I left for culinary school," Jenise told me. "Now I can't go a morning without it." I thought of all the pork belly we'd had that night, the ribbons of *jamón ibérico* she'd slice at work—leaving me a single ribbon on a baguette to try—our nights of whiskey sours and bitter craft beer. That she had devoted her career, her life, to this particular kind of decadence felt almost transgressive. Food was complicated for both of us, our door into a new world. We both danced with the pleasure we sought and denied ourselves, loved food and drink fiercely, and feared our own appetites.

"My parents love me, but they don't understand anything at all about my life, or why I have rejected theirs. The cook's life could not be more sinful. But I know it's right for me. It's almost like it chose me."

"You're such a good cook." I knew that wasn't the point. But it was true.

"I never want to judge anyone the way my family has judged me."

"You won't." To me, Jenise seemed the least judgmental person in the world. "You're worried about Justin because you care about him. That's not the same thing."

The sun sank slowly behind a mountain. In its glowy wake, Jenise looked like she was on fire. There was no check. We left our collective cash on the table for a tip and sat in the two Adirondack chairs in the restaurant's garden, waiting for Justin to finish work. We were full, a little bit tipsy, and deeply content. The sky turned grey and then coal. It was too cloudy for stars.

Jenise's food was a sort of offering to the people around her, customers and friends. It was the path to her freedom from a family that saw the world as a fundamentally different place than she did, full of temptation that would bring damnation. In her friendship, I found her generosity so deep it bordered on need. That perfect pesto, that candy-sweet peach, that buttery clafouti—to share those things was a way to something like salvation.

For Justin, the food was pride. Was it an escape from addiction or its own addiction? The loop of cook, drink, cook, drink, was all-consuming and relentless. I saw how that loop played out for my friends and coworkers endlessly, a sort of trap. My friends who were line cooks and hosts became sous chefs and managers; they worked harder and drank more. It was a *really* hard way to live.

"*Advent* means 'coming.'" Jenise broke our silent vigil over the patch of herbs and curlicue sweet pea vines. "They think Jesus Christ will return to earth any minute now. It's sort of optimistic."

"Do you think that's true?"

"How would I possibly know?" We watched the cooks and servers head into the night. "I envy their certainty."

Finally, Justin appeared, can of beer in hand. "How was dinner?" he asked us, but he looked far away as we told him how lovely it had been, that the scallops tasted of honeysuckle.

"Do you want to go for a swim?" Jenise suggested, but Justin said he was spent. We could go back to the Coop and share a joint.

"Are you okay?" she asked him, there in the garden. He still had a bandanna tied around his forehead. He jiggled his can; it sounded empty.

"I'm the same," he said, resigned. "I came all the way across the country, and I feel the same."

"There's no subway here. No subway and the ocean." Jenise gestured, but it was too dark to see its expanse ahead of us.

"You know what they say: 'Wherever you go, there you are.'"

"I'm so glad you're here." Jenise touched his arm. "We love you." Jenise and Sophie, they loved Justin. I didn't love Justin, but I loved Jenise. I loved the island.

When they hugged, I felt like I was watching something I shouldn't, a private moment, but Justin said, "Bring it in, Hannah," and the three of us stood there, arms around each other, until we started laughing—little people on a little island under a big sky.

Tony

Winter 2014/2015

I started chatting with Tony on a dating app called Hinge. I swiped right. He was super cute and had the warmest smile.

The last guy I had dated, also via Hinge, was a math professor with an Israeli accent and lots of muscles. We had been out first for a glass of wine in my Harlem neighborhood, then to ramen near his place downtown. He made me laugh and was sort of freakishly perfect on paper—Jewish, brilliant, accomplished, and kind. But there was something off about him, something emotionally removed.

On our fourth date, I slept with him in his studio apartment. It was just getting cold outside and his apartment's heating pipes clanged and clapped violently. Afterward, I couldn't sleep. In the morning, he pressed fresh juice from carrots, oranges, and ginger. He cooked eggs with all sorts of veggies and herbs. I was impressed with breakfast.

But something was nagging me. It seemed the distance between us was gigantic. "Listen," I said, putting my fork down between bites of scrambled eggs and leeks. "Ultimately, I'm really looking for someone I can share my heart with, and vice versa."

He didn't skip a beat. He looked into my eyes. "Oh, I can't do that," he told me. His lips looked nearly blue in the early morning light. I thanked him for breakfast and said goodbye. That was the last time we spoke.

I was only twenty-seven, but I felt like I had dated half of New York City. My lineup of bad boyfriends felt, if not objectively long-winded, definitely exhausting. My heart had been broken and healed and broken again.

Between my ill-fated attempts at love, I went on dates that left me depleted. On one date, a guy in a tie hammered out so many questions about my five-year plan and my ten-year plan that I left feeling more depressed than after even the most disappointing job interview. Who were these people, and how would I ever meet not just a decent person I liked spending time with, but *my* person? Would I be alone for all of eternity? I reminded myself that my life was pretty great and full—that my own company was better than the wrong person's. I took breaks from the dating apps, which by then had become the ubiquitous way to meet anyone, and then I'd log back in, some lonely night or another.

But when I first saw Tony's picture, I wasn't feeling dejected. It was Christmas Eve, and I was alive with a rare glimmer of romantic hope. He had the most gorgeous eyes and a dusting of freckles across the bridge of his nose. He had a grown-up job in financial technology and his own enviable apartment in Brooklyn Heights.

The next day, I spent our traditional New York Jewish Christmas with my family—another movie and Chinese food. My romantic mood had plummeted. I snapped at my dad when he asked me how dating was going over veggie dumplings. "It sucks," I said. I meant it.

I was nursing a weird combination of cynicism and hope as I rebooted my dating app that night. I was back home in Harlem. My roommate was with her family, and the place felt empty and eerily quiet. I turned on some music and—to my delight—there was a message from Anthony:

How's your festive season going?

I told him about the movies and Chinese food. It turned out that Anthony was from the UK and lived in NYC. He was staying with his parents for the holidays, near Birmingham. He messaged me about his own family Christmas traditions: smoked salmon and champagne for breakfast, port and Stilton for dessert. The cheese talk intrigued me.

It was late in England, and he initiated his exit by saying he had to "climb the wooden hill." I had to google the phrase; apparently it means "go to bed." I fell asleep with a smile on my face.

The next day, there was another message from Anthony: What did I say when the kid threw a wheel of cheddar at me? . . . That's not very mature! He knew arguably bad cheese jokes. Apparently, the way to my heart. This guy was promising. The more I learned, the more I wanted to meet him. He was smart, and cute, and funny, and well traveled. We exchanged numbers.

Tony texted me when he was back in town and we made plans to meet up. Part of me was dying to get together, another part of me didn't want to get my hopes up. I had been bruised so many times before.

On our date night, I woke up feeling sniffly, headachy, and awful. I thought maybe I'd rally if I stayed in bed that morning, but by afternoon I felt worse. I texted Anthony to see if we could reschedule. His message back was sweet and kind. We moved our plans to the next week.

That next week I got invited to an event about food trends for the *Wall Street Journal*. I was eager to meet Anthony, but the invitation to the event seemed too good to pass up. I called my mom for advice. I can't remember what she said, but I left the call figuring if I'd waited this many weeks to meet a guy, I could wait a few days more. I cringed

33

as I wrote my second message asking to reschedule. I was worried he was going to give up on me.

He texted back right away, and it was both better and worse than I'd expected. Better because he didn't seem to be giving up on the whole thing. Worse because he was heading off on a business trip to London for six weeks. Six weeks is like six years in dating time. I had missed my chance, it seemed, but I'd made my choice.

The event was completely disappointing—I was hoping to network, but only ended up talking to a peppy donut influencer (that's a thing) and a grumpy older writer; almost immediately, I knew I had made the wrong decision. Tony and I kept sending messages. I was working on a story on New Haven pizza, and I texted Tony a picture of my clam pie (it was everything I hoped it would be, with a chewy crust topped with sweet-salty bites of fat clams). He texted back a magazine story about his friend's new bar in London that he had plans to visit that night.

He sent another cheese joke: What's Jay-Z's favorite cheese? Brie-oncé! On the subway, I giggled out loud.

When Tony was back in town, I invited him to a wine tasting in Tribeca. This is how the evening went down:

6:00 PM: Finally! I was actually going to meet this mysterious, cheese-joking man. I left myself plenty of extra time. It was the height of the so-called polar vortex—New York was so cold it hurt, blowing brutal winds into everyone's faces, so I made sure to wear my extra-warm coat. I didn't wear a hat—I had just blow-dried my hair and I didn't want to ruin it.

6:30 PM: At West 4th Street, the dreaded muffled announcement came over the subway sound system: "We are delayed due to a sick passenger."

6:45 PM: We were still not moving. I wanted to text Anthony and let him know, but I didn't have cell service.

6:52 PM: The subway was back in motion, crawling along. I messaged Anthony that I was running a few minutes late. He said he'd saved me a seat and the tasting was starting.

7:00 PM: I got off the train and looked for the wine shop. The little dot on my Google Maps kept jumping around. I only had three blocks to walk, but it was so cold I lost feeling in my ears almost instantly.

7:04 PM: Frustrated, I jumped in a cab. It would only take a minute, surely. But the driver sounded confused. Out the window, I saw we were driving up Broadway into SoHo, the wrong direction entirely.

7:15 PM: Somehow, we found the wine shop. I paid the cabbie and ran into the place. The presentation was in full swing, and everyone was quietly hunched over their rows of red, intently focused. On my way to the seat Anthony had saved for me, I knocked over a whole row of wineglasses with my puffy parka. They crashed to the ground, red wine flowing onto the floor and glass shattering. Everyone turned to look at me. My face felt as red as the wine I had spilled.

7:18 PM: They cleaned up the mess, I apologized, and now I turned to say hi to Anthony. He was even cuter in person. We got shushed for talking during the presentation. I couldn't focus on the winemaker or his PowerPoint. I swirled the wine in my glass and stole glances at my date.

8:00 PM: We headed to Terroir Tribeca and shared a bottle of bubbly, Brussels sprouts, and anchovies. We talked about Brussels sprouts (often soggy and sad in the UK). We discussed New York City and so many other things that we were the last people in the place. When the bartender started flipping chairs onto tables, we got the hint: it was time to go home. Anthony walked me to the subway, a true gentleman. He even lent me his hat. It was so unbearably cold—I didn't even worry about hat hair. As I headed up the steps at 145th Street, back in my neighborhood, there was a lovely message from him. I didn't want to get my hopes up, but the first date had absolutely been worth the wait.

Tony and I didn't kiss until our fourth date, walking across Central Park on the very first day that hinted at spring. There was still snow on the ground, but sunshine shimmered on the reservoir. We held hands all the way to Penn Station, where Tony dropped me off—I was heading to visit a friend's new restaurant in Jersey City. I made my way through a gorgeous cheese plate and a glass of Albariño, but I couldn't stop thinking about Tony, the way his hand felt in mine, that kiss.

◆ ◆ ◆

A little more than a year later. Everything was right about the proposal except for one thing.

The things that were right were the things that mattered. Paris, first. It was New Year's Eve and we had booked a table at a tiny restaurant on the Christmas-light-strewn Rue de Richelieu, up a narrow spiral staircase. I wore a dress and Tony had shaved for the first time in a month. We ate foie gras sandwiched between sesame crackers, and oysters wrapped in parcels of smoked cabbage. We drank champagne and blackberry red wine from Spain. We held hands across the table.

Conditions were perfect but I thought, *Don't get too excited; enjoy this dinner.* If I got too excited and he didn't propose, I would be devastated.

We took a walk along the Seine after dinner and I thought: *He is going to propose.* And then: *Maybe he just wants to take a walk.* We had feasted all week long. For breakfast: chèvre and ham and *pain au chocolat*, grapefruit juice and café au lait. Hot chocolate and bottles of Kronenbourg 1664. Kir Royales and steaming bowls of French onion soup, which was just called onion soup since we were in France. After we scooped up garlicky escargot from their shells, we drenched our baguettes in their parsley-flecked butter. When we weren't eating, we walked and walked. A kidney bean–shaped blister on my pinkie toe blossomed and popped. Tony stuck a Band-Aid on the raw skin left behind.

It was cold, and he had bought me a hat from a street vendor with a pom-pom on top for fifteen euros.

"Do you want my coat?" he asked.

I stuck my hand in his hand, and then directed our two hands into the pocket of his wool coat. I was happy.

"Do you want my trousers?" he joked.

We walked along the water. The Louvre was all lit up. The city was all lit up, and I understood why Paris was the City of Light.

Tony had told me about the Pont des Arts, the bridge over the Seine that was once covered in padlocks, symbols of love. The padlocks had accumulated until they weighed tons, and the bridge's structure struggled under hundreds of thousands of pounds of love. So the padlocks were no more, but still it was the Love Bridge. From it, we could see the Institut de France and the Eiffel Tower if it was a clear night, which it was not. Instead we saw a hazy, beautiful scrim.

We walked onto the bridge and Tony let go of my hand and slowly descended onto a knee and I thought, *This is it*. And it was it. Even in my new pom-pom hat, I was cold, my nose was cold, my eyelashes felt icy. There were plenty of people on the bridge. It was still hours until midnight, but it was only us.

Tony said something like, "I love you. You are perfect and I want to spend our lives together. Will you marry me?"

A bunch of happy, shrill sounds came out of my mouth and I pulled him up off the cold ground of the bridge and buried myself in him. We had to sit down on a bench because I was crying and laughing and crying and choking.

There was something else: a ring. It was simple and funky and not a ring I had seen before, a sideways rectangle of a diamond set in rose gold. I hadn't even wanted a diamond until that moment. It was stunning. I loved it. Later, I would come to love it even more when I learned it was "baguette cut." Of course I loved a diamond named after a baguette.

But there had to be one thing—not only did the ring not fit on my finger, it didn't even *almost* fit on my finger. Here I was, five years into eating disorder recovery. Those five years were rewiring my brain in terms of how I thought and felt about my body. But I had logged a lifetime of eating disorder baggage before that, and it was impressively persistent. There was still a pesky voice that told me I was not allowed to enjoy all those croissants, that I was not thin enough for love, for this big moment. That's what my eating disorder did—robbed me of my joy. Here I was with this man I loved, indulging in the fantastic tradition of food that I felt so connected to, and still I could hear that voice chime in.

The ring didn't even fit on my pinky finger. It was a perfect moment, and my body or my paranoia about my body was messing everything up, again. My body was too big, even down to my chubby fingers. My body had betrayed me.

I told that voice to shut up, but I still remember it.

"You said yes, right?" Tony asked, his arm around my shoulder, his body shielding me from the hissing wind. So far I had only made weird blubbering sounds.

"Fuck yes." I couldn't wait to marry this man. He wiped a tear that had made it all the way to my chin.

We sat there on the bench on the Pont des Arts and smiled and said, "Oh my god, we're going to get married. We're going to get married! Married!"

But the ring. "I thought it might not fit," Tony admitted, "but I wanted to see if you liked it before we got it resized. After all, you will wear it forever."

Forever. An impossible amount of time. How could I wear something forever when I couldn't wear it now?

We sat there until I lost feeling in my nose and fingers, even with my hands entangled in his. Tony hailed a cab back to the hotel. There was a lot of New Year's traffic and security, so we had to walk a few blocks. A security guard patted us down. I remember wishing I had my ring on. Instead, it was back in Tony's pocket.

"We just got engaged!" Tony told the cab driver.

"She's going to marry me!" Tony told the security guard.

"We're getting married!" he said to the hotel desk clerk.

When we arrived back at the small hotel room, it overflowed with long-stemmed red roses and chocolates and champagne. We called my parents and Tony's parents and everyone was overjoyed. We called my best friend, Ursula, who was at some sort of new age sound meditation event and had a horrible connection, but she squealed in joy, too. Tony put the ring back in the hotel safe. We finished the champagne and ordered more because why not, you only get engaged once. We watched the fireworks on the little TV. We could hear cheers coming from outside. We kissed and kissed.

Tony and I had a train to catch in the morning, but I didn't sleep all night. Eventually, Tony started to snore. I watched him sleeping and my heart felt too big for my body. I was sure it would burst. I tried to write in my journal, but my hand was shaking and my brain was fuzzy. I ate the chocolates. I looked at my too-big hands. I thought this was almost storybook. My fucking hands.

◆　◆　◆

Three and a half years after our first date at the wine tasting, we got married. My parents consented to a pig roast, even though we are Jewish. We decided to have the ceremony in their backyard by the Delaware River, where Pennsylvania meets New Jersey, and the party under a tent. When I told this to Tony's English family, they were confused. (In British English, a yard is like a junkyard and a tent is something you camp in.) Translation: the ceremony would be in their garden, and the party under a marquee.

There would be fairy lights and a band that got everyone dancing. There would be really good food. We looked into fireworks, but the price tag shocked us. Who needs fireworks? We didn't need fireworks.

Reader, the night was magic. Tony's family came from England and Denmark, and mine came from Baltimore and South Dakota, and friends came from everywhere. There was no feeling like walking out into the backyard and seeing all the people I love in the world, their soft smiles and flowy dresses. My heart exploded into heart dust.

The sun peeked out of cotton ball clouds right as we said our vows under the chuppah my dad had built for us. The river was right beside us, and we made another river of happy tears.

Even though my strapless dress had been tailored not once or twice but three times, Ursula still had to safety pin my bra into its stiff fabric.

She used fabric tape, too, just for good measure. Miraculously, it stayed up the whole night.

Our friend Leigh made us a cheese platter and a lemon cake with strawberry jam and buttercream frosting. Our friend Rena wrote us a poem. We had not just delicious-for-a-wedding but actually delicious food. The music was so electric that our friends and family spilled off the dance floor, out of the tent, and into the night. The moon's reflection danced on the river.

Paola

Somewhere over the Atlantic I started to feel the fluttering of butterfly nerves in my belly. I was flying from New York to Oslo to attend the Parabere Forum, which takes place in a different European city every year and brings together women food activists, farmers, chefs, and sommeliers. I was excited about meeting new people and learning how they were reimagining and changing the food world. Superstars Dominique Crenn and Alice Waters were going to speak. But *really*, I was going to see Chef Paola Martinenghi.

When Paola told me about the Parabere Forum, I knew I wanted to go. "Seriously," she said, "I've been going for years and it fills my soul for the whole year after. All those amazing women. You are going to love it." I wanted to see what the conference was about. But it was an excuse to meet in real life this particular amazing woman I had a connection with, to see if the connection was real.

I had only met Paola over Skype and WhatsApp, but she felt like a friend. Or, I wanted her to be a friend.

When my coworker Carole had asked if I wanted to take a cooking class with her via Skype, I was less than enthusiastic. We were going to make risotto. I am a little bit of a snob about risotto—already convinced mine is the best. Carole and I edit a food and wine website together— she's in charge of videos, I'm responsible for the words—and the cooking-class company had reached out to us for a potential partnership.

But eventually the idea grew on me and I got excited. It sounded like a fun way to spend a dreary New York afternoon. We were also going to make bruschetta and poached pears, a delicious meal. Before the class, we gathered the ingredients between the two of us—carnaroli rice, fat tomatoes, a big hunk of Parmigiano-Reggiano—and spread them out on the counter of Carole's little Upper East Side kitchen. We perched her laptop on top of the microwave and dialed up Chef Paola. Outside, sirens whizzed by.

Paola gave us a tour of her home in Vergiate, about an hour outside of Milan in Italy's Lombardia region, via the camera on her laptop. Her place was full of wooden beams and decorative bronze lamps that she and her mom craft and sell under the umbrella of their family company, Il Ferrivendolo. In her kitchen, her pots and pans hung in a neat row above her stove top. There was so much space! Most of it seemed to be full of jars of spices and jams, bowls of fresh fruits, a long island with piles of little espresso cups. She seemed very far away from the Upper East Side, where we barely had enough room for the two of us and our ingredients. We had to duck past the bike Carole had mounted on her wall to squeeze past each other. I had kitchen envy.

"Let's get started," Chef Paola said, friendly yet in charge. Carefully following her instructions, we roasted the tomatoes until they were just soft enough so we could pop off their skins, then let them marinate in salt and olive oil. We dropped cinnamon sticks, star anise, and strips of lemon zest in prosecco and let the whole thing simmer and perfume the kitchen, placing in our pears for poaching. (Chef Paola tried to teach me a handy way to zest the lemon, where I peeled it in one long, continuous strip with a veggie peeler, but I couldn't get it.)

It turned out that taking a cooking class by Skype is a sort of genius idea.

"How much wine?" we asked when it was time to deglaze the toasting carnaroli rice.

"Show me," Paola instructed, and we angled the laptop toward Carole's stove.

"Pour, pour, pour . . . now stop."

She could tell us precisely when it was time to add water—not stock—to the risotto.

"Why not stock?" I asked, suddenly doubting her expertise. To me, water seemed blasphemous.

"With the prosecco and Parmigiano-Reggiano, there's a lot of richness already. Water makes for a cleaner flavor."

Although we set off the fire alarm and burned our first round of bruschetta bread in the broiler, we ended up with a lovely lunch. We toasted to Chef Paola and snapped the laptop shut, then ate our meal on Carole's couch. Paola was right, the risotto tasted bright and clean. It wasn't missing a thing. We feasted and drank the rest of the prosecco.

By the time I left, the day had become less dreary, and I decided to walk home to the West Side across Central Park. My stomach was full, and I felt buoyant. I had felt a connection with Chef Paola, but it was something more than that.

At that point, I'd worked in food for more than a decade. At first, getting paid to sell uni so buttery and briny it gave me goose bumps felt like a dream. The first time a box of cheese arrived at my apartment, I was so delighted it may as well have been Christmas. I got to travel to meet ranchers in Colorado, olive oil millers in Crete, and dairy farmers on the French-Swiss border. I got to spray stinky cheese with cider, watching and smelling it ripen into something miraculous, like a locker room that hasn't been properly cleaned for a very, very long time, but a million times more delicious.

Does it get better than that? My answer remains: not really.

But sometimes a calling (which it is) feels more like a job (which it is as well). Most days involve me scrambling to meet deadlines in my pajamas. I probably really need to wash my hair, but I'm not expecting to meet any actual humans. I'm happy to wax poetic about cheese for a specialty food importer, but when it comes to describing cheese number seventy-four, I find myself totally out of adjectives. I keep checking my in-box, waiting to see if an editor has answered my pitch. I keep checking my mailbox, waiting for a check that never seems to come. Anxiety is my constant state.

Cooking still breaks through the noise in my brain. It reawakens me to my senses: the slick of eggplant in my hand, the rhythm of chop-chop-chop, the sizzle of a knob of butter in a hot pan. That thrill is where it started for me.

But all of this escalates to a whole new level when it's not just me alone in a kitchen. It's sharing a laugh with Carole and Paola. It was my mom, commanding the hub of our house, and my dad, stationed at the sink, washing dishes, and me, drying. It's knowing there is a former attorney who quit her job to raise goats and turn their milk into snow-white rounds of cheese, which she wraps in wax paper until she begins to lose feeling in her fingers. It's the farmer who gets up when the rest of us are tucked happily away in our beds, grabs a mug of coffee, and sets out on her tractor, the sun rising over her shoulder. It's the baker whose forearms are ropy strong from kneading thousands of loaves and who can see bread as a path to social justice. It's knowing we're all sharing this collective creation together. Sharing that afternoon with Paola, I felt deeply connected to her, and to her rustic kitchen, and I knew we'd speak again.

◆ ◆ ◆

When I mentioned the Parabere Forum to Tony, he said, "You have to go. It's decided."

The tickets were sold out. I emailed and asked about press passes; they wrote back and said no. And then two weeks before the conference I got a message in my in-box: a ticket had become available. I booked my flight that day.

I messaged Paola to ask where she was staying. She wrote back right away: I'm bringing my dad and our family friend. We're getting an Airbnb near the center of town. If she was traveling with family, maybe I should, too. I asked my mom, who had recently started working for herself, if she could swing a last-minute trip. She was in.

The red-eye was packed and choppy, but I managed to sleep for a few hours. We were meeting Paola, Papa, and Tonino, the father of Paola's best childhood girlfriend, for dinner that night, and the nerves in my belly felt like I was preparing for a first date.

Chef Paola was thirty—almost exactly a year younger than me—and very pretty. I had a bit of a friend crush on her. She had told me that she'd lost nearly ninety pounds several years ago. I always think of myself as someone who *struggled* with food and my body. For years, living with an eating disorder made me feel like I was fighting a constant war with myself: messy binges with crumbs I'd find everywhere, even days later, crying jags that left my whole face puffy—my disorder seemed to define my life for those years. It was tempting to see kinship in Paola—a passion and devotion to food, a need to change her physical appearance. But Paola told me that she always liked herself, at her biggest and at her thinnest and everywhere between. She felt undefined by her body in a way that I couldn't relate to. Her confidence feels deep-seated. Maybe that's what makes her so magnetic.

Everything in Oslo was eerily clean. When my mom and I arrived, it was garbage day; even the trash bags were neatly organized along the sidewalks in what looked like those big bright plastic sacks you get from Ikea. It was cold, with a steely drizzle that threatened to turn icy. The silver sky was boundless. Early March in Oslo is definitely not tourist season.

My mom and I arrived at the restaurant Sentralen first. Paola and I had messaged each other back and forth with long lists of places we wanted to eat—we had landed on this one. In the theater next door, there was a salsa festival going on, and women wore parkas over swirly skirts and sequins. My mom and I ordered two glasses of bubbly and tried not to yawn in our stiff-backed chairs—the jet lag was suddenly catching up with us. It was Saturday evening, and we hadn't slept properly since Thursday night.

Be there soon, Paola texted me, along with a picture of her, Papa, and Tonino with beers raised high, eyes crinkly from their big smiles.

Then Paola and her crew waved to us through the window. I had traveled across the Atlantic to join someone I had never met for a conference I knew nothing about, but when I saw her, my nerves turned to excitement. I was suddenly sure I'd made a very good decision.

Paola, Papa, and Tonino had already been touring in Oslo for a few days. "We walked and walked," Papa told us. He made two fingers walk across the table to demonstrate.

"You must be ready to sit down. Where would you like to sit?" my mom asked, but he just looked at her and shrugged.

Papa only had a few words of English—Tonino had none—and Paola had to translate for her guests. "Don't worry, I'm used to it."

The conference would hold presentations in French and Spanish. I would rely on the translation headphones they provided to understand everything, but Paola had no trouble with French and Spanish, just as she had no trouble with English. Her first language is Italian. Listening to her switch effortlessly between just Italian and English as she kept the conversation moving, I began to feel like quite the dumb American.

We ordered almost everything on the menu: smoked beets made spicy with horseradish and creamy with egg yolk, tiny mussels with a garlicky mayonnaise, mackerel with mustard and some kind of roe. The waiter urged us to double up on some dishes for the table, so we did, and still we all laughed when the food arrived on small plates, looking like delicate play food. The mussels were fantastic, briny and sweet, but reaching into the small pot, we each got only one.

"This would be, like, snacks in Abruzzo," Tonino said, as translated by Paola. Paola explained that he lived on a vineyard there. He told us about the hillsides full of grapes that slanted toward the sea, and the meals they'd savor of chitarra (a sort of pasta), porchetta, and as much red wine from their own harvest as they could reasonably imbibe. Right then I hoped very much to visit. Outside, the rain turned into hail. We toasted to new friends.

◆ ◆ ◆

Later, Chef Paola and I traded stories about our time in restaurants. I was curious about her career, what had brought her to the classes she was teaching online. It turned out that Paola had a familiar story to tell.

Chef Paola's first job out of college was in the same field she'd studied: PR and communications. She worked for a university in Milan.

"I had always lived in the countryside of Italy, in this beautiful little town where I live now again, Vergiate," Paola told me. "When I went to university in Milan, it was like—yay—I'm going to Milan! The big city. And then I was in the metro station, everyone was like this"—Paola pulled the corners of her mouth down into a scowl—"just very sad and grey. I wondered: *Why? You're in such a beautiful city. Are you not excited to be here?* I promised myself that if one day I became like them, I would do something to make my life sunny and beautiful again.

"After five years of living there, I fell running to catch the metro one day. The next train was in just two minutes, but I was so upset. I got back up and saw my reflection in the metro glass, and I knew it; it had happened. I resigned from the university the next day.

"My boss asked, 'What are you going to do?' And I told him, 'I'm going to become a chef.'"

The day Paola fell and resigned was in 2012. Paola decided her life "needed a breakthrough." She thought about what really brought her joy, and she kept coming back to eating and sharing food. "It was always something more than just eating for me," she told me. I understood. Since I could remember, the kitchen seemed to be the most promising, wonderful place. When my mom cooked for dinner parties, I had always wanted in on the action.

Paola wanted to learn more about her own food culture, Italian food culture. She researched culinary schools and found ALMA, the International School of Italian Cuisine. She liked that the school was not only about mastering culinary fundamentals, it also focused on the history and culture of Italian food.

"I followed an instinct," Paola said. "I was not a small child prodigy of the kitchen, and I did not have a grandmother who cooked or an old aunt from whom to steal the techniques of the trade. I started from scratch in January 2013, when I wore the white uniform for the first time." From her very first class, an introduction to basic techniques, she was hooked. Holding her knife in the gleaming professional kitchen, listening to the chef instructor shout and soliloquize about the right way to chop an onion, she felt fantastically far away from her old office. She knew she was exactly where she was supposed to be.

At culinary school, Paola spent a lot of time in the library. She studied sauces and soups, poaching and braising, plating and presentation, but it was the history and the stories, the theory behind the food that kept her up late at night, brainstorming, excited. "Other chefs wanted to be cooking all the time. The more time in the kitchen, the better. For me, it was more about learning, studying, and researching. Reading, and studying, and more reading." I knew that was another reason Paola and I hit it off instantly—we were unabashedly nerdy. We were overachievers with the drive to learn more, do more, know more.

Paola graduated at the top of her class. She had a new shiny prize and a prestigious culinary education, but she was hesitant about heading to work in a restaurant kitchen. She envisioned monotony and loneliness; she knew she'd be one of very few women. She knew the work would be physically demanding, even backbreaking. Still, it was what she had been training for. Like an athlete heading off to the big tournament, she began work in the Michelin-starred Ristorante L'Erba del Re in Modena. Modena is a culinary mecca, the birthplace of *aceto balsamico di Modena*, Parmigiano-Reggiano, and sparkling Lambrusco.

Her apartment was in the same building as Osteria Francescana in Modena, one of the best restaurants in the world. Ristorante L'Erba del Re was a competitor, and only a five-minute walk away. Perched on a postcard-worthy square in Modena, the restaurant was minimalist yet welcoming, with white tablecloths and light that poured in until sunset. Ristorante L'Erba del Re served elegant renditions of classics from the region, like risotto infused with pine nuts, black garlic, and rosemary. The plates looked like abstract works of art, strewn perfectly with flowers or microgreens or tiny dollops of brilliant-green or orange sauces.

There were parts of the job that Paola loved. She got to visit the market every morning to buy produce for the evening's service. In the kitchen she was encouraged to experiment with fancy, gorgeous ingredients. "One time a guy arrived with a little bag, and it was full of fresh truffles. We just stood there for a moment, smelling them, inhaling the beautiful smell." The smell carried her through her long, strenuous shift that night. It was a marathon of prep, carrying loads of ingredients from the walk-in to her station, checking off items from a never-ending list of sauces and spice blends and veggies, followed without any break by a whirlwind service, where she'd assemble, sauté, flip, stir, and plate until she started to ache down to her toes. There was hardly time to catch a breath, pee, or get something to eat.

The work was grueling, but Paola experienced joy in it. Listening to her recount the adrenaline-fueled dance of a busy service reminded me of the years I spent working in restaurants, mostly in the front of the house. There was plenty I didn't miss, but listening to Paola describe her fierce focus—"the need to always be careful and alert, because miss a moment and you are in the shit"—I remembered how a long night would pass by in a beat. How the world would shrink to the distance between my tables and the hot kitchen.

Paola sometimes cooked for Ristorante L'Erba del Re's catering arm. One day they catered a party in Milan for Salvatore Ferragamo, the posh shoe designer. It was a flashy see-and-be-seen sort of event in their sumptuous high-fashion store on Montenapoleone, what's known as Europe's most expensive street. "I was running under the fine drizzle in Corso Montenapoleone, between women in Prada and Ferrari," she remembered. "I was there with my uniform, my apron, and my hat. And I felt beautiful. I felt just right for the occasion. I felt like I had hoped to feel my whole life."

The chef appointed Paola to work in his cooking school on weekends, where she got the chance to share some of her knowledge with home cooks. It was there that Paola understood she wanted to "give something more than the dish." Food was just the beginning. She discovered a love for sharing what she had studied and experienced, and she found connecting with others face-to-face more satisfying than cooking for them, hidden away in a restaurant kitchen, where the only sign of a job well done was the satisfying return of a clean plate.

But Paola's job mostly took place in that kitchen, and it was brutal. More than a job, it was a life. "I was proud to be part of the team, like a warrior. We would do anything for this Michelin star." The way the restaurant industry functioned in Italy was different from anything I'd experienced in the States. And the more lauded and exceptional the restaurant was, the more it seemed like a calling, a devotion, instead of a workplace. Paola explained to me that "in Michelin-starred restaurants in Italy, they don't pay you. We worked seventy hours in a week and didn't get paid at all. You don't even have a contract. They give you food and a bed, but you are paying the restaurant to be there. And yet they own you."

I thought of my summer internship, where I had happily worked twelve-hour shifts for experience and zero cash at a Midtown restaurant, peeling buckets of carrots and baking endless sheets of *tuiles* that would garnish more complicated desserts. There was cold beer at the end of service, and the relief in unbuttoning the starched white jacket in the stifling heat. I thought of the cooks and the bussers and the dishwashers and their minimum wage, their cash off the books. Suddenly, things didn't seem so different.

Paola was the only woman in the kitchen. "I don't even want to explain where I was sleeping, because it was such a terrible situation," she said. The cooks bunked together. At night, Paola's fellow cooks would routinely sneak into her bed. She would shove them out in anger, and then they would do it again. She was living under a constant threat of assault. She couldn't get any rest. Things became so desperate that she asked her family for money to help rent her own apartment nearby. They were happy to help.

The harassment was relentless. "In the kitchen, they would touch my ass. It happened all the time because it was allowed," Paola told me. "I just pushed them away. I was tough," she said. She wanted to be tough. She wanted to be able to do the job that was asked of her, to be part of this group of restaurant workers constantly fighting to keep their Michelin star, to achieve culinary greatness. But it wore on her, and it would wear on anyone, as that same behavior and environment wore on me.

"Has the Me Too movement changed Italian restaurant kitchens?" I asked, unsure how I'd answer the question for restaurants in the USA. Since October 2017, when the *New York Times* published its bombshell news on Hollywood producer Harvey Weinstein's decades of abuse, women in virtually every industry came forward with their own stories. The hospitality world, famous for its bro culture, was no exception, and reports of sexual misconduct brought down some of the most powerful figures in the restaurant industry, like Mario Batali, Ken Friedman (my former employer), and John Besh.

I had known I wanted to work in restaurants the first time I ate at Babbo, Mario Batali's temple to Italian food in Greenwich Village, New York City. I was fourteen and angsty; we had just moved and I hated my new school. My mom thought a night out might cheer me up, and she was right. There at the bar, in a crowd of downtown cool, I had an epiphany with my first bite of beef-cheek ravioli, pasta yielding to the meltiest, meatiest beef beneath a shower of pecorino and black truffles. All these years later, the allure remained. And yet, I had been shouted at and talked down to and touched uncomfortably. I knew my industry was fundamentally broken, and suddenly the world seemed to be acknowledging that.

Finally, society was having a conversation about things that had been brushed under proverbial rugs for, well, ever. That was an important beginning, but there was a mountain of work ahead.

She laughed. "No way. This masculine culture is very strong in Italy, especially in the kitchen world. Not in the near future. But hopefully one day."

The women she knows who still work in restaurants have made moves in their careers to cook under women chefs or have moved away from Italy altogether, where the machismo is deeply ingrained. But most women have simply left the restaurant industry, as Paola has. At the Skype cooking school, The Chef & The Dish, Paola teaches from her own kitchen in Vergiate, on her own time. Her life has changed completely. She lives right next to her parents, her sister, her brother-in-law, and her nephew, in the country, with her big kitchen and candles that smell of cloves and warmth. She gets to connect with students from all over the world. But she has aspirations to push her career further. Big things are brewing. Paola is working on bringing fresh-baked focaccia to Saudi Arabia and teaching kids around the world about the joys of seasonal ingredients.

Entrenched misogyny was a big reason Paola left restaurant kitchens, but it wasn't the only one. "It wasn't my life; it wasn't my story. I didn't have the chance to talk and share about food. I didn't have time to go to the library. I didn't have time to travel, and for me traveling is the most important thing in the world."

◆ ◆ ◆

Each morning in Oslo, my mom and I got up early to drink coffee and eat smoked fish on fresh, dense bread. Out the window was snow and grey. Then she'd go explore the city and I'd walk to the old civic building filled with chatty chefs and bakers and food writers, my gloved hands deep in my pockets for maximum warmth. At the Parabere Forum, we listened to a twenty-one-year-old Sámi reindeer herder talk about saving the Arctic from oil drilling before it's too late for the land, the reindeer, and the people who have lived there for countless generations. We heard a British baker detail her efforts to turn Parisians—for whom bread making is close to religion—on to sourdough. We met a pickle maker from Berlin and a French lady who was trying to get funding to open an empire of fancy cheese shops in South Korea. There was a private chef who worked for royalty in Dubai and a sommelier from Sydney who sold only wine made by women and indigenous Australians. But mostly, Paola and I talked to each other. We whispered and commiserated and laughed and shared *lefse*, little rolls of sweetened flatbread, and *svele*, flat pancakes served with inky coffee.

On the last night, the conference participants rode a boat from the Nobel Peace Center to Vippa, a trendy food hall on the docks. We filled the whole boat with happy laughter. A natural winemaker poured everyone glasses of bubbly. Paola and I sat near the bow and drank our wine.

The event was sponsored by the Norwegian Seafood Council. We were greeted by the dinosaur-like limbs of red king crabs and buckets full of stony oysters on ice. There were blue mussels from Trøndelag and fried cod skins with smoked roe. We ate raw prawns from Lyngenfjord, grilled langoustines the size of our outstretched hands, and crunchy fried cod tongues. For dessert, spoonfuls of ice cream made from the milk of cows in a village called Fannrem, on the Orkla River, were drizzled in caramel. Then we went back for more fried cod tongues, which tasted like a silky take on fish and chips.

Paola and I decided to walk home together. It was cold and clear and the streets were eerily quiet. We took a wrong turn at some point, distracted by the conversation and champagne and the abundance of the evening, and wandered into a construction site. We made our way out, back to downtown. We had met amazing food women from Brazil and India and Monaco. We had met each other.

We talked about what we would do next—each of us had tons of ideas, from a chain of baked-to-order focaccia stands in the Middle East to an interactive cooking show, but it was clear we wanted it to be something together.

"See you in Vergiate," Paola said.

"See you in New York," I said.

Walking back to the hotel alone, Oslo gleaming and austere, I felt almost high with new ideas and new friends. It was freezing, but I felt warm. Despite the patriarchy, these women in food had seen new possibilities and carved out paths to do meaningful, creative work, to nourish each other and the world with food and purpose and potential.

Sweet Pea

I was pregnant. The pregnancy app said the proto-baby growing inside me was the size of a sweet pea, and so this is what Tony and I called her (always *her*): Sweet Pea.

I had just stopped taking birth control pills, which I had started some time in high school and ceased only at the age of thirty-one, six months after getting married to the man of better-than-my dreams—a tall, dark, and handsome British man with a scary knowledge of obscure trivia and a talent for cooking steak. Tony is kind, brilliant, and funny, and when I wake up in the middle of the night, next to him and half-asleep, I still cannot believe my good fortune.

I'd assumed getting pregnant would be a challenge, like getting into college or writing a book. Most big things in life were hard, why would this be any different? My good friends were on their third round of in vitro fertilization, and the process was expensive and painful (so many injections), and when it failed, heartbreaking.

I'd resolved not to take a pregnancy test just yet. I wanted to wait another few days, or a week for good measure. But earlier that day, at my therapist's office, I'd mentioned that my boobs were throbbing in a strange, persistent way like they never had before, and that the frisée and chicken thigh salad I usually treated myself to before our appointment had tasted like wet cardboard.

"Why don't you just take the test?" she suggested.

I couldn't think of a good reason why not. I splurged on the digital ones—as per her suggestion, "The cheap ones can be hard to read, and this is not something you want to be confused about"—a two-pack, on the way home. I watched as the first one blinked and then spelled out PREGNANT in all caps. It felt unreal, impossible, so I peed on the second stick for good measure. A pause. PREGNANT.

I had been trying all my life not to get pregnant, and switching my intentions so abruptly was disorienting, as if I was being disloyal to my former self. I stood there in my apartment staring at the two sticks. My hand was shaking a little. I felt high. The sun was too bright coming in through the windows. I picked up my phone to call Tony but then hung up before the first ring. He was at work, in an open-plan office, and it seemed like the wrong way to convey such epic news. I started to dial my mom, but then I stopped myself again. Tony should know first. I wanted to tell Tony first.

I took out a piece of paper and wrote him a note. *I may be a writer, but I can't even begin to explain how excited I am right now. You are going to be the most amazing dad.* Then I sat there on our sofa and bawled messy, happy tears.

We had planned to have dinner that night with a group of my former coworkers. One of them had taken a job in a serious wine shop, and we had picked a BYOB Chinese restaurant so she could supply our dinner with a lineup of bottles she loved. Tony and I had arranged to meet at the restaurant across town on the Upper East Side and he was heading there right after work, so there would be no chance to tell him the news beforehand.

It was the longest dinner I have ever had. The wine guru decided to order one course at a time to better pair with her bottles. We started with dumplings and sparkling rosé, then moved on to an Alsatian white that was all perfume and springtime in a glass, complementing our humongous salt and pepper shrimp. I took just a sip of wine and passed the rest on to Tony, acutely aware of something new and wild happening inside my body. If anyone noticed my teetotaling, they didn't say so.

For stretches of time, the dinner felt like any dinner with friends. I got swept up in the conversation, laughed at a joke, and then it would hit me again and again—*I am pregnant*—and everyone felt out of focus, on the periphery although they were sitting right next to me. As if there was a schism in my reality.

Under the table, Tony squeezed my hand.

"Should we get one more course?" my cheese friend asked after the waiter cleared the remnants of our sticky ribs.

"One more," the group chimed.

"We still have another bottle!" the wine friend pointed out. The dinner started to feel interminable.

I was floating by the time we got home. I'd left my letter for Tony beside one of the PREGNANT sticks on our kitchen counter. I watched his face as he registered the tableau and its meaning.

I'll never forget the way Tony smiled then. It was as if his entire being smiled, the hugeness of it. His feet may have left the floor. That's when it felt real to me. We hugged and we cried. I tasted our intermingled tears when I kissed him. "We're going to have a baby," we kept saying, as if we couldn't quite believe it, which we couldn't.

◆ ◆ ◆

I was seven weeks pregnant when we left for an epic trip. The trip's impetus was Tony's friend's wedding in Surrey, in the blindingly green

English countryside. Tony and his friend had grown up together in England, and they'd reconnected when they both moved to New York City about a decade ago. The groom and his bride—she was from New Jersey—were the first friends of Tony's I had met when we started dating four years before. That night, they had welcomed us into their home and cooked a traditional Sunday roast, with leg of lamb, mint jelly, and little mounds of Yorkshire puddings. I have liked them ever since.

At seven weeks, we had told only people close to us about the pregnancy: my mom and dad, a few close friends. The night we arrived in England, we broke the news to Tony's parents. Tony's mom, Christine, is subdued and proper in this very British way, yet she nearly screamed with happiness. It felt like I had a sort of new superpower, to be able to make people so jubilant, to act so outside their usual selves.

Tony and I had decided to take advantage of the trip and spend a week in Italy before the wedding. We would be tourists, eat a lot of pasta and gelato, and visit Paola. I mourned all the spritzes and Chianti I would miss. Tony would have to enjoy them for me. It would be worth it.

After visiting with Tony's family for a few days, we took a plane from Birmingham to Milan, and then a train to Venice. It was both of our first times there. I had been told the city was touristy and strange. We spent the weekend getting lost in the tangle of canals and ogling fresh fish at the market. I fell in love. It was touristy and strange indeed, and also magnificent. We ate plates of sea urchin–flecked risotto and I took sips of Tony's Soave, which also somehow tasted of the sea. We rode gondolas.

Next was Florence. It rained so hard when we arrived that the water in the Piazza Santa Croce came nearly up to our ankles. Tourists cowered in their ponchos. We took shelter at the Mercato Centrale Firenze, where Paola told us we had to try a *lampredotto* sandwich, a classic Florentine street food made of tripe. We watched as the vendor scooped a tangle of pot-marked brown tripe—which comes from the muscle wall of a cow's stomach—from a big pot of braising liquid onto a soft roll. He doused the meat in chili oil and a bright-green sauce made from parsley and garlic before giving it a quick dip in the braising liquid. My pregnancy app said tripe was on the verboten list, so Tony ordered one and I took a single, exultant bite.

We texted Paola a picture of the sandwich with a starry-eyed emoji. I couldn't wait to see her again. Tony and I decided we'd tell her the news when we went to visit her on the last and final leg of our Italy journey.

At the Accademia Gallery in Florence, I had to use the restroom. I walked past the statue of *David* on the way to the bathroom and felt a surge of awe: how magnificent he was in person after seeing pictures my whole life, how forceful and magnetic. When I wiped myself, I noticed a smudge of brown on the toilet paper.

I was aware that spotting was a thing that could happen in pregnancy—I had been dutifully reading pregnancy books and articles and apps—yet my initial reaction was a wave of fear. We called Tony's mom, Christine, who had worked as a midwife. She said it was very normal and told us not to worry. We heard the same from my mom, my general practitioner at home, and most of the pregnancy apps. But the OB-GYN in NYC said something different: she told me to go to the hospital right away. I cried when I hung up. Tony tried to calm me down. We sat in our hotel room and weighed all the advice we'd gotten. It was already nighttime in Florence. We were on our way to see Paola the next day. She could help us navigate the Italian health system, if we needed it. If not, we could wait a few days until we were back in the UK. We decided against a trip to the hospital.

By the time Paola picked us up from the train, the bleeding had stopped. When we told her the news, she double-kissed me and then Tony, holding our faces in her hands. "You're going to be amazing parents," she said, even though she and Tony had just met five minutes ago. I could tell she meant it.

We had never been to Vergiate, but I felt totally at home. We ordered pistachio gelato and walked around Arona, on the southern shores of Lake Maggiore. Paola pointed to the other side of the lake, where the Swiss Alps rose like in a storybook. We drove around the lake and picked out which villas we would buy when we became rich. I chose one with a turret and arches, filled with big windows that looked out onto the water, which sparkled in the sun.

We went for *aperitivo*, one of my favorite Italian traditions. Paola ordered me a Crodino, a bitter, thick nonalcoholic drink the color of Orangina. The three of us debated the best spritz ingredient: Aperol or Campari. We munched on olives and talked about food, culture, and family.

I wanted to hear everything about Paola's fiancé, Abdul, who lived in Saudi Arabia. They had just bought an apartment together in Dubai, on the forty-seventh floor of a still-rising high-rise. It would be finished in two years. Maybe they would live there; maybe it would be an investment. Everything seemed to be exciting and ripe for change. Outside, the bar owners' kids kicked a soccer ball in the cobblestoned town square. Sometimes the ball rolled under our table and we lobbed it back their way.

Back at Paola's house, in her kitchen that had become famous—if just to me—she began to cook us risotto, this time with asparagus and Gorgonzola. She used the special rice we had snagged at the Parabere Forum—where each individual kernel had been aged for a year in refrigerated silos. We munched on real Fontina Val D'Aosta from cows that graze on 6500-foot-high Alpine pastures down the river, and local Taleggio while she cooked, and Tony opened a bottle of wine. I drank sparkling water from a turquoise ceramic cup Paola had brought home from a trip to Fez with Abdul. My nerves from the past few days intermingled with deep satisfaction. I looked from Tony to Paola and felt my heart might explode with love.

◆ ◆ ◆

On the flight back to Birmingham, in the little bathroom with a wad of stepped-on toilet paper on the floor, I noticed khaki-colored discharge. I had to stop myself from going to the bathroom every five minutes. The color was changing every time—now it was pink, now rust-colored, now the scariest hue of all: bloodred. We made an appointment for an ultrasound scan for the next day in Solihull, a pretty town near Birmingham, where Tony's family lives. It was the first open slot. It would be my first ultrasound, my first chance to see what was happening inside me. I tried hard to pass the time by taking many deep breaths until then, but it passed slowly.

We waited a long time for the ultrasound appointment. I played with my phone, scrolling distractedly, until Tony pointed out a sign that said, **No Phones, Please.** We flipped through a real estate catalog, but I couldn't focus on the symmetrical houses and their supple green lawns. There was one other nervous-looking couple in the waiting room. We didn't make eye contact. It felt like forever before they called my name.

I lay down on the medical table and Tony sat beside me. Everything was angled toward the huge screen. Years before, I had been told I had a tilted uterus at an OB-GYN appointment, and I was sure that I was weird, broken, so it was an amazing surprise when a little blurry blob popped on the screen, the wand cold and gooey on my belly, Tony's hand warm and clammy in my own.

The doctor smiled. "There it is." She sounded proud of us, like we had just run a marathon or found a cure for some awful disease.

I felt relief rush over me, like fresh air. There was its heartbeat. A hummingbird.

"There are no guarantees," the doctor said, "but everything looks just as it should. Now, did you say the baby will be born in the US?"

"Yes! In New York."

"A New York Christmas baby!" she exclaimed. "How wonderful."

Sweet Pea would be a New York baby. Our New York baby. I couldn't think of anything more fabulous.

"What about the spotting?" I asked.

"It happens. We can see in the ultrasound that you are having a healthy pregnancy, so now we know there is nothing to worry about."

They sent us away with a printout of a picture of Sweet Pea: a blob, a Rorschach test. I texted it to my parents and to Paola. **We're going to have a New York Christmas baby,** I typed out on my phone with shaky fingers.

◆　◆　◆

The ultrasound had been on Thursday. I remembered the doctor's words a few days later, on Saturday night at the wedding, when crimson drops of blood dribbled into the toilet. *There is nothing to worry about.* I repeated them to myself as I returned to the dance floor. The bride was holding her niece/flower girl in her arms as they twisted and shouted to the music.

We joined them. I kicked off my heels. I put my hands in the air. *There is nothing to worry about.*

It had been an unusually gorgeous day for the wedding, and cows had gathered from a nearby pasture after the ceremony to say hello. Everything was green. I had worried about my outfit of choice, a black jumpsuit, wondering if it was appropriate to wear to this British wedding, but there were plenty of women in jumpsuits when I'd arrived, and I felt unoriginal instead. The night was coming to an end, and the dance floor thrummed with the last of the happy revelers. Outside, it had grown too dark to make out the cows, but they still mooed softly.

I was low-grade mad at Tony because he had gotten two drinks from one trip to the bar—a beer and a whiskey. I was sipping my tonic (tonic and tonic, which looks like gin and tonic if you don't examine it *too* closely), feeling a little achy and sorry for myself. I wasn't asking him to forgo booze entirely, but two drinks just felt like rubbing it in.

We hadn't yet told these friends I was pregnant. It was still such early days, plus we didn't want our news to distract from the festivities. Pregnancy hadn't made me nauseous, at least not yet, but it had made me tired. I'd get these waves of bone-aching exhaustion. My breasts continued to ache and throb. Touching them was like touching a fresh bruise. Pregnancy also made my emotions feel even more acute, which is saying a lot, for me. I'm the first one to cry at a cheesy commercial or, well, a wedding in normal times.

British weddings are usually longer than American ones, and thus filled with even more drinking. I felt a little lonely, being sober and exhausted with a secret. It had been a long day, and it was nearly midnight. The celebration was almost over; I told myself to suck it up and enjoy these last few songs. *There is nothing to worry about.*

And then I felt something odd and terrifying—warm liquid gushed through me. I put my hand down to my jumpsuit to see what was happening and when I picked it up, it was covered in blood.

"Tony," I urged. He was only holding one drink by then. "I'm bleeding."

"Don't worry," he said. "Remember the doctor said it was normal."

"No." My heart lurched in my rib cage. I held up my hand. "Look." I could feel the blood dribbling down my legs. I remember feeling relieved I was wearing black.

"Okay." He seemed suddenly calm and sober. "We're going to the hospital."

"Should we talk to Cassie?" Cassie, another wedding guest, was the girlfriend of Tony's good friend Gavin. She also happened to be a midwife back in New York. We hadn't told her, but surely, she would know what to do in this situation.

"Cassie's dancing. Let's leave her be. We're going to the hospital."

The cab we had arranged earlier to take us back to our Airbnb had already arrived in the parking lot outside. The driver stood outside his black car, arms folded across his chest. Tony talked with the driver—we had been planning to return with a group and going to the hospital was a change of plans—while I retreated somewhere inside myself. There was a horrible battle going on in my abdomen. My face burned. The blood kept rushing out of me, which felt bizarre and excruciating. I was desperate to reverse its flow, to make it go back inside me. Fuck gravity.

Tony somehow made the driver understand that this was an emergency. Suddenly we were careening down narrow, windy, hedge-lined roads. I closed my eyes and felt my body bleed and tremble.

"Do we need to go back and get my ID?" I asked Tony as the cab whizzed forward. I had forgotten to pack a clutch for the trip, so Tony had stashed only my phone and lipstick in his suit pocket for the night.

"We're fine," Tony reassured me. I was so glad to be with him. When we got out of the cab, there was a puddle of blood where I had been sitting.

I was grateful for the NHS that night. Tony gave his family's address and our names to the receptionist, and I only had to stand in the ER lobby for a few short minutes, feeling the blood drip down my jumpsuit over my chunky heels and then, horrifyingly, onto the shiny tile floors, before we were shown to a room.

What I noticed as I sat on the examining table, waiting for the doctor to come in, was the cadenced, furious trembling of my thighs. Tony loosened his tie.

A nurse came and took my vitals: my pulse was fast. I could have told them that. I felt my blood racing through my arteries and between my thighs.

She mentioned that we were the best-dressed patients in the ER that night. I was wearing the same dangly earrings I had worn to my own wedding.

The nurse gave me a diaper-looking contraption and told me to change into a robe and pee in a cup. On the way to the bathroom, I left a trail of blood. I peed, but it just looked like lumpy clots, crimson and black in the little plastic vial. I felt a strange sense of calm as I wiped up the mess on the toilet bowl and floor with a wad of paper towels and tied the paper robe around my waist.

But back on the table, my legs kept shaking.

I felt calm answering the doctor's questions. He looked like he was fifteen years old, but he was serious and kind. We told him about the scan just two days ago, about the spotting. He asked if I wanted Tony to stay while he examined me, and I said yes. I didn't let go of Tony's hand.

"There are three possibilities," the doctor said. "One is you've already miscarried. The second is you're miscarrying now. But it's also possible that this is what they call a threatened miscarriage, which means the complication is elsewhere, and the pregnancy is still viable. I'm trying to see if your cervix is open or closed, but it's neither all the way opened, nor all the way closed. So it's very hard to tell."

It felt crystal clear to me that something was very, very wrong.

The doctor left, and Cassie and Gavin were there, all of a sudden. Cassie's arms were around me. She smelled like shampoo and champagne. Later I would learn they'd told the hospital staff they were family.

I remember so well her whispering in my ear: "It's nothing you've done. No exercise. No alcohol. No traveling. No coffee. No nothing. Nothing you've done. Nothing you could have done." I felt self-conscious about crying into her long, pretty hair, but there was no way I could stop.

Cassie talked to the doctor in an I-mean-business voice I had never heard from her before. We filled her in on what had happened. A few hours ago, we had been barefoot on the dance floor together. Now her eyes were gleamy with focus in the fluorescent hospital light.

"You're going to need a scan to know for sure," said Cassie. "That's the only way to be positive about what is going on."

The thing was, it was 2 AM on a Saturday night and there was no ultrasound person on staff.

"Is there an ultrasound machine in this hospital?" Cassie asked the doctor. "Can it be wheeled in here?" She knew how to use the machine. She could take care of it herself.

There was no way the hospital would allow that, but I was grateful to have her there, insisting. A medical professional and my friend. I would have to come back Monday, during business hours. We were waiting for the results of my blood test and for my pulse to go down before they would let us go home—back to our Airbnb. It was 2 AM, and then 3, but I no longer felt tired. I thought of the other eight friends who were staying with us in the big barn we'd rented. This wasn't the way I had planned to share the news of my pregnancy.

"I'm really anxious," I said, to explain the racing of my heart.

"Of course you are," said the doctor.

"How could you not be?" said Gavin.

Tony squeezed my hand. He looked exhausted in the stiff industrial chair.

"Can you rub my legs?" They were starting to hurt from all the shaking. He did. I took long, slow breaths so that my heart rate would return to normal, and soon it did, and we were allowed to leave. I cried and cried, for Sweet Pea and Tony and everyone who had been so happy at our happiness. And for me.

The nurse gave me a soft robe to wear home, and a few of those diaper pads, for which I was also grateful. I was still bleeding. I stuffed my soggy jumpsuit into the biological waste bin. Somehow Gav and Cassie had gotten a cab, which was waiting for us. It was almost dawn. My head pounded. I felt seasick and empty. I also felt strong.

Ace

I had my first prenatal doctor's appointment scheduled for the morning after Tony and I flew home to New York. I called the office from Heathrow to let them know it would be a different kind of visit after all. "I'll give the doctor your message," the receptionist told me after I explained the gush of bleeding and the uncertainty of the British ER doctor. But when Dr. Chen opened the door to the antiseptic room where Tony and I waited and reached out her hand for us to shake, she had no idea. I told the story once more. Her eyes were tired and sympathetic.

She wheeled an ultrasound machine into the exam room. It was Tuesday morning. Sunday after the wedding, we had driven to London, checked into our hotel room, and canceled our plans to see friends. I spent all afternoon and evening under the covers, falling in and out of a shallow sleep while Tony flipped through the channels. We ordered room service, but I was too bereft to eat. Tony pushed the full-ish tray back into the hallway. I bled through the last of the gigantic pads from the hospital. Tony went to the pharmacy to get more.

Monday, I felt well enough to walk through Hyde Park before we had to head to the airport. It was dizzyingly sunny, almost anti-London weather. We walked and walked. We went to the rose garden, although the roses were only naked buds—they wouldn't bloom for another month. I sat on the side of the Diana, Princess of Wales Memorial Fountain and watched the water swirl and bubble over the granite. Kids splashed in the flow. I took off my sandals and felt the cool water between my toes. When it was time to leave, I didn't want to go back home, back to real life. I didn't want to know.

The next morning, at Dr. Chen's office, Tony sat in the plastic chair next to me. I wiggled out of my underwear. The doctor tilted the sonogram screen so that we could both see it. Tony and I peered at the image as the cool gel of the wand spread over me. I'm no expert, but I could tell there was nothing in my uterus besides a bunch of sad squiggles.

"That's just some residual tissue," she explained. "I'm so sorry."

There was only static. There was no flutter of a heartbeat. There was emptiness.

I knew I had lost Sweet Pea, I had felt it. But it stung to confirm that she was gone. I wanted her back desperately. Couldn't I just turn back time to Thursday, when I had cried with relief? I would do anything to hear the pit-a-pat of her tiny heart instead of the loud hum of silence.

Dr. Chen answered all our questions. Like *How could this have happened?* "I don't know how much you remember from biology class." *Not very much.* "But when the egg and sperm meet, chromosomes pair up. Usually miscarriage is due to a chromosomal complication. Cell division is a complex process with a lot of things that can go wrong—and when something does, this is your body's natural reaction. In a way, it knows best." I took this to mean that Sweet Pea wasn't meant for this world.

"Having a miscarriage doesn't mean you're more likely to have another one," she said, which felt reassuring, or almost reassuring. She told us, "It's 2019. If you want to have a baby, you are going to have a baby. Where there's a will, there's a way. I hope the next time I see you, it's happy news." Leaving the office, the sun tilted onto our faces. I walked Tony to the subway—he was off to work—and kissed him goodbye.

I bled for another week, and each time I wiped the brick-colored stuff from between my legs, my chest ached. I missed Sweet Pea more than I thought was possible.

It was Tony's idea to say an official goodbye to Sweet Pea. We did it the very next day. He found a beautiful box adorned with butterflies, their wings wide and shiny. We each wrote her a letter. We told her how much we loved her and how much we missed her. We said we'd always remember. We promised the love wouldn't go away. We read the letters to her and to each other, crying so much our mouths turned dry. Then we put them in the box, along with her ultrasound picture and the positive pregnancy test that had been sitting on our bedroom bookshelf for the last month. We closed the lid. For a long time, we hugged and cried, and hugged and cried.

◆ ◆ ◆

I wanted Sweet Pea back. Since that wasn't going to happen, I wanted to get pregnant again as soon as possible. That very instant, ideally. Waiting has never been my strong suit, and I carried around a hollowness so extreme it hurt. The emptiness was visceral. I dreamed I was pregnant and woke up angry with the blow of reality, the loss fresh again each morning.

I had planned to tell my coworkers at the wine website I edit that we were pregnant over the fancy dinner we had every season or so—the occasion would have aligned with the start of my second trimester. I had pictured the whole thing: glasses clinking to toast the new baby-to-be, smiles twinkly in the dim restaurant light.

Instead, I ordered a manhattan. At the restaurant sixty stories above Lower Manhattan, we squinted to see what would have been a spectacular view if the night was not dense with fog. There was plenty to discuss: One of my coworkers had just moved to Jersey City. The other was dating someone who just might be a keeper.

I had different news—Tony and I had thought about getting a puppy for months, but after getting pregnant, we decided it was best to wait. In the past weeks, I'd channeled my grief into a frantic search for someone furry to love.

◆ ◆ ◆

The dog, we had decided, had to be hypoallergenic since my mom is terribly allergic; a few hours in a canine-occupied home leaves her wheezy and swollen. I did a lot of research. Our best options were breeds that didn't shed: Havanese, poodles, Portuguese water dogs, schnauzers.

We went to a big pet adoption event in Union Square the weekend after the miscarriage. It was a warm day and the sun beat down on long lines of eager pet moms, dads, sisters, and brothers that formed in front of each trailer. Kids pressed their faces up against the little glass crates, where dogs slept, barked, or gazed out into the commotion. I crossed all my fingers about coming home with a sweet furry creature.

We decided to choose a line in the shade and park ourselves there. Immediately, I felt discouraged. We were handed a clipboard and I filled out the paper version of a form I had already filled out online, to no response. A grown adult in front of us started screaming, "I want that dog!" while pointing to a panting creature with pointy ears. The volunteer asked her to wait in line and fill out the form—just as everyone else was doing—but her screaming didn't stop. "I want him! That's my dog. That's my baby." The sun was in my eyes; I had forgotten to bring my sunglasses. We waited in that line, and then another. The volunteers said they'd call us if something came up, but I didn't feel hopeful. The lady from our first line was still screaming—we could hear her from across the street. "That's my dog!"

I was parched. I missed Sweet Pea. I started to cry. All these desperate people and all these homeless pups. Why did this feel so hard? Where was our dog? Where was our baby? Tony had to calm me down. He bought me an iced tea and slipped his sunglasses on my face against the glare. I pressed the icy drink up to my face.

We visited a handful of shelters around Manhattan and came home empty-handed. At the ASPCA Adoption Center on the Upper East Side, a woman with half of her head shaved and a big smile listened to our request for an allergy-friendly dog and then took us around to meet the canine residents. They were all very cute. Every single one of them was a pit bull or a pit bull mix.

"Are any of these dogs hypoallergenic?" I asked after we had met the last one, Snoopy, who wagged his tail and gave us the most poignant puppy-dog stare I could imagine. I wanted to bring Snoopy home that instant.

"Can I be honest?"

"Please."

"You're not going to find that sort of dog in a shelter in New York. Those are all designer breeds." Snoopy rested his head on his front paws. Part of me thought, *My mom will just have to use her inhaler,* but the other part of me was still reasonable. When we turned to leave onto East 92nd Street, I looked at the little reception area and willed the waiting families to go home with Snoopy, with all the pit bulls and their strong bodies and sweet eyes.

At night, I'd swipe and swipe on Petfinder and a bunch of other pet apps. I filled out forms and applications. I emailed breeders and rescues.

"Sorry," I kept hearing, "Penelope has found a family in Michigan." Or, "We'd love to add you to our wait list. You will be number sixty-seven."

It was Tony who found a breeder in Yonkers online. They had good reviews, and when I called, they had several poodle-mix puppies available. On a weekday, my mom traveled with me to the end of the 1 subway line, where we caught a cab to meet the litter. On the way back, I had a four-pound Maltipoo in my arms. He was the color of cream, besides his brown ears. He barked and nuzzled and gnawed on the hem on my jeans, and he looked like a teddy bear. I fell for him instantly. My mom kept him company on our couch while I ran to Petco for supplies. I had to ask the nice woman at the store what we needed for a new puppy. I rushed buying nearly as much as I could carry, treats and a leash and chewy toys and bowls for food and water; I couldn't wait to get home to him.

◆　◆　◆

After we ordered lamb chops and Dover sole at my work dinner, I showed the three women pictures of Ace from my phone and told them about our newest family member. Tony had thought of the name, and it stuck. I had wanted to name him after cheese, maybe Taleggio or Roquefort, but those felt like cumbersome names for a little dog to carry. Everyone told me they thought he was very cute, maybe too cute. He could be a puppy model!

Ace peed in the kitchen and in the bathroom. He pooped by the hallway, next to the door, which we thought may be a good sign—he was on the way outside, sort of. We put a Wee-Wee Pad in the kitchen, but he thought it was a toy—he'd pick it up and run in circles around the apartment with it clutched in his jaw. Each time, we had to yank it from his teeth before he tore it into a million pieces. Once he found a tissue box and created a pretty impressive mountain of tissue confetti.

We walked him around the block over and over again, down and up Riverside Park in all its glorious springtime splendor. He'd sniff every tree and every trash can, want to play with every passing dog and person, gaze in rapt attention at every bicycle and garbage truck and kid on a scooter whizzing by. But he wouldn't go potty. Then the moment we'd give up and walk back into the apartment, he'd pee on the carpet inside our front door. We got rid of the carpet. Still, he'd go to the bathroom inside as soon as we got home. I knew he wasn't messing with us, but it sure felt like it.

We had lived in the building for almost two years and met pretty much nobody, as per New York City apartment etiquette. Sure, we'd exchange the occasional cordial *hello* or *have a great weekend*, but that was the extent of my relationships with our neighbors. The moment Ace came home with us, all that changed. People wanted to know his name, his age, his breed, and where we got him. They wanted to invite us to a dog parade or tell us we were using the wrong leash. We got business cards from dog trainers and invitations to puppy playdates. We met people's kids and their cousins who were visiting from Connecticut. We heard all about the building gossip and the rivalries on the co-op board, about who was allowed to decorate the lobby for various holidays.

Ace was cute, but he didn't sleep through the night for a month, and neither did we. I had a full-on nervous breakdown one morning when Ace started barking at 5 AM. I had taken him out at 10 PM, and 3 AM, and I had *just* managed to fall back asleep. Tony had walked him at midnight. My body felt sore from exhaustion, as if each limb weighed a hundred pounds. I am someone who really needs her sleep.

I was grateful for the work dinner; it was a delicious distraction. The lamb chops were charred on the outside and brilliantly juicy. We talked and laughed until we were the very last table in the dining room.

On the subway home from the restaurant, a friend texted to say she was pregnant and due around Christmas. I was happy for her, of course I was, but an acerbic anger welled up in my chest. That she got to keep her baby while mine had been flushed down a British toilet—the whole thing felt unthinkably unjust.

Wow, congrats, I texted her. I'm thrilled for you! I followed it with a string of gleeful emojis, but by the time I came home to my amazing husband and my sweet, crazy puppy—not just his tail but his whole body wiggling in a fit of elation upon my return—I had cried off my mascara and bitten off my lipstick.

◆ ◆ ◆

It turns out we were puppy helicopter parents. We enrolled Ace in not one but two puppy training classes, one via an app and one at Petco. We practiced sitting and lying down and coming when called. We tried crate training with mixed success. But mostly, it was potty training all the time. I took work calls while circling the same route, up the hill to West End and up to 102nd Street, hoping the repetition would do the trick. We kept a detailed log that felt infuriating:

Wednesday
5:00 AM peed outside
7:00 AM peed inside
8:00 AM pooped outside
9:30 AM peed inside
(and on, and on)

One day I cried when we ran out of paper towels. My exhaustion made every little thing feel worse. I used a dish towel to wipe up a small puddle of Ace's pee.

Most of the time, I could work from home. When I had to leave for a day of meetings, or a weeklong barge trip through Bordeaux, we booked Ace a dog-walker who'd text us pictures of him playing in the park or hunched over his dinner in concentration. Still, leaving the apartment to get groceries or go to the gym or meet a copywriting client for coffee filled me with dread. I'd gather his toys, his chewy sticks, some treats. He'd start barking frantically the moment I headed toward the door. I'd stand outside the threshold, waiting for it to stop. Sometimes his barks would turn into a soft, sad whimper. Sometimes I'd be running late and have to go, and the noise of his distress would echo in my head even as I walked to the subway and turned up the music on my headphones.

I would feel an edge of anxiety until I got home, hoping Ace was okay, that he was happy. I kept waiting for him to be sullen, or mad, but there was never a time when he wasn't so overjoyed to see me upon my return that his whole body didn't vibrate with a tail-wagging, body-squirming exuberance. Reader, I have felt a lot of delight in my life. But there is little so perfect as coming home to Ace. When Ace comes in for a cuddle, pressing the whole weight of his warm little body against my hip or my leg, maybe resting his face on my foot, my heart still does a little happy throb.

I was falling behind with my work, which I was usually so on top of. How could I handle a baby when I could barely handle a puppy?

"It's really very similar," said a nice neighbor with two kids in a stroller and a basset hound on a leash who stopped to chat when Ace ran up to first the hound, then the babies. Ace jumped up to lick one of the baby's feet. The baby squealed with delight.

The Petco trainer recommended a fancy spray that would inspire Ace to pee. We were desperate; we bought some. When he did go outside, we celebrated with the recommended thirty seconds of praise (that's a long time!) and multiple treats. Nothing seemed to work. I was taking the failure personally. Here was more proof of my lack of patience.

And then one day, lots of rolls of paper towels and exasperated tears and sleepless nights later, something clicked in Ace's puppy brain. We went outside and he peed and peed again. We went outside a few hours later and voilà. I nearly screamed in excitement. We slept through one night, and then another. We slept through until 5 AM, then 6, then 7. On the weekends, we'd go to the dog park, and then next door to share calamari and beer at the café outside. Ace would stop to play with sticks and other dogs, dig holes in the dirt until his creamy fur was dusty brown. Tony and I would talk about the future and how much we loved our little family. It was so much love it tingled, it was dazzling and abundant, it was more than I could wrap my head around.

Wendy

I hate the word *miscarriage*. The prefix *mis-* brings to mind *misplaced*, *misstep*, *mistake*. Many women who experience that type of loss feel guilty that, because they lifted something too heavy, or had a drink before they knew they were pregnant, or struggled with anxiety or depression, they somehow provoked the pregnancy loss. But these incidents don't cause miscarriage. They just don't. Yet even with that knowledge and reassurance, a nebulous feeling of responsibility can linger. Miscarriages are common, and often completely inexplicable. But I kept thinking about how my body had failed me, had failed the proto-baby growing inside me. It had failed my husband, and my mom, and his mom, and everyone who had been thrilled for us.

The clinical term for miscarriage is *spontaneous abortion*. That's certainly no better.

The month after my loss, I felt pregnant. I knew it. It was my boobs; they were that same kind of terribly achy as before. Smells on the street were amplified: a lady smoking deeply by a bus stop, the stale piss scent on the subway platform, our neighbor down the hall burning bacon in the morning. These scents repulsed me but also gave me hope.

I learned that people called a baby born after a miscarriage a rainbow baby.

Dr. Chen had said there was no need to wait to try to get pregnant again. In fact, some studies show couples are more fertile after an early miscarriage. I hadn't stopped taking my prenatal vitamins—the gummy kind. They tasted like red Jolly Ranchers. I bought another jar and a set of pregnancy tests at the pharmacy. I didn't say anything to my therapist or Tony this time. I went straight to the bathroom and peed.

NOT PREGNANT.

Then once more, for good measure. NOT PREGNANT.

But what about my breasts? My poor breasts! I knew some women's breasts got tender before their periods, but mine never had. I obsessively read everything about pregnancy tests, which measure HCG (human chorionic gonadotropin) hormones. If you test too early, there may not be a high enough concentration of HCG in your urine for the test to detect. I thought I'd wait and see.

Did I mention I am no good at waiting? But oh, how I tried. I waited until my period was one day late, three days late, and when it had been almost a week, I tested again, first thing in the morning, when my pee was supposed to be its least diluted. I stared at the stick while it blinked. Then: NOT PREGNANT.

The next day, I got my period and with it, a sinking sadness. I touched Sweet Pea's box when I walked by it on the way out of my apartment. I wanted to reverse time. The day ahead of me felt endless.

"You'll get pregnant," my therapist assured me. I placed the fuzzy pillow from her couch onto my lap. "Maybe next month, maybe in six months, or a year, but it will happen." She said it with such certainty. She suggested I put the whole pregnancy thing aside and think about it in fall. It was June. I wiggled my toes in my sandals. Though I thought it was an excellent idea, I doubted I'd be able to pull it off. When I really wanted something, I clutched on to it with an out-of-proportion ferocity. Patience is not my strong suit.

I told her I was afraid that the next pregnancy would be tarnished with my fear and the remnants of my grief. It would feel somehow less pure than it had with Sweet Pea. She didn't try to convince me of anything different.

Think about it in fall became a sort of mantra.

I had sex with Tony with a renewed urgency. Lying with my head on his shoulder afterward, I tried not to go down the rabbit hole of hope and frustration. I concentrated on his soft skin and the rise and fall of his chest. I was focused on other things, too, like writing the proposal for this book and finding a new apartment—we were trying to buy our first home in Brooklyn. The idea of owning our own home felt to me fabulously grown up. At first we'd assumed we could never afford it, but it looked as if that might not be the case.

On the weekends, we traipsed through people's homes. We trudged up to fifth-floor walk-ups and took circuitous routes around the city when subways were rerouted for construction. We peeked into their closets, full of plastic dry-cleaning sleeves and mysterious workout contraptions. We stood in bedrooms the size of closets and breathed in the smell of fresh paint and other people's lives.

In each apartment, I wondered, *Will our baby grow up here?* And, *When?*

An apartment, a book, a baby. Wanting, wanting, wanting.

When my period was about to come, I got antsy. I tried to distract myself. I took Ace to the dog park just because, and said yes to invites to mochi pop-up previews and bourbon tastings (tasting would be okay, I figured, even if there was good news). I wrote extra-long emails to my friend in LA. I did face masks. I took on extra work projects.

Ace tore up giant swaths of our living room carpet—little mountains of carpet fibers started to pile up in every corner of our apartment—and I obsessively researched dog-friendly rugs for our new apartment, which did not yet exist. I couldn't bring myself to vacuum, though, unless someone was coming over. Then the vacuum overflowed with puffs of carpet that Ace had turned to carpet snow with his incessant chewing.

Then I got a *really* welcome distraction, an invite to attend and write about a barge cruise through Bordeaux in July, only a month away. I didn't pause, I just responded, **Yes!!** If and when we had a baby, it would become more challenging to go on last-minute European barge cruises. I was in. At times I still felt goose bumps that taking wine cruises through France for work was actually my real life.

The cruise company sent along a waiver to sign, and as I skimmed it, I noticed the mention of a guest.

I wanted to invite Tony, but we had the rest of his vacation days for the year all planned out between our friends' wedding coming up in Spain and our plans to visit his family in England. But the opportunity to share the trip through Bordeaux with someone who'd love it as much as I would was too much to pass up. I asked the coordinator if I could bring my mom. The barge lady said yes. My mom said hell yes.

I was still deeply sad about Sweet Pea, and my mom was sad about Sweet Pea, too. I hated that she was sad. But I understood. What better than a French getaway to cheer us up?

We started our trip with a few days in Paris and a night in Bordeaux. We ate snails dripping in garlic butter, fluffy omelets green with herbs, and drank mineral rosé.

I worried about Ace—I missed him, he was still so little and helpless—but a dog-walker came twice a day when Tony was at work and sent us updates and photos of our puppy with his favorite lamb toy hanging from his mouth. In most pictures, he was blurry from moving. Ace never really sat still, unless he lay splat in puppy sleep.

From a sleepy canal in French wine country, I could check on Ace pulling up the grass in Riverside Park and making puppy friends. I missed my boys already, both the human one and the canine one, but the human assured me the whole point was for me to have as great a trip as possible.

If there is a downside to the amazing opportunity to travel for work, it's that the conferences and barge excursions almost always occur in the off-season, when the weather is uncomfortable or the scenery less resplendent. This had seemed like a particularly amazing opportunity (France in the summer!) but France was experiencing a heat wave—not just any heat wave, but a string of the hottest days on record, ever—and I spent most of the trip unbearably sweaty. By noon, the temperature creeped above 100 degrees. I craved iced coffee, which is a decidedly un-French thing. It seemed impossible to find an iced coffee, cold brew, or an iced latte, anywhere. Most coffee shops and restaurants just didn't have ice machines, so they couldn't even make one if they tried. At a Starbucks in Bordeaux, I willingly sacrificed my worldly cred for an iced latte with extra ice. I knew I was playing the part of an uncouth American perfectly, but my head had started to ache and I could actually feel the individual beads of sweat dripping down my back. Immediately, I regretted not getting a gigantic *venti*. I wished I could jump my whole body into that iced latte.

My mom and I, too hot to eat real dinner, took a baguette, a few pieces of cheese, a fat *saucisson sec*, a little tub of pâté, and artichokes resting in a bath of olive oil back to our hotel—plus a bottle of champagne we picked up for only a handful of euros. We waited until the sun set and there was a semblance of a breeze to unfurl our bounty in the hotel's courtyard. The champagne wasn't quite cold, and we didn't have a knife, so we had to tear off pieces of the baguette with our hands and scoop into our wedges of cheese with plastic forks. It was a perfect dinner.

The next day, Peter picked us up from the Bordeaux train station. Peter Carrington and his wife, Wendy, are the owners of the *Saint Louis*, a tiny hotel barge on a tree-lined canal. I realized I had been given no prep for our time on the barge. I had no idea who these people were, but Peter put us at ease instantly. He was a small, rakish man with silver hair and jokes that kept coming.

It was yet another drippy, sweltering day in Gascony (that's southwest France), but when we reached the barge, Captain Wendy Carrington looked perfectly put together in her pressed blue shirt and crisp white shorts. Wendy was elegant, blonde, and petite. She left her usual spot, the helm of the *Saint Louis* barge, to greet us with her charming Irish accent. The group was small—Stephanie, who had invited us on the trip and helped run the barge company, Prachi, a travel writer from Mumbai, my mom, and me. Stephanie greeted us with hugs. She had a big personality and a big laugh; I liked her instantly. The boat was gorgeous, but the best thing was that it had air-conditioning, not super common in France and a true miracle in the stifling heat.

I had never taken any kind of cruise, and certainly not a barge cruise. The moment I stepped onto the *Saint Louis*, I took a sort of existential exhale. Wendy had greeted us with flutes of champagne. The cook emerged with little compressed globes of watermelon and fresh goat cheese. On the boat, the space was tiny but elegant. There was face spray and night cream in the bathroom of our cabin (I'm a sucker for fancy cosmetics), and the towels were cloudlike. I had a good feeling—this was going to be an excellent few days.

Press trips are often packed with as much as possible: visits to more and more cheesemakers, olive mills, vineyards. Writers would start the days early and end them late and exhausted, notebooks full of scribbles I would struggle to decipher later. This was something else entirely.

A day on the *Saint Louis* started whenever I liked. If I felt inspired to wake up early and join Peter for a croissant run to the bakery in the postage stamp–sized nearby town, great. If I wanted extra time in my comfy robe in my comfy bed (I was officially claiming it as mine!), that was another perfectly sound option. The Wi-Fi was spotty, so I had no choice but to forgo checking my email in favor of reading my novel on the reclining lounger on the sundeck, the canal stretched in front of me, bisecting fields, forest, and blue sky. I had brought my journal, but it remained untouched. I've always been a touch-and-go journaler. If I wanted, I could stroll or bike along the shaded path that stretched alongside the canal. This was best done in the morning, before the day began to blister. Prachi and I would walk together, talking about being a freelance writer in Mumbai versus New York City, or how to know which press trips were wonderful and which were a waste of time. Or if I preferred, I could stay right where I was on the sundeck and help myself to another espresso.

In the morning, Wendy invited us to try our hand steering the barge. The wooden wheel was larger than she was. To make the smallest turn took all my strength, and I had sudden appreciation for Wendy, this small woman with so much grace and power. In front of us, the sleek boat's deck was dotted with pink and purple flowers in bloom. Tree canopies draped the narrow canal for some welcome shade. As a New Yorker, I was instantly fascinated by the quiet. Besides the occasional bird chiming in, the day was almost loud with silence.

Wendy did not set out to pilot a barge, or even a boat. She grew up in Ireland. Her background is in art and design. Through the design world, she met her husband, Peter, a fellow creative soul and food and wine lover.

"About fourteen years ago, school friends of mine invited us to a family barging holiday on the Canal du Midi [in the Languedoc, in southern France]," Wendy remembered. "Peter was not keen, but the food, the wine, and the region won us all over. We were then not boat people and had no idea what to expect, but needless to say, we loved the whole experience." The seed had been planted.

Fast-forward eight years, and Wendy and Peter's kids had grown up, their retail business was feeling the strain of the financial downturn, and their friend's wife had passed away from cancer. The friends decided it was time for a new project—they would leave their lives and their country to buy and run a hotel barge in the south of France.

"It all seemed perfectly sensible—our friend, who had never piloted anything bigger than a hire barge would pilot, Peter would be chef (though a very good cook, he had never worked in a restaurant), and I would be hostess without ever having worked in hospitality!" It sounded like a wild plan, but they went for it. Why not?

Peter, Wendy, and their friend took over the business in 2014. They haven't looked back. "I'm known for my determination," says Wendy. "When our friend had remarried and could no longer pilot, I decided that I would step up, gain my professional license, and become our pilot. I've always been a bit of a behind-the-scenes kind of person. It's difficult to pilot behind the scenes, and piloting has helped me grow my inner confidence and step out from the shadows. I love the fact that I'm doing something really different and challenging, and that I own my space." It was hard for me to think of a nicer office.

France is intersected by an intricate series of antique waterways of canals and rivers meandering through the countryside. Once used for transporting cargo, the barges have been reoutfitted as floating boutique hotels. They sail at the leisurely pace of about four miles an hour (that's quite slow!), perfect for biking or walking alongside, or watching the tiny towns and lush farms roll by from the deck.

The barge is a home base from which to explore the region. The *Saint Louis* sails two routes along the canal in Aquitaine and Gascony. Each day, Peter took us to see tiny cobblestoned towns, old churches, postage stamp–sized bakeries, a generations-old Armagnac producer, and Latour-Marliac, a remarkable garden of water lilies.

The lily garden was like a painting—actually, it was where Monet first got his inspiration—and it looked unreal. Stephanie had urged us all to dress up; she wanted to take pictures of us in the garden, and she wanted to wear her brand-new dress. Stephanie's former career was owning a plus-sized clothing boutique, and she was *tres chic*, with long dark hair and a smile that took over her whole face. Now she had joined her family barging business, started by her mom and run by her sister, which coordinated and sold trips to barges like the *Saint Louis*. These days, Stephanie channeled her talents into marketing amazing experiences rather than beautiful ensembles. I put on one of my favorite summer dresses, and almost immediately felt it dampen and sag with the brutal humidity of the day and my own sweat.

I walked very slowly through the garden. We carried umbrellas to shield us from the sun, but there was nothing to do about the unrelenting heat. It baked us and started to shrivel the lilies, even in their water beds. I wanted to jump in, although the water was certainly tepid at best. When Stephanie urged my mom and me to take a picture by a fountain, we obliged—first us, then her, then Prachi, a pretty Indian woman who wore flowy dresses and big sunglasses. We left our umbrellas for a minute under a tree. In the photos, we're squinty, my hair has frizzed into a poof, and our foreheads are shining with sweat. It is an accurate representation of how I felt in that moment. I made it to the other end of the garden, where they sold Diet Coke with ice, found a spot in the shade, and tried to think cool, calming thoughts as the ice cubes melted and my drink turned lukewarm. My mom joined me, reminding me that I never did too well in the heat, propping our umbrella up near our feet since we had found shade. Getting back into Peter's air-conditioned van was sweet, cool relief. The windows fogged up immediately. My skin still felt scorching to the touch. I angled the vents toward my face.

"How do you still look so great?" I asked Prachi, who had continued to pose for and take photos with Stephanie while my mom and I hid in the shade. Her hair was still shiny and fresh.

"I'm from Mumbai," she said. "I'm used to it."

I was not used to it. Even as the heat sucked all my energy away, I knew each stop was a place I would not have stumbled upon otherwise as a tourist, and the journey was made even richer with Peter's colorful stories. He knew about the sweep of history, the weird owners, the town gossip. In the evening, we returned to canapés and then a four-course meal from the barge's chef, featuring local ingredients and paired with wines from the *Saint Louis*'s six-hundred-bottle cellar that had been curated by an expert in nearby Saint-Émilion. It was a revelation to eat this way, salads peppery with radish and creamy with goat cheese, oysters briny from the sea, meaty crêpes, perfect profiteroles with red strawberries for dessert, simple but extraordinary. A four-course meal every night felt unbearably decadent to my eating-disordered brain, but I knew this was only a few exceptional nights of my life. Was this real life?

One of those four courses was, each night, without fail, a cheese course. The cheeses were familiar to me: Roquefort, Buche de Poitou, and Valençay, served with homemade jams, fresh berries, and crusty baguettes. But each offering was also entirely new, amped up, funkier, runnier, milkier, as if they were the cheeses I knew so well on steroids. We can't get a lot of the good stuff in the US because the FDA stipulates raw cheeses must be aged at least sixty days. Pasteurizing cheese is certainly not bad, but it can rob the final product of much of its nuance. French cheesemakers often produce a totally different product for the American market. The good stuff they keep for themselves in order to meet the regulations. And that was what we were diving into as the night wrapped us in perfect stillness.

The boat Wendy and Peter had originally bought had been a bit old-school and stuffy, with wood paneling and dark colors, and the couple had slowly transformed the look into something classic yet totally modern over the past five years. Off-season, when the barge is not booked with guests, they get to work making sure the boat is perfect, inside and out—that means oil changes, mechanical repairs, and furniture reboots. The work showed. Rich creams and dusty blues gave the boat a light and airy feel. Each room had white orchids and cloud-soft sheets. Wendy created a different table setting for every night—she used tablecloths, jacquard linen napkins, candles, and fresh flowers to design a backdrop that echoed each night's menu. She put Martha Stewart to shame. Her inventive eye for design was everywhere. She even repurposed the former curtain rods to be used along the bar as a footrest.

Everything felt so pretty and effortless, made for Pinterest. But it turns out that piloting a barge is the opposite; Wendy's daily work entails "managing a hundred and forty tons of steel in changing conditions, maneuvering a ninety-nine-foot barge into a hundred-and-one-foot spaces, and having guests join me at the helm to steer short (straight!) sections of the canal." Wendy is a small person, and it takes—as I witnessed—a lot of physical strength to command the boat. After the first season, the whole right side of her body ached. By the time we'd met, she'd gotten used to the work, mentally and physically. Through all kinds of weather, her job requires constant concentration. There's no such thing as a moment to tune out. The safety of her crew and guests rests in her hands. It's demanding work.

When Wendy first began driving the barge, she was "very aware of the reaction of people along the canal to the fact that a woman was piloting. More people watched a woman pilot maneuvering, more so than any male pilot. Some bystanders, mostly men, had advice to give, even though they were not necessarily pilots themselves, and the round of applause once a difficult mooring was completed or some other skill demonstrated was somewhat condescending. Peter would always say something like, 'What did they think you were going to do, leave it in the middle of the canal?'" But the barge world is small, and by the time I visited, most everyone we passed knew Wendy, Peter, and the barge. They waved and we waved back.

I had a realization sitting around the dinner table after the foie gras course had been cleared. Prachi was telling stories about the life of a travel writer, missing her husband during her endless trips, rushing to file a story as a flight attendant urged her to put away her laptop for landing. My mom wanted to plan an epic vacation with my dad to celebrate their fortieth wedding anniversary, which was coming up that year. Prachi suggested a ferry from Helsinki to Saint Petersburg.

"It's once-in-a-lifetime stunning," she told us.

Stephanie, of course, suggested a barge cruise, maybe to Burgundy or the Scottish Highlands.

The rich livers had been served with ripe slivers of nectarines flambéed in Armagnac from a producer we had visited earlier that morning—a woman in a flowery dress and her ninety-year-old father who lived on the vineyard above the barrels of the brandy they pressed, fermented, and distilled, just as his own father had done. She'd poured us a bottle of Armagnac straight from the barrel of Tony's birth year—I had an embarrassing moment where I couldn't remember if it was 1983 or 1984—then sealed the bottle by melting wax over a burner. The foie gras and that Armagnac! It was sweet, savory, meaty, and full of happy depth. It was paired with a miraculously not-too-sweet Sauternes.

I slipped into my cabin to go to the bathroom between courses. When I slid back into my seat, I noticed something: I wasn't wearing any shoes. Neither were my dining companions. It was standard procedure for a boat, but novel to me. I had never had foie gras without shoes on, until that night. Or a four-course meal paired with local wines on a gorgeously set table in my most comfy gym shorts and a T-shirt I like to wear to bed. Outside the window, bright-green tree canopies rustled in a soft breeze. Inside, I wiggled my toes. The whole thing felt sort of radical . . . and really, really good.

I shared my revelation with the group—we were "barefoot in Bordeaux." So catchy! It could be the name of an article, or a lifestyle brand.

At night, I called Tony from the cabin I shared with my mom—she was reading on the balcony—and Ace barked his hello into the phone.

Our apartment search had continued while I was away. We had made an offer on a small but sunny two-bedroom in Prospect Heights, Brooklyn, on a leafy street. I had daydreamed about our lives unfolding there. But someone else had offered more, and more cash, too. Tony had been to see a few more places, and he sent me photos: exposed brick walls, high and low ceilings, new open kitchens, and dated galley kitchens. He made a list of pros and cons. The whole thing felt both exciting and unreal. Would we find a place to live at all?

Outside was the bright light of beauty. Inside I felt trapped in a liminal, hazy space. A home, a book, a baby. Wanting, wanting, wanting.

Wendy had once lived a busy life in Northern Ireland. Now, this was her life. So many people share the fantasy of skipping town and maybe kneading dough in a pocket-sized bakery by an ocean or piloting a luxury barge through the French countryside, the sun shining on our faces. Wendy had made the fantasy her reality.

Was it everything she had hoped? Barge life was not without its challenges—from marketing and booking the boat each season to dealing with the arcane system of licensing in the French territories that they traversed all spring, summer, and fall. But the challenges only made the whole thing feel more rewarding—journalists and their moms sipping Sauternes on the sleek raw-wood dining table she had found, refurbished, set, and would help her staff clear and clean later that night. The next day, she'd wake up before the sun and do it all again.

At the end of the day, it's the community that Wendy loves being a part of. And for the guests—they usually stay for a week, and a lucky few return every year—getting to visit this other world of canals crisscrossing the verdant landscape of Bordeaux, of time becoming as languid as the water, is what makes the experience so extraordinary. "*Saint Louis* is not just a barge holiday," Wendy explains. "It's an insight into another life where the focus is on personal connection and relationships. Very often our guests leave us reflecting upon their experiences on board and the friendships made."

My time on the *Saint Louis* was the opposite of what I had imagined a cruise to be; the stereotype had led me to expect the commercial and generic. Barging with a crew—a family—is an intimately personal experience. It unfolded slowly, at four miles an hour over an espresso or a Diet Coke or a glass of champagne or Bordeaux, with lots of conversation and laughter, and sometimes just birdsong and the old, brilliant-green trees out the window. Stephanie, Prachi, my mom, Wendy, Peter, their lovely chef, and I became our own sort of makeshift family on the water for a few days, a blink in time.

At its best, travel gives us more than aspirational Instagram posts and stirring stories. My experience is rooted in the meals I get to share, the moments of connection over cheese from the local Saturday market or pastries flaky with butter. The food comes from a unique moment, a place, a set of hands, a culture. It comes with its own stories, and then I get to add my own memories to the mix. My world intersects with people like Wendy or Prachi for a meal, a few days, a week, and it is richer for knowing these women. We come home a little bit changed. I love my life in New York City. I don't know what I would have to do in order to live a life that was "barefoot in Bordeaux" all the time, but I know myself well enough to know I'd get restless. I thought about Prachi, a dedicated food and travel journalist like me who freelanced, traveling three out of four weeks to write stories about rooftop bars in Hong Kong and avant-garde design in Helsinki. Her life sounded thrilling. But it also sounded a little bit lonely.

When it was time to say goodbye, nobody wanted to leave. On the one hand, I wanted to lie back on that recliner again and feel the nighttime air on my skin for just a little while longer. On the other, I couldn't wait to be back in Tony's arms in our New York City apartment (our *for now* apartment), the traffic screeching by outside, the soft fur of my puppy's little head resting on my leg. For me that cliché always rings true. I love travel, I am enormously lucky to get to see so many different places and meet so many incredible people as a food journalist. But the best part for me, hands down, is coming home.

◆ ◆ ◆

When my period was a day late, two days late, I remembered the last month. The sinking disappointment of NOT PREGNANT. I remembered: *Think about it in fall.* It was August, and I was back in New York, where I had immediately reestablished my iced coffee habit. New York was so hot my iced latte had become a room-temperature latte in the time it took to wait for the subway to come banging down to the platform. I pressed it against my sweaty forehead in vain.

It was Monday. I told myself that on Friday I'd take a pregnancy test. The week dragged and dragged. Every time I went to pee, I looked for blood. When Friday came around, I was too nervous to find out. I'd wait one more day. It would be the weekend, and Tony could scrape me off the floor or jump up and down with me, depending on what it said on that plastic stick.

Saturday morning, I woke up fully alert. I went straight to the cabinet where I had an extra pregnancy test. I peed in a cup, just to be safe, and reread the directions that I could have recited by heart. Then I read them again. I dipped the absorbent tip into the cup and set the timer on my phone for ten seconds. I couldn't quite trust myself to count to ten. I turned the stick over and placed it gingerly on a paper towel. I stared at it, not blinking while the cursor blinked and blinked.

Reader, I was pregnant.

I was PREGNANT.

My heart flipped into my stomach. Tony was still half-asleep in our bed, his left cheek gently creased from the pillow. Our humidifier puffed humid air. I jumped onto the mattress with that stick and held it up for him to see. Together, we smiled and cried, and the whole weekend went by like that in a haze of joy and disbelief and worry. We didn't tell anyone the news, not just then. We kept this tenuous moment to ourselves.

Rachel

Fall 1991

Days off from preschool did not make me happy. It was on such days that my mom, Rachel, would leave me at the mercy of her father.

My mom had gone to graduate school to study social work and then worked for nonprofits, advocating for rights and equity for people with disabilities. During my childhood in Baltimore, she worked hard, long hours. She ran group homes and then worked at Sheppard Pratt, Baltimore's biggest mental health care system. They had a Gothic-looking campus on a green hill with an imposing gate at its entrance. Before cell phones, I remember the beep of her pager at all hours, in the car, on the weekend, late at night when I was supposed to be asleep. Her whole body seemed to clench in response to that dreaded sound.

I liked the cool, manicured lobby of Pop-Pop's apartment building. I also liked pushing the button to rouse the elevator. But as we'd ascend the six floors, I'd grow teary, holding tight to my mother's legs, amassing dread for apartment 6C. My mom was sympathetic, tucking a loose strand of hair behind my ear, but impatient to get to work. Pop-Pop's apartment was a different universe from the glossiness of the uniformed doorman and soaring flower arrangements downstairs. Pop-Pop smoked a lot of cigarettes while watching golf or the local news, and his place was thick with that smoke and the TV droned. The dark familial antique carpets trapped the leathery odor of tobacco and old man. So, somehow, did the waxy green plants that he and I would water later to assuage our midafternoon boredom, his speckled, wrinkly hand clamped tight over my small one to steady the pitcher.

Pop-Pop would answer the door sheepishly, in his robe and slippers. "You're early," he would say to my mom. "I need a minute, I'll get dressed." My mom would roll her eyes and check her watch. I would will her to have a change of heart, call in sick from work, and liberate me from a never-ending day in Pop-Pop's custody. But she never did.

Mom would escape with a hug and a requisite *Be good*, although I never understood what being good entailed, or that an alternative path existed. My anxiety would swell as I sat alone on the couch, swinging my legs furiously. But when Pop-Pop arrived eons later—everything happened unnervingly slowly in apartment 6C—he would have shed some of his just-roused-from-bed grumpiness. He'd tuck in his checkered polo, fasten his belt, and run a comb through what remained of his wet hair, grazing his freckled scalp. Sometimes he'd switch off the TV and turn on the radio, hum along to a soaring symphony. Sometimes he'd attempt a hug, which he treated as an elaborate and uncomfortable production, as if it were a foreign practice he had observed but never himself attempted. He would squat to my height, stiffly, his behind sticking way out, and offer up his arms without opening them wide enough for me to wiggle between.

Pop-Pop and I made an odd couple. Even at the age of devotion to *Mary Poppins* and my raggedy teddy, I was keenly aware of the awkwardness between Pop-Pop and me. He had been entrusted with an enormous burden: a whole day with his granddaughter. A few decades before, he had played with his children only sporadically (a fact my mom attributed to his generation more than to his character). I think my mom felt a little guilty leaving me with him. Since my grandmother, his wife of thirty years, had died just six weeks before I—his first grandchild—was born, he had spent the vast majority of his days alone. That seemed to be how he liked it.

A few years after his wife's death and my birth, Pop-Pop sold their house near Boston. They had settled there after being pushed up and down the East Coast for years by his job as an engineer for NASA's first space missions. He did work on the trip to the moon, and later for missile defense. He had loved being part of the space program, the hugeness of it, the possibility, but when NASA's budget was cut and cut again and he found himself designing obscure military parts, he lost any joy he had once had for his work. Pop-Pop had been relieved to retire.

I wish I could have gotten to know Helen, Pop-Pop's wife, my grandmother. I'm named after her—her Hebrew name was Hannah. My parents wanted to name me Emma, but when Helen passed, they decided I should get hers, as per the Jewish tradition of naming your kids after a dead relative. They *really* thought I was going to be a boy named Max. My dad said that after my mom's long Rosh Hashanah labor, "When the nurse cried out, 'It's a girl,' we had sort of forgotten that babies came in different kinds."

So all I have from Helen is a slim pencil skirt that she knit, my mom's stories, and a few pictures in black and white of her looking stern. Recently, my mom cleaned out some closets and found the letters she wrote home from college to her parents, Helen and Joe, but the saved notes were only from her side of the conversation.

I've always loved the Helen stories. My mom says Helen could usually be found on the couch with the TV on, a book open on her lap, some knitting going, and a cigarette hanging from her lip. Helen was the original multitasker. Her house, it turns out, had always been thick with cigarette smoke, which my mom blamed for her and her brother's asthma. She'd have a martini and be knitting a scarf or a sweater. This is how I picture Helen—elegant but antsy, educated but bored, in a fog of smoke.

Apparently, she read more than anyone in the world. She read books about philosophy and feminism. She read romances and women's magazines. She read through libraries faster than they acquired new books. She kept big piles of unreturned library books that quickly accumulated late fees that she intended to pay but never got around to.

She had multiple sclerosis. She was constantly sick as she grew from child to teenager to young adult. The doctors decided that the stress of knowing about her disease would make her condition worse, so they urged her family to keep mum. In retrospect, it seems cruel. Isn't it more stressful to feel horrible without any explanation?

Helen grew up tough if not happy. As an adult, she expected those around her to have the same type of fortitude. She may have always been depressed, but she liked her life in Queens. She attended the opera and the ballet and the theater. She took my mom and David, my mom's little brother, to Bloomingdale's. My mom was fitted for dresses and David for suits. Helen wanted her family to look like the Kennedys. She got dressed up in dresses with cinched waists and went to fancy parties with endless cocktails. Her dream would have been to move to the Upper West Side. Instead, Helen and Joe moved their young family from Queens to Horsham, Pennsylvania, when my mom was in middle school. I have Helen's city love in my blood. And her book love.

But the deepest, darkest enclave of the suburbs was where Joe's job took them, and so they went. Helen hated it. She felt isolated and lonely and detached from all the cultural hubs that had made her feel a part of something bigger.

Criticism was Helen's love language. "Getting pregnant with you was the only thing I ever did right in my life according to my mother," my own mother told me. My mom always knew her mom loved her, but she was unrelentingly hard on her.

After Helen died, newly alone, Joe moved to Baltimore, where his daughter had a house, a job, a husband, and a toddler. But Pop-Pop kept a remarkable distance from my mother's life—soon our life—considering the proximity of his apartment and his newness to the city. Once a week, he'd show up dutifully to my parents' house for dinner. He liked cake and we rarely ate dessert, so he'd bring a crumb or coffee cake in a box from a bakery. I liked the cake. Other than that, Pop-Pop's presence felt unremarkable to me.

Things were different when I visited him. I was in his territory. He and I, we were responsible for each other. A hug from Pop-Pop could not have possibly broken any ice between us, and he proved entirely inept at the banter adults learn to offer to children, usually in the form of a series of questions about lost teeth and birthdays. I don't know how we first arrived, miraculously, at an activity we both enjoyed. It must have brought him tremendous relief.

The French toast was a dance. We'd make a production about the decision to make it, as if the possibility of its preparation had to be, each time, freshly conceived. *Have you eaten?* he'd ask. I hadn't. My answer was always the same, independent of whether I had ingested a bowl of Cheerios an infinite hour before. I'd watch as he'd scour his kitchen for the potential makings of a breakfast worthy of his growing granddaughter, perhaps mumbling something about the ineptitude of his daughter for having failed to feed me. Laminate cabinets were opened and shut, the fridge—naked except for a single snapshot of me sporting a baseball hat and holding a mini golf club—meticulously raked. One by one he'd assemble the components of our meal: eggs, milk, vanilla, cinnamon, and the crucial stale challah. *What could we possibly put together with all this?* he'd muse. First with prompting and later with none, I'd suggest French toast.

One morning, there was no challah. He cursed his indefensible failure as he extracted a loaf of cinnamon-raisin bread from his bread box. "Your mom didn't tell me until last night you were coming," he confessed, "and the Jewish bakery was closed." I excused his failure to keep up the charade of the French toast's spontaneity. By now, challah French toast was tradition.

"We could make pancakes instead," he offered. But I insisted on French toast, with or without the chewy challah. As always, he instructed me precisely. "Put the butter in the pan. That's not enough butter. That's too much butter. You just want to coat the pan." He taught me to crack the eggs every time, as if he had never taught me before. "Flick your wrist, not your arm. Hard, like you mean it." The batter had to be half egg and half milk, or else it would be too watery or too eggy. He put the fork in my fist and wrapped his own leathery palm around my hand. It was important to whisk the batter, not stir it, and my hand would tense up in his concentrated grip as we slammed and clopped the fork together back and forth across the bowl. It was important to let the challah soak up the egg and the milk. It was important to wait for the butter to get bubbly and hot. If a drop of water spattered in the cast iron, he'd hold up the pan close to the range and I could transfer a thick piece of sopping bread from the bowl to the hot surface, adding a final sprinkle of cinnamon. But not *too much* cinnamon. Flipping the toast at the precise moment was his job, as years of experience had endowed him with intuition to know when the bread had acquired the perfect golden skin.

We would set the table before we cooked, real maple syrup and butter, knife with the sharp part facing in, so we could eat as soon as our flawless breakfast was ready. Pop-Pop slid the finished steaming challah right from pan to plate. He taught me at each meal, as if he had never taught me before, to use a knife and fork properly, switching hands to cut, then to eat, perhaps mumbling something about the ineptitude of his daughter at having failed to teach her daughter proper table manners.

My mom told me her happiest childhood memories of Pop-Pop were from when she was a little girl in Sunnyside, Queens. He was going to school for engineering at Brooklyn Polytech during the day and working a night job changing the tubes on one of the first-ever computers—a building-sized beast, in the MetLife building in Manhattan. After work, he'd stop at the bakery, which would be just opening, for fresh crullers and hot rolls. Back at home, he'd wake up Rachel for breakfast, scrambling eggs to eat with their bakery bounty. It was their time together, before Joe would wake up Helen and fall into bed for some much-needed rest.

Pop-Pop was picky, but he admitted that the cinnamon-raisin bread made perfectly acceptable French toast. Maybe even delicious French toast. Maybe. Next time, though, I should make sure my mother gave him plenty of warning that I was coming. Or at least that she call before the bakery closed at eight.

◆ ◆ ◆

I knew I wanted to live in New York City the first time I visited. I was eight, and my mom and I stayed with her brother on Jane Street in the West Village. I slept on the couch, which felt decadent. Mom took me to Broadway to see *My Fair Lady*, my favorite musical of all time (I watched the film with Audrey Hepburn and Rex Harrison at least weekly). I thought I had ascended to actual heaven. When we went to Radio City to watch the Rockettes high-kick their way through the Christmas Spectacular, I found it unbearably boring.

Mom explained that Macy's in Herald Square was the very first Macy's ever, a mesmerizing fact, hard to wrap my kid head around. To me, Macy's were ubiquitous fixtures in malls everywhere. This one was different. This one had a wooden escalator—proof of its history. We rode it up to the top, where we sipped hot chocolate in the holiday shopping din. Mom let me watch the children wait in line to sit on Santa's lap, even though we didn't celebrate Christmas. Their faces were luminous in a sea of confetti snow and shiny lights that blinked on, off, on, off.

But it was walking through the Village that made me feel that I was both somewhere very, very far away and that I was home. There were women in tan coats sitting outside of cafés with long cigarettes in their lipsticked lips. A man with a billowing cape tapped his cane as he walked. Shops sold chess pieces and musical instruments and buttery croissants. People spoke all kinds of languages on the sidewalks, and the streets circled back in on themselves. There were secrets, and possibility, and promise.

A street vendor hawked puffy scarfs and hats in bright rainbow colors. I wanted one, and bad.

"Can we stop?"

"Sure." Mom seemed happy there, too. After her time in Sunnyside, Queens, Pop-Pop's job took her family to Maryland, Massachusetts, and Pennsylvania. She became an expert at being new in school and learned to enjoy the suburbs in a way her mother hadn't. But she loved New York City. They had all been happy there.

I tried on a scarf the shade of Pepto-Bismol. It looked sort of like a giant cotton ball, with hundreds of little and big pink fuzzy cotton balls affixed. I thought I would never find a scarf like that in Baltimore.

My mom haggled with the street vendor and bought me the scarf. I was surprised and moved by her spontaneity, generosity, and negotiating skills. It was as if the city had brought out a sparkly side of her.

"Look." The scarf vendor's voice was deep and throaty. "It doubles as a hat." He wrapped the monstrosity around my head. He handed me a hand mirror to examine the look.

I loved it. I thought I looked funky, unique, urbane.

I assumed everyone would check me out as I walked through the streets in my crazy new accessory, but no one batted an eye. It was New York: everything was allowed, nothing was weird.

"When I grow up, I'm going to live here," I told my mom. Her smile was as bright as the city at night, all lit up. I meant it.

◆ ◆ ◆

My parents met during college at the University of Chicago, before she went to social work school and began her career in nonprofits. For a long time, she earned more money than my dad. My parents have been married for more than forty years, yet I remember her telling me, "Never be financially dependent on a man." When I was in her belly, she took me to DC to march for women's rights. I always think of her as a good feminist.

My freshman year of high school, we moved from Baltimore to Princeton, New Jersey. My dad had accepted a new job running technology for a pharmaceutical company, and my mom found herself not really knowing what to do. She had a new part-time job consulting at a school for kids with special needs by the Jersey Shore, but it still left her plenty of time and flexibility, something she wasn't particularly used to. In Baltimore, she had been a big deal. In New Jersey, she was a newbie. She wanted a change from her go-go-go days, to let go of the pager, but it was a struggle to fill that extra time.

My mother and I were driving down route 1 on a sunny afternoon when we saw a sign—Whole Foods was opening in Princeton. They were hiring. "You and your dad made fun of me," she remembers. "You said I may as well get a job at Whole Foods because I would be spending all my time there anyway." I've definitely inherited my mother's outsized love for groceries and great food stores.

On a whim, we stopped by and she filled out an application for the prepared foods department. They called her back the next day—she had an interview with the team, including several former restaurant people who had pivoted to grocery in search of more humane hours. Mom is an excellent cook. She cooked with Helen from Craig Claiborne's *The New York Times Cookbook* and baked with her grandma Sarah—Joe's mom—in her tiny Brooklyn kitchen. Sarah made rich German Jewish food. My mom remembers rolling out dough for *lokshen* (egg noodles) and puff pastry in her apron, standing on a step stool to better reach the layers and layers of dough, and the smell of sour cream coffee cake and kugel baking. She remembers how much the rest of the family loved the goodies, and how proud she felt at having helped make them. The family dynamics could be complicated, but the food was a bright spot, pure joy.

Days after the interview, Whole Foods called and told her she was in. Her new foodie career was about to begin.

Although, it wasn't *entirely* new. As a high school student in Framingham, Massachusetts, my mom had lied about her age to get a job waiting tables at the Copper Kettle diner. "I had a uniform like nurses wore then, with a little dress, white shoes, a white hat, and a black apron." Sadly, she told me there is no photo documentation of this. She worked the overnight shift so it wouldn't interfere with her school schedule—"I went straight from there to school in the morning." The diner was painfully slow, so she didn't make too much money, although she did "talk to a lot of depressed people."

She lied again to land her next gig at an Italian restaurant called La Cantina, also in Framingham, this time by telling them she had more experience than she did. Every table got bread, soup, and salad, plus often cocktails—it was a lot of timing to manage. "I was always in the weeds," she said. "I couldn't get the rhythm."

When the owner sat her down and told her, "You have a bright future ahead, but it won't be in waiting tables," Rachel remembers shaking her head, holding back tears, and insisting, "Yes, it will!"

She was determined and stubborn. There were other reasons that kept her waiting tables, too. She loved getting paid in a wad of cash at the end of the shift. Something about the work felt energizing and gratifying. During a shift, she wasn't stuck behind a desk, and she genuinely enjoyed meeting people she otherwise never would have crossed paths with.

My mom told me about her waitressing past while she and I were sharing some meze in Brooklyn, a few months after my miscarriage. We had just been to more open houses, and we ended the long day dipping puffy pita into baba ghanoush and labneh. I recognized her reasons as almost completely the same as my own. I had applied to my first restaurant job on Craigslist at the age of eighteen and fallen in love with the energy, the pace, the people and their outsized personalities, this other world I entered when I zipped up my black hostessing dress.

When Mom moved to Chicago for college, she looked for another restaurant job. Her parents could help her out with tuition, but they didn't have the means to cover all her costs. She landed at a Greek restaurant called Kaffenio, where one night, the owner sat her down.

"Do you see her?" He pointed to one of Rachel's fellow servers. "She is like a ballerina. You are like an elephant." It seemed, perhaps, her future wasn't as a waitress.

My mom moved from restaurants to bars, where she worked as a cocktail waitress and a bartender. Turns out she was a truly amazing cocktail waitress. "I had an uncanny ability to look at someone and remember what they were drinking," she told me. "It was simpler than waiting tables, plus usually people were drunk and grateful."

Rachel had some really "dark days," as she calls them, at college. She had just been through an agonizing breakup. My mom has always been incredibly smart, but she hadn't had the sort of high school education that adequately prepared her for the rigors of the University of Chicago, and she struggled in many of her classes. A professor once scribbled on her final paper, *You have a great personality, but you're not University of Chicago material.* In her sophomore year, someone broke into her apartment and tied up and raped her and her roommate. She felt like everything was coming unraveled.

On top of that, there was trouble at home. Her mom's physical and mental health were declining—Helen had tried to kill herself. She had been to the hospital for a mysterious "operation" that she refused to share any details about. Helen urged my mother, despondent by the loss of her then boyfriend, to come back home to Framingham for a while.

Mom refused. "My life is here." She had grown up tough like Helen had insisted.

So Helen flew to Chicago. But almost as soon as my grandmother arrived, she came down with a torturous migraine. She curled up in her daughter's bed and didn't leave for about a week, until it was time for her to fly home to Massachusetts.

My mom needed a change, but going back home to a life that was in tumult and held no prospects for her future wasn't even an option. She thought living with a bunch of people in Chicago would feel better and safer. A friend told her there was a room available at a socialist collective called the Winter Palace in Hyde Park. She described the palace as a "big, beautiful mansion with a lot of hallucinogens and a game of Dungeons and Dragons that went on for a year and a half."

Soon after she moved into the Winter Palace, Rachel got another waitressing job, this time at Ciral's House of Tiki, also called "The Tiki." The Tiki bar had opened in 1962 and thrived for almost forty years before it closed, serving stiff, sweet rum concoctions in tiki heads and piña coladas in fake coconuts to a colorful cast of "cops, students, sex workers, and locals," according to my mom. The signature drink, the Zombie, was made with six shots of five different rums, with an obligatory umbrella on top. Wicker monkeys hung from the rafters, and blowfish lamps glowed late into the night.

When the campus bar closed at 1 AM, the rush started at Mom's new job, which stayed open until 4 or 5 AM on Saturdays. My mom remembers the cops storing their guns behind the bar before ordering their first drink at The Tiki.

Bea and Ted, a warm older Jewish couple usually outfitted in Hawaiian shirts, owned The Tiki, and they created a sort of substitute family for my mom during this rough time. Her dark days were literally dark. When her shift ended in the small hours, she'd go out for breakfast with her fellow waitstaff—career servers, not students—then head home and get some rest, missing daylight entirely, and then repeat the whole thing again. Her classes suffered, but The Tiki was a warm bamboo-curtained respite in the cold Chicago winter. The tips were pretty good, too.

High on acid one shift, Rachel had a moment of blissed-out joy "marrying" the ketchup bottles (combining the contents of two or more near-empty bottles to create a full bottle, a piece of side-work I've spent many hours of my life engaged in). "It just seemed so absurd, but in a sort of great way."

The chef, an older Black man who had come from the South during the Great Migration, cooked a family meal for the staff every night—my mom ate her first collard greens at The Tiki. The menu featured pupu platters and, strangely, fish and chips, but the family meal was straight soul food. "Everyone took a lot of pride in their work" and looked after each other. At The Tiki, Bea and Ted weren't about to tell my mom to move more like a ballerina. "They worried about me, but I knew as long as I showed up to work, was honest, and did my job, I wasn't going to be fired."

But Mom eventually decided she needed to focus on school. Leaving The Tiki was a bit like leaving a family. She had just given her notice when she met my father in a Psychoanalytic Interpretations of Literature class. She was a senior, and he was a junior.

"Marty saved my life," she told me that afternoon as I finished asking the waiter for more pita. I had gone my entire life without realizing that.

I *had* known what attracted her to him—he was a nerdy Jewish boy who could replace the engine in the beat-up truck he used to deliver the student paper without breaking a sweat. They went to see *An Unmarried Woman* and then to Due's for pizza.

After their first date, my dad asked my mom for her number.

"I wasn't going to sit around waiting for him to call," she told me. "So I asked for *his* number."

"I knew that trick," Marty remembers. He thought he was getting a polite rejection, but she actually called.

Two years later, they were still together, living in a basement apartment on the north side of Chicago. My dad needed a suit for a job interview, and a department store was having a big sale. They went together and realized the store didn't sell men's clothes. Still, they browsed before they left and noticed there was a sale on jewelry. My mom found a ring she loved and they brought it home.

Later, my mom called Helen and updated her on their day—the suit, the ring.

"Is it an engagement ring?" Helen asked her daughter.

"Hold on," my mom said, covering the phone with her palm. "Marty!" she called across their apartment. "Is the ring an engagement ring?"

"Sure," he said. And that was that. They've lived happily ever after.

In her twenties, Rachel embarked on a short-lived catering career. She and my dad had just moved from Chicago to DC, where she'd landed a prestigious presidential internship after graduate school. One of her friends, who had also moved from Chicago, was about to get married.

"Is it okay if I just serve champagne and Brie?" this friend asked Rachel. The year was 1983.

"No! People are coming to celebrate; you have to feed them," my mom told her. She offered to cater the affair as her wedding gift. She twisted puff pastry cheese straws and whittled veggies into crudités. She steamed shrimp with the shells on and assembled a cheese platter. "It was the eighties; I made three different kinds of phyllo triangles," she told me. "I really, really enjoyed it."

It was hard work, but it was extremely satisfying. At her government job, there was no concrete beginning, middle, or end to her work. Catering was entirely different. She must have had a knack for the job, because two wedding guests asked if Rachel could cater big events they were planning. My mom said yes.

She dreamed up the menus and budgeted her ingredients "like a real caterer," she recalled. The next wedding was at a public park. My dad helped her set up tables and supplies—there was a lot of grunt work. Rachel did the bulk of the prep in their tiny apartment kitchen. She made a Thai beef salad and stained the pages of her *Frog Commissary Cookbook*. Again, the night was a success.

"I remember sitting on the front porch at the end of the night with your dad, counting the cash and drinking a cold bottle of beer. It was such a great feeling."

Years later when I was in elementary school, Rachel auctioned off kosher Indian dinner parties for some fundraiser at our reconstructionist synagogue in Baltimore. This was a happy time in our household—I got to taste-test trial runs of puffy, hot garlic naan and cumin-scented cauliflower. She tried out her new dishes on us—tandoori chicken, coconut soup with lemongrass shrimp, mushrooms and goat cheese that would turn gooey and blister under the broiler. Our kitchen smelled like ginger and percussed with the popping of mustard seeds.

As for me, when I hit thirteen, I was full of resentment. My teenage angst was a full-time job, and I channeled it all into the injustice that was our move to the dreaded suburbs.

After Jewish preschool, my liberal mom and dad had intended to send me to Baltimore city public school, but a trip to the elementary school down the block changed their minds fast.

So they drove me each morning to a fancy all-girls' school in leafy Roland Park, the only private school that had a spot for me so close to the start of the school year. Everyone wore ponytails tied with crisp pastel ribbons and scratchy blue uniform skirts.

I was one of the few kids who arrived from Baltimore city and not the neighboring pristine suburbs or pony farms. Almost all the girls had moms who stayed at home. I was jealous when they got picked up in SUVs right after the day ended; I had a few hours to kill at the after-school program, which meant a quiet study hall with breaks for microwaved popcorn and when it was nice out, trips to the playground.

"This is where the slaves used to live," we learned during a fifth-grade field trip to a classmate's historic home. Her house had a name. "They liked it here."

When I told my mom at night, she rolled her eyes.

I was painfully ready to get out of my preppy school, ready to stop feeling like an outsider, ready for a change of scenery. My planned escape route was the Baltimore School for the Arts, a high school in an old, chandeliered hotel in the pretty part of downtown. In my thirteen-year-old mind, everyone there was a brilliant artist. They sang and danced in the hallways. Once a slightly more than indifferent cellist, I began practicing daily, religiously, as my acceptance rode on a single audition. I watched *Fame*. I was sure this school would be exactly like that. I practiced some more. I got in.

Suddenly, my world was sparkling with grand prospects. I would be a cool and urban artiste. I occupied myself with fantasies of my new friends, my new wardrobe—after eight years in a uniform, this was no small thing. The Baltimore School for the Arts sat on a cobblestone road, near my favorite coffee shop and Peabody Square. Things were looking up.

But I knew my dad was looking for a new job. I knew he was looking in New Haven and Austin and Boston. I was terrified.

We weren't alone in Baltimore. Pop-Pop was there, just a short drive away in a new development called Cross Keys that smelled more like air freshener and less like old man, home to the famous French toast. On one of his visits to our house, over cake from the white bakery box, I told Pop-Pop about Baltimore School for the Arts.

"Are you sure you want to be a musician?" He was skeptical.

"I'm sure," I told him. I'd drag my music stand to the living room and play something on the cello for him. He'd nod. Never praise, but sometimes a smile.

The summer before high school began, my parents broke the news of our departure to Jersey in my favorite Chinese restaurant. I cried into my garlicky string beans. Rage bubbled up below the surface of my skin. I hated my dad for doing this to us and my mom for letting him. They looked miserable. I wouldn't let them hug me. Instead, I plotted my escape. I was full of teenage bravado. I would live with a friend, on the street. I would stay there, in the city where I belonged.

My one childhood move had been from a Charles Village row house to an old Mount Washington home on a hill just a few miles away. I had stayed at the same school. In Mount Washington, there was an exotic new acquisition: a backyard. We were no longer on the route to the hospital, which meant new, eerie, siren-free nights. But Princeton was a whole different story. I was opposed to the suburbs, aesthetically and morally.

But at fourteen I had little choice in the matter. I visited Princeton with my dad. He was plagued with guilt but trying to put an optimistic spin on the situation. We ate pizza and walked around the town. It was tree-lined, lovely, hard to hate in the sunny spring.

"The youth orchestra here is a big deal," he told me, as if that would be reassuring. "It's supposed to be the best in the state."

I auditioned. Carefully, I played the same song I had rehearsed about a million times for the Baltimore School for the Arts. The conductor spoke in a thick Russian accent and kept slapping his hand against the wall and my chair, as if giving them a good spanking. He scared the shit out of me. I cried when I left the building, a squat cement structure that was fluorescently lit, and again when a call came a few days later to inform me that I did not get in. I knew I had reached the depths of agony, and that life in Princeton was destined to be wretched. This was a sign.

Pop-Pop was sick. He had lung cancer. He had quit smoking just a few weeks before his diagnosis, as if he had known something was going on.

He had smoked since he was a teenager, but when the doctor asked if he was a smoker, his only answer was no. After all, he hadn't enjoyed a cigarette in two weeks.

In our new New Jersey house, Pop-Pop took the master bedroom. My parents set him up with a good view of the TV for golf and news. It played constantly and loudly. Sans cigarettes, the Pop-Pop smell I was used to was missing. The room's sterile cleaning-supply odor signaled looming death. Pop-Pop was feeling worse and worse, wheezing more. His already hunched-over body seemed to curl into itself. He was perpetually spiraled. My mom took time off from her new jobs to drive him to the hospital for tests, and then for chemo. His trips downstairs—usually to the kitchen—became increasingly difficult ordeals, and then increasingly rare. He watched CNN, heavily medicated as airplanes hurtled into the World Trade Center exactly a month before his death. Pop-Pop became obsessed with devising intricate ways to shoot down the planes, ways to strike back. His missile-defense experience, engineering skills, and drug-induced distance from reality spurred constant, wild scribbling on a yellow notepad. He asked for a calculator, and I happily sacrificed my ninth-grade geometry home-work. Watching him poke at it aggressively and incessantly scared me, though. I excused myself from his room.

My mom began to bite her nails, though she'd never been a nail-biter. "He's really losing it," she said to me, my father, and anyone who would listen. She begged Pop-Pop to hand over the pencil, but Pop-Pop was proudly stubborn. Then my mom arrived at a solution. This was our first time with cable TV, and we stumbled upon a new, wondrous thing. It was the Food Network, a station of endless cooking shows. Pop-Pop shifted his obsessive fixation from bombs and missiles to *Emeril Live*.

"Bam!" I heard all the way from my bedroom across the hall. I sprawled on my bed, reading Ginsberg poems and listening to sad music; the cooking show sliced through my focus.

When Pop-Pop couldn't bear lying in bed any longer, propped up or not propped up, he would venture downstairs to the kitchen. At first, he would make himself something to eat. As his health deteriorated, he still wanted to be in the kitchen. It was where the action was.

On one of his last trips out of his room, all the way downstairs, the two of us spent a rare few minutes together.

"Can you make me some scrambled eggs?" he asked in his gravelly voice.

"Sure. Will you tell me how to do it the way you like them?" I knew Pop-Pop was exacting. He really loved eating; it was his great comfort. But as his illness progressed, he started to lose his appetite. He longed for his favorite foods, but couldn't actually stomach them, or much of anything.

He barked orders. "Keep the eggs moving," he corrected as I put down the spatula, the kindness from our earlier days of French toast gone from his voice. "They should be wet, but not too wet. You have to keep stirring or you'll mess the whole thing up."

"Damn it," he said, stunning me with his anger. "You overcooked them."

He left me and the bungled eggs behind and ever so slowly ascended the stairs to his room. I spooned them onto a plate and sat down alone at the kitchen table. To me, they tasted delicious.

"He's never going to get out of that bed again," my mom said, and I hated her for making it sound so dramatic. But she was right. Death is dramatic, and I refused to consider that it should be treated as such. We'd bring him meals from downstairs when he wanted to eat, which wasn't too often. That his decline was fast was lucky only in the way that one wishes for miserable things to be brief.

I didn't want to talk, but I'd work next to my mom in the kitchen, chopping garlic and picking parsley leaves off their stems, helping her make dinner. Her feet hurt and her back hurt from her new Whole Foods job.

Rachel worked at Whole Foods for several months. They had a system—everyone started with the very cheapest ingredients, making the coleslaws and potato salads, and worked their way up to proteins and fancier veggies. Her coworkers were all from Mexico, and Rachel spent the time that she wasn't shredding cabbage and peeling carrots helping them with their immigration paperwork.

She wasn't as fast as the women and men who worked beside her, but just like catering, she found satisfaction in her work. The food was fresh and high quality, and she made it with her own two hands.

It was physically demanding, too. At the end of a shift, her whole body ached. Rachel graduated from cabbage to eggs, chicken, and fish.

The Jewish holidays were coming, and she had to pick the bones out of a mountain of whitefish sides. "I had a sort of Marxist moment,"

Mom said. The task was thankless and took all day. "Whitefish salad was something like eight ninety-nine a pound, and I was getting paid about ten bucks an hour. If I was going to do this, I was going to either organize or make money for myself." She made as much in one hour as a consultant as she did in one day at Whole Foods.

Still, she felt like she had to stick it out for a bit. She made it to six months before giving her notice. When it was over, she missed the store discount. She didn't miss the constant pain in the arches of her feet.

At home, the kitchen was her happy place. But it was a weird time. "I have an idea," I'd say about her newest dish, that she should add some cumin, or some caramelized onions.

"Those things don't really go together," she'd retort, trying to be gentle about it, but I took it as an insult. I'd leave the cutting board and retreat to my room.

Pop-Pop's room began to smell like detergent and piss. "You have to go say hi," my mom told me. "It will mean a lot to him. It's not so bad. He's dying." Having no choice, I'd approach him tensely, perch on the big tacky chair by the side of his bed that we had brought from his Baltimore apartment.

"How are you?" I'd ask.

"I'm okay," he always said. "Hanging in. How is school?"

"It's good," I lied. Being new in high school was no fun. One of the reasons we had moved to Princeton, instead of a nearby town, was the excellent public school. I had never been to public school before. I knew the school was fantastic on paper, but it didn't feel that way to me. At Princeton High School, there was no dancing in the hallways. There were a lot of rules that seemed to exist for no particular reason, and the hundreds of faces I saw each day were unwaveringly uninterested in my existence.

At home, I wondered how Pop-Pop and I had both grown even worse at handling the awkwardness, unrelenting and heavy between us. We would sit for a while, in silence. The TV would flash its cooking shows, pots and pans and close-ups of Giada's lips around a fat strand of noodle. Then I'd leave to do homework, or whatever it was that I was actually planning to do—spend hours pinging old and new friends on AIM. I didn't have too many places to go, but I wanted to be anywhere but home. There was a coffee shop in town where I could do my homework and read the zines I loved. I spent all my allowance on mochas at Small World, and watched college students study in groups, and blind dates scope each other out. I wondered if my loneliness could choke me.

My mom was having her own struggles, but she would try to cheer me up. She took me to New York City to eat at Babbo. My mom thought a night out might lift my spirits, and she was right. She let me try her Barolo. The downtown crowd seemed to undulate and buzz. We felt forever away from Princeton High School in the best possible way.

At night, I called my friends from Baltimore and cried. I burned them mix CDs full of sad songs. If only I were home—Baltimore would always be home, I swore, until I could make it to New York City—all the adventures we would have! But they were having their adventures without me.

Slowly, I accumulated new friends. A Russian boy with a shaved head who chain-smoked in the basement, a girl who had just moved from Milwaukee and wanted to talk about Kant all the time, a guy named Joe with a compulsive lying problem and an impeccable fashion sense. When they came over, we would stay downstairs. We walked to Small World and drank our coffees in a cemetery down the street. We spent hours in used bookstores—I'd fill my backpack with finds from their dollar box. We planned out the rest of our lives. I didn't want them to know Pop-Pop existed. I liked having them around. They were a distraction, and distraction was protection.

◆ ◆ ◆

The last fight was about a tomato. Pop-Pop wanted a tomato with his bagel and whitefish salad. The fact that we lived in a house without a tomato was not only unacceptable but unfathomable to him, ridiculous. He was dying and he imagined the perfect breakfast—a tomato with his whitefish and his sesame bagel, toasted but not too toasted.

Through the closed door of the bedroom, I could hear the low groan of his voice and the pain in my mom's.

"We have a new home and new jobs and a miserable teenager, and we are taking care of you the best we can. But we don't have a tomato."

I couldn't make out his response, only hers: "I'm sorry. I'm sorry. I'm fucking sorry."

When she emerged, my mom's face was streaked with tears. I followed her to the kitchen.

"Hannah," she said, almost in a whisper, "bring Pop-Pop his breakfast." She handed me a tomato-less bagel and whitefish atop a tray.

"Where's your mother?" Pop-Pop demanded before I even presented him with his meal.

"I'm sorry that we don't have tomato," I told him. I felt sad for my mom. When I was a kid, my dad lifted me onto his shoulders, and coached our neighborhood basketball team. He taught me to shoot hoops. He sang me silly songs. I couldn't imagine having Pop-Pop as a dad.

"I don't want it," Pop-Pop snapped in a gruff whisper. He turned over in his bed. For once, the TV was off. The house's silence was merciless.

In the kitchen, I set the tray down and put my hand on my mother's shaky shoulders. She sniffed back tears and shook me off.

"I'm sorry," I said to her.

"It's okay," she lied, and I let it be.

Mom was schlepping him to and from doctor's appointments. She was consulting for a school that taught kids with autism, and worrying about me. She took an essay class and wrote personal stories, and helped sell Pop-Pop's apartment at Cross Keys in Baltimore. Nothing was under control. She felt so much guilt. Her husband was busy at his new super-stressful job, Pop-Pop was always angry and dying, and I was depressed.

Pop-Pop asked Marty to put a pillow over his head. He asked Rachel to give him drugs that would kill him. They both knew it was time for him to die, but they didn't want to kill him, couldn't do it.

My mom hoped Pop-Pop would have a flash of insight at the end of his life, or maybe just a moment of kindness. That he'd want to talk about her childhood or his, about his wife, his triumphs and despair. But the only things he seemed to care about were scrambled eggs, tomatoes, vanilla ice cream—things that were both easier and also not easy at all.

Food was an imperfect medium for sharing our love and healing from pain, even though it was sometimes all we had. It could bring us together, but it could also keep us apart. I thought about Pop-Pop's cake that he used to bring to family dinners, the French toast lessons. But more than that, I thought about his disappointment with us, his family, the plate of uneaten eggs, the whitefish salad. It was around this time that my own eating disorder started to escalate, this impulse to turn one of the things I loved most against myself, starving myself all day and then bingeing on cookies (my favorite) until they turned to chalk in my stomach and threatened to choke me. I thought of my mom rolling out sheet after sheet of puff pastry with her grandma. Food could make us whole, even if just for a minute, and it could break us into pieces.

Avocado

As soon as I was pregnant again, I was scared. I didn't know if I could handle losing this pregnancy the way I had lost Sweet Pea. I read everything I could find about miscarriage.

"The thing is," Tony reminded me, "there's really nothing we can do."

I had been so careful to do everything right the first time: I took my prenatal vitamins every morning. I didn't eat lunch meats or sushi or drink more than one cup of coffee in a day. And what had it mattered?

I was afraid my joy—I was full of joy, just as I was full of fear— would jinx the whole thing. I also understood that the world doesn't really work like that.

There is a Jewish superstition that stems from the idea of the evil eye, the *ayin hara*. A person with ayin hara is not just someone who can't be happy for another's good fortune but someone who actually gets distressed when happy things happen for their friends. Their spiteful gaze can bring bad luck. This is why many Jews traditionally avoid having baby showers, and even buying clothes or furniture for the baby before she is born. All that fuss, even a small fuss, for an unborn baby might bring a *kinehora*, the Yiddish word for a jinx. (The expression comes from *kayn ayin hara*, literally "not the evil eye.")

My therapist, who is also Jewish, says it's like holding up an umbrella all day on a sunny day, just in case. Your arm is going to get awfully tired. And you'll miss that glow of the warm sun on your face.

I knew from experience that tamping down your present happiness doesn't create a bulwark against future despair. So why did I keep trying? But I distrusted getting too attached to the cells multiplying inside me. I knew now too well that anything could happen.

We had another European wedding coming up. Sam and GG, Tony's two close friends from university, were getting married to each other in Xàbia, Spain, a little coastal town on the Mediterranean. Sam and GG had been friends throughout college but hadn't started dating until many years after. Since they lived in London and we lived in New York, I had only spent time with them on a handful of occasions, yet I still felt as if I were the one who had known them since college. They were both warm, and quick to laugh, and nearly always the last ones lingering at a party.

Our plans were looking a lot like they did at the last wedding we had attended—we would see Tony's family and go to our niece's christening; we would have a brief but beautiful vacation in the north of Spain; and we would conclude the trip with Sam and GG's celebration by the ocean. It was "not a wedding but a party," it said on the invitations, which we got via email. There would be college friends. Tony had been a pretty serious rugby player until he needed a second surgery on his knee, and several of his rugby buddies would be there. The cava and vermouth would flow all weekend long.

I knew it didn't work this way, but I worried going to a wedding—even an un-wedding wedding—at nine and a half weeks pregnant was a bad plan. I replayed what happened at the last wedding we had attended. There had been so much blood. I thought about the ayin hara. It felt too symmetrical.

But the wedding was not a question, and so neither was the trip. We loved these people and we wanted to celebrate with them. They had made the journey from London to New Jersey for our wedding just a year ago. In fact, when Sam told me about her own engagement, she asked, "How do you feel about celebrating your one-year anniversary at our wedding in Spain?"

I told her I couldn't think of anything better, which was the truth.

◆ ◆ ◆

I've hated my stomach since I can remember. My poor stomach. What did it ever do, besides digest my food and help me live my life? When I was in the throes of restriction, it grumbled and twinged unhappily with emptiness. When I binged, stuffing myself until I couldn't physically eat any longer, it went to work, breaking down all the foods in the weird, manic combinations I frantically put inside of it into nutrients. During those times, it felt tender to the touch; it ached and pleaded with me to stop, but I ignored it, and it did its job anyway. It never let me down.

I hated it for its softness, its stubborn roundness. Even when I swished way past the limits of my own boredom and exhaustion on the elliptical machine, even when I signed up for extra Pilates classes and counted one hundred sit-ups, then kept counting for good measure, even when I skipped dinner, it remained convex. Even in the worst days of my anorexia, when my hip bones and clavicle started to emerge as if rising from the ether, when I stopped getting my period and lost whole stretches of time to daydreaming about frozen yogurt and nothingness, I never quite had a flat stomach.

In yoga class, when the teacher said put one hand on your chest and one hand on your belly, I would cringe at what I felt under my leggings with my fingers: the bulge of my tummy above my underwear. Something about it disgusted me on a visceral level. I daydreamed of slicing it off with a knife, freezing it off with some sort of radical technology. How free I would be with the pancake flatness of some imaginary perfect stomach!

Accepting my body has been the slowest part of my eating disorder recovery. First, I stopped the frenzied middle-of-the-night binges. Slowly, I eased off on the more insidious restrictions—there were so many weird games I played with myself, waiting until I was lightheaded before allowing myself a meal, not eating carbs at one meal or for one day, so I could "compensate" with a chocolate-chip cookie after a long day at work. Slowly, slowly, slowly, I've stopped classifying food as "good" or "bad." I've started listening to the subtle but persistent voice of my body.

Yet I'm shocked at the absentminded way my friends smile for bikini-clad pictures without seeming to give it a second thought. I still need to give myself a sort of pep talk when I see photos of myself, and my very first, unadulterated thought remains: *Oh my god, am I actually that fat?* My first feeling is like being gut punched.

I know my eyes are broken; I know I cannot see myself clearly. I am grateful for the way my body takes me through my life, carries my laptop and groceries around New York City, powers me through spin class, hugs friends and throws toys as far as I can for Ace, and wraps itself into Tony. But I cannot yet, in good faith, say I love the way it looks.

On a good day, I accept it. I know it is the home of my mind and my heart. I know I'm stuck with it, so I may as well extend it some kindness. But that year, with the miscarriage and this new pregnancy, it had taken on a fresh role. It was doing something unfathomably big: it was making a person. Each Wednesday morning, I watched the little video from my app with Tony in bed before we got up. It narrated the baby's development. One week, the baby can hear. The next week, the baby has all four chambers of its heart. If our baby is a girl, all of her eggs are fully formed in her tiny uterus. It seemed more like science fiction than real life. I practiced touching my belly and trying not to wince.

I checked it in the mirror as my future baby grew from the size of a peppercorn to a cherry to an apple in my uterus. I lifted my shirt and gazed downward at my reflection. I turned to the side. I didn't see anything. I recognized the pudge of my belly as the same old pudge as always.

One day, I thought my jeans felt tighter than usual. But the next day, they fit just fine. Maybe the dryer had been too hot.

I asked Tony if I looked pregnant. At the beginning he dodged with "You look glowy," or "You look beautiful," or "You *are* pregnant." And then one day he squinted a little, right at my stomach, and said, "I can see Avocado."

"Are you sure?"

He was sure. I couldn't see anything at all, but I knew I was no good at seeing myself.

In that week's pregnancy video, just before we left for our trip to London and Xàbia, the annoyingly chirpy host said that fetuses respond powerfully to belly touches—rubbing your belly probably makes them feel good. So I rubbed my belly, and I cried. My poor, innocent belly. The home of so much loathing, and for no good reason. Under its supple flesh, something miraculous was unfolding.

I called a friend in recovery and cried to her about my paunch. Why couldn't it be cute and perky like the photos women shared on the pregnancy app? Instead it just felt meaty.

She had been pregnant, too. Now she had two small children, a boy and a girl. She never thought her belly was cute, either.

"Have you tried talking to your baby?" she asked me.

It seemed hokey, but I tried it anyway.

"How are you doing?" I asked when my tummy rumbled. "Are you hungry, too?"

I sang to her in the shower. When I got on the subway or into a car or a train, I told her exactly where we were going. When we arrived, I said, "We made it."

I had started taking a prenatal yoga class on Sunday mornings. The room was full of pregnant women. The heat was overwhelming, and I felt the cold air from the cracked window as relief. We sat cross-legged on cushions and lifted our arms skyward and cat-cowed our backs.

We stretched our necks down to our chests. "Now look at your belly," the teacher said, in her soft yoga-teacher voice. How many times had I avoided catching a glimpse of the center of my body? I looked.

"Take a moment to appreciate your bump. Is it bigger today or smaller? Does it feel soft or hard? Thank your body for the amazing things it is doing."

Thank you, body.

In the morning, or alone for a moment, or in the bathroom, I began to put two hands on my belly. I looked at it without looking away. *Hi there,* I said. *I hope you're happy in there. I hope you're comfy. I hope you're growing. I hope you know how deeply I love you. I hope you never learn to hate yourself.*

◆ ◆ ◆

If I had been tired during the first pregnancy, this time around I felt nearly crippled by exhaustion. One night, Tony and I ordered in Indian food and I fell asleep between bites of garlic naan and saag paneer. Keeping my eyes open was just not a viable option.

We preferred to take night flights from New York to London, usually one that left around midnight and arrived late morning in Heathrow—it just seemed the most civilized option with the time change and the schlep. We would have a day at Tony's parents' home in Solihull, where he grew up, before heading to my sister- and brother-in-law's house in the countryside west of London for our unreasonably cute six-month-old niece's christening.

On the plane, I arranged myself with my head on Tony's shoulder and his sweatshirt wedged between us for a pillow. I fell asleep moments after we boarded. There was a buzz of people wedging suitcases above their heads and quieting their children, but I barely registered anything. Being awake was almost painful, so I drifted off. I wasn't quite comfortable, but I was content.

I had stayed like that for about an hour when I vaguely registered some announcement about "mechanical issues." We needed to deplane. Everyone looked weary and exasperated. But I was too zombified-sleepy to be anything but befuddled. Tony gathered up our stuff and I unballed his sweatshirt from beneath my head.

Back at the gate, a baby wailed, and a flight attendant rolled out a cart of apple juice and Cheez-Its. A horde gathered around the snacks. An unrelenting announcement about the broken Airbus played on repeat. Our flight was delayed, they said, and delayed again. We waited for an hour, then two hours. A lady screamed at the poor employee at the gate and the rest of the crowd stared. I was drained but too anxious to fall back asleep.

I had been plotting how to deliver the pregnancy news to Tony's family. The first time it had all felt so easy. Tony had sweetly announced that he was drinking for two to his parents during our visit and they had immediately lit up. We had toasted—I'd raised a glass of tonic water—and it felt as if we were standing in front of a fireplace in winter, bright and warm. But what would they say now? I felt like we had somehow lost claim to our own unfettered joy, and to that of others', too. Just as we had made everyone happy, we had robbed them of that happiness. I *knew* it wasn't my fault, I kept reminding myself, and yet I still felt responsible.

I was also worried about the logistics of telling Tony's family. We'd visit with his dad, his little brother, and his brother's wife first (they lived close to Solihull). Christine, Tony's mom, would already be helping Anna, his sister, get ready for the christening. But we couldn't really tell them first without telling Christine, right? Or could we? I didn't want to share the news during the event—the spotlight did not belong to us. The next morning, they'd drop us off at the train station and we'd head to Bilbao. Then our chance would be over.

But it seemed that planning had been looking too far into the future. We couldn't even get across the Atlantic. They announced our flight was delayed once again, and they had started offering comped hotel stays for out-of-towners and cabs home for locals. But what would we do at home? Nobody knew what was going on. More people were shouting now. A toddler was having a full-blown temper tantrum. The apple juice and Cheez-Its were long gone.

We waited in a line to talk to someone from Delta. The line snaked around on itself multiple times and into the hall, where all of the shops and bars were closed for the night, chairs stacked neatly on tables. It was two-something-AM. The two ladies ahead of us were also on hold with Delta customer service. "You should call them, too," they advised. "We've been waiting for more than an hour, and nothing is moving."

It turned out another flight to London and two flights to Paris were also delayed, and delayed, and delayed again that night. When a Delta employee announced that one of the flights to Paris was actually leaving—it had been scheduled to depart seven hours before—he seemed genuinely shocked. We heard him turn to his colleague and ask, "Really?" And again, "Are you absolutely sure?"

The line cleared up enough that we got to someone. It was after 3 AM. My head was throbbing. I let Tony do the talking. We were trying to understand what was going on. We wanted to get to London ASAP, obviously. We'd wait for our plane if it was actually going to leave. If not, we needed another plan. We were having trouble getting a straight answer when the drained-looking Delta lady looked us in the eye and said, "I would suggest you book another flight." We nabbed the last two seats on the next flight to Heathrow that afternoon—it was already the next day.

On the cab ride back home at 4 AM, we finally got a text alert that our original flight had been canceled. Without traffic, we cruised through the city, all empty and aglow. At least Delta had paid for the cab ride. Our apartment felt weirdly empty without Ace. I fell into a shallow, dreamless sleep curled up next to Tony. That morning, we had enough time to eat some bagels and lox before we took another cab back to JFK. Out the window, déjà vu.

Our new plan was to go straight to the christening. We'd have time to check into the place where we were staying—a little inn above the town pub—and hopefully take a shower. I hated how exhausted and groggy I felt before we even left. All these years of knowing them, I still wanted to make a good impression on Tony's family.

On the plane, my pregnancy nausea crept up. I puked a few times in the bathroom, but the next time, the urge to throw up came over me so suddenly I had to use the paper barf bag stuffed into the pocket of the seat in front of me. My forehead was clammy. I was shivering but hot. A few minutes later, I was freezing. The nice flight attendant brought me a giant bottle of water and an extra blanket. I wrapped myself tight like a sausage. I tried to take deep breaths.

I had to run to the bathroom after we landed to throw up again, but customs was a breeze. At the baggage carousel, Tony's suitcase arrived right away. We watched the colorful luggage drop and circle around. We had gotten a set of new suitcases for a wedding gift, and I noticed that his already looked beat-up. It was a good problem to have; we were lucky to get to travel so much.

My suitcase didn't come. At the Heathrow desk, the lady explained that instead of being rerouted onto our new flight—as they had explained would happen to our bags—the bag's tag had been deleted from the system. We filled out a lot of forms. We would get fifty euros a day reimbursed until our bag arrived. In preparation for this exact situation, I had packed my toothbrush and even an extra dress for the christening, which was in a few short hours.

At the airport pharmacy, I bought some tinted moisturizer, mascara, and makeup-remover wipes. Somehow, my purchase totaled nearly fifty euros. I texted Christine to see if I could borrow a shawl or a wrap—it was chilly outside, and the sweatshirt I'd traveled in didn't seem christening appropriate.

We had to splurge for a car to take us to the small town where Anna and her husband, Sandy, lived; there were no good public transport options on the weekend that would get us there in time. The roads were twisty and I've always been prone to car sickness. Tony was worried, asked if I thought my sickness was pregnancy or motion related, but I had no idea. I was just sick.

"I'm so sorry," I had to say to the cabbie multiple times, "can you please pull over?" He wore a cap and opened the windows. The air tasted of oak and just-cut grass.

Neat hedges lined the roads and green hills rose and fell in the middle distance. The sun was shining in a very non-English sort of way, bright and resolute. I thought, *This is a beautiful place to puke,* as my stomach heaved and I threw up into the lush fields, over and over again. There was nothing left to throw up, but my body kept at it. The driver handed me a tissue and another bottle of water. People could be so nice. Back in the car, Tony held my hand and I turned my face to gulp in that clean, cool air. I sent a message to what was happening inside me: *Please, be healthy. Please be okay.*

Our room wasn't ready for us at the little inn yet, and I tried to play it cool. All I wanted, desperately, was to lie down. I could use a shower, too. The innkeeper invited us to order breakfast and Tony tucked into his favorite—a full English breakfast, complete with the British back bacon Tony insisted was superior to the American kind (I disagreed), black sausage, and a sea of slimy beans. I couldn't look at it without my stomach capsizing. I ate two pieces of sourdough toast with a lot of butter, then found a couch in a quiet spot in the lobby and fell into a wobbly sleep.

Things that I spent my whole life loving—scrambled eggs, crispy-skinned roasted chicken, green Thai curry—suddenly made my insides churn. One night, Tony and I had ordered some calamari to share. Who doesn't love crispy fried calamari? The idea sounded delicious. But when the bowl arrived in front of us, the fryer-oil smell and lumpy bread-crumbs sent a wave of revulsion down my spine. I pushed the calamari over in Tony's direction. I couldn't even look at it.

All I wanted was carbs. Bagels for breakfast. Maybe bagels for lunch, too. Grilled cheese sandwiches turned golden brown from but-ter. Pasta, rice, popcorn, and toast.

I woke up in a foul mood. My neck was scrunched up on the side of the couch. I wasn't sure if I was going to puke again. I was embar-rassed to see my in-laws for such an important event in such poor form. I asked the innkeeper if there was an update on our room. When he motioned for us to follow him up the stairs, I felt a surge of relief. I had time for a quick shower—I couldn't get the water hot enough, but I didn't care—and swiped on my new mascara.

Apollo, Tony's dad, came to pick us up. He greeted me with a big hug. We had a few minutes before we had to be at the chapel, so he and Tony ordered frothy beers (water for me). We sat outside in the perfect, bitsy town, the post office and not much else across the street, the hills undulating in the distance, the sunshine making the whole scene gleam. We told him about our apartment search, he gave us some family updates.

I sat up front by Apollo on the short drive to the chapel, grateful to feel, for the first time in a day, not awfully nauseous. I didn't need the shawl, after all. It was unseasonably warm and all the women, the sisters and sisters-in-law and mothers, were dressed in flowery dresses, big sunglasses, and bigger smiles. Thea, our niece and the woman of honor, smiled the biggest of all as she was passed around to different doting relatives. This was only the second time I had met her, and yet how I loved her.

Tony's brother Charlie and his wife, Sarah, pulled up with their brand-new baby, William, my nephew, and immediately, upon sight, I loved him, too. He was drowsy from the car ride and impossibly tiny. "Can I hold him?" I asked, and he sunk into the nook of my arm.

I've never been one of those people who loses themselves over the mere sight of a baby. I think babies are cute, but I've never felt a reaction like my friend Alexandra, who squeals with joy and starts to cry, "My ovaries are aching," as a baby approaches. People say it's different when it's your own, and I believe them. When we would see Avocado on the ultrasound, yawning or wiggling, her arm behind her head, my heart would leapfrog in my chest.

◆ ◆ ◆

During my first pregnancy, I no longer felt a secret thrill from skipping breakfast, then waiting as long as possible for lunch. For the first time in as long as I could remember, it felt natural and normal and good to feed myself and the creature growing inside of me. I wanted overripe pineapple and grilled cheese sandwiches and yogurt with berries (who craves yogurt?). I didn't want to binge until I felt the food welling back up in my throat. I thought, *This is how normal people must feel around food.*

When I lost the baby, nothing—least of all food—sounded good anymore. I'd make myself a bowl of oatmeal for breakfast, the way I like it, with plenty of cinnamon and apples, then let it get cold. Then slowly, my appetite returned. It helped to write about food for work. I'd be at an Israeli wine lunch and a plate of fried eggplant covered in tahini and *amba*, a piquant mango relish, would arrive, and suddenly I'd find myself smiling. Or I'd be talking to a cheese importer at a meeting of the WICHes, the Women in Cheese, and someone would hand out creamy, salty spoonfuls of Gorgonzola dolce drizzled in wildflower honey, and I'd remember all over again why I had pursued this career, and how lucky I was.

I stopped weighing myself way back in my early days of recovery, something like eight years before the pregnancy. Early into recovery, I

had called my first sponsor in a fit of tears one morning after weighing myself and seeing that dreaded news—the number moving in the
"wrong" direction, up. I could not metabolize this information. I felt
like an utter failure.

She didn't tell me that weight fluctuates with hormonal cycles and
sodium intake and when you last pooped. She didn't tell me that bodies are always in flux, not arbitrarily stuck at some fixed moment. She
didn't tell me to eat less carbs or spend more time at the gym or never
eat after 8 PM.

Over the phone, she asked if we could try to breathe.

"Let's breathe together," she said. "In. Out. In. Out."

I sat like this, inhaling and exhaling into my phone at my little
table, rush-hour traffic sounds whirling outside, not caring that I was
going to be late to work. I felt my jagged gasp turn into some semblance
of breath.

"Is this information you get from the number on the scale, or
ammunition?" my sponsor asked, although I knew she knew the answer.

"Ammunition, absolutely."

She didn't tell me to never weigh myself again, or that weighing
myself was a destructive emotional trigger, or that my merit as a person
could not be measured in pounds. She said, "Why don't you do some
writing about that?"

She said, "Just because you've done something in the past doesn't
mean you have to keep doing it. Just because something served you
before doesn't mean it serves you today." She suggested I ask my fellows
if they weighed themselves, and how that went for them.

I wrote; I asked; I listened. Some people did and some did not. I
heard stories about the freedom of not associating every occasion and
life event with a number. I thought I felt my shoulders relax when I
heard this. I thought of the anxiety that precluded every step I took
toward any scale. Maybe I'd give the not-weighing-myself thing a try.
If it didn't work out, the scale wouldn't go anywhere.

I feared, of course, that I would grow and grow and grow until I turned into some sort of amorphous half human, half blimp.

But in recovery, I learned a new way of thinking about the world. I listened to people say things like, "My body is God's body," and "I trust my body's innate wisdom," and "It's not my job to control my food or my size." These things sounded foreign, mysterious, and strangely compelling.

"What do you do when you go to the doctor?" I asked one of these friends.

"It's simple. I turn around so my back is to the scale. It's called a blind weigh-in, and people do it all the time."

"Do they give you a hard time?"

"Never," she said. "If they did, I'd find a new doctor."

For as long as I can remember, I've hated going to the doctor. I wondered how much of this was tied to the inevitable click, click, click of the back-and-forth weights on those big old-fashioned scales, the judgment of the number staring back at me.

Still, I was initially embarrassed to ask the physician's assistant at my annual checkup about the blind weight. I wondered if it would mark me as some sort of damaged patient with more baggage than could be tallied on any sort of machine. But she didn't even bat an eye. "Of course," she said, and scribbled something on her clipboard after I stepped onto the scale, facing away from whatever verdict it showed. That was that. Then she wrapped the cuff around my arm to take my blood pressure.

I texted my sponsor to tell her how it went. I had tried something different, and it felt pretty great.

One of the things I worried about, being pregnant, besides all the growth and change itself happening to my body, was being so closely weighed and monitored. I heard horror stories—to me they were horror stories!—about women being reprimanded and shamed by their doctors for gaining too much weight as they grew a baby. I couldn't imagine all the emotions and hormones surging through me, my own eating disorder history lurking in the background, and a health-care professional castigating my body. Or I *could* imagine it, and I knew it would sting.

My sponsor and my therapist told me what I had learned to be true: I could do what I, by then, had been doing for years—ask to not discuss my weight. If my doctor gave me a hard time, I could go elsewhere, to another doctor who honored my wishes.

Tony couldn't go with me to the first doctor's appointment, so I brought along my mom. I had been embarrassed to ask her, but I didn't want to go alone. She was happy to join me, anyway. It was the first appointment in the morning, and still we had to wait in the waiting room. I got Rachel and myself cups of water, even though my mom said she didn't want any. When they called my name, I asked for the blind weight as usual. No fuss.

The doctor was professional and to the point. We listened to the heartbeat below my navel and I let myself smile with relief. She handed me a schedule of my appointments, first every four weeks, then every two as the pregnancy progressed, and every week as I got closer to April 15, my due date. They would need to take a lot of blood at this initial appointment. And good thing I'd had all that water—I'd have to pee in a cup.

"Do you have any questions?" The OB-GYN's teeth gleamed in the fluorescent light of the exam room.

"Where do you deliver?" my mom asked. I was grateful for her calm presence in the corner of the room.

"Mount Sinai on the Upper East Side."

"We're moving to Brooklyn in a few months," I chimed in. "Do you think that's too far away?"

"It's your first birth, so labor should take plenty of time," she said. "You'll be fine."

"Is there a birthing center at Mount Sinai?" my mom asked. It was a perfectly good question, but one I felt too nervous to ask.

"No." Did she smirk a bit? "There are labor and birth facilities. It is a hospital in Manhattan. An acclaimed hospital in Manhattan, but there are no bells and whistles. You're not going to find bathtubs or scented candles." At least she was honest.

◆ ◆ ◆

After the christening, which was a short and lovely service that Thea smiled and cooed through, we went back to Anna and Sandy's house. They lived on the property of the boarding school where Sandy was the director of athletics, and the whole thing looked to be out of a movie set to me, bordered by rugby pitches and thick forests interrupted by muddy fields.

We sat on the lawn and ate couscous and curried chicken salad studded with currants. Like every English event I've ever attended, the wine and beer flowed and flowed. I found some elderflower tonic and poured it into a wineglass. We had been married for almost a year, and Tony's family was slowly starting to feel like my own. (He consistently corrected me when I called them *your family*: "They're our family.") Everyone wanted our life updates and I wanted to know about theirs—what was it like to be a parent? Miraculously, I didn't need to sneak away and puke. I felt the warmth of the day cover me like the sunshine.

After the plates had been cleared away and Thea had been photographed with the pink-and-white cake and the sun was beginning to set behind the low brick buildings, Tony turned to me and said, "I think we should tell them," and I nodded my consent.

I was afraid to ruin this perfect day. I was afraid they wouldn't be happy for us, or that the happiness would be so muted behind the sorrow of what had transpired before that it would register as worry instead.

But instead I watched as Tony's mom's face broke into a smile—what a pure, beautiful smile—and she hugged first me and then Tony.

Tony's brother Charlie saw the interaction and guessed, a tentative "Congratulations?" and soon everyone heard the news and had hugs for us that felt like the best hugs in the world, totally spontaneous and not perfunctory or somehow, like I had worried, tarnished. I started to tear up and didn't even try to fight it. I was too happy even to feel exhausted anymore. I needed that shawl when the sun went down, after all, and a blanket too, and someone made me a peppermint tea. The babies were getting grumpy from the ebbing excitement of such a big day. We sat and talked for a long time. The sky darkened and then brightened with a big moon.

◆   ◆   ◆

The un-wedding was nestled by the Mediterranean Sea in the south of Spain. My bag finally arrived—it met up with us in the Alicante Airport, and how beautiful it looked! My travel sweatshirt felt grubby. I had packed shorts, summer dresses, and bathing suits. Xàbia was a beach town, and it was supposed to be hot and sunny. Instead, a rogue hurricane had blown through just a few days before the big event. When we arrived, the sky was slate grey and still dense with unrelenting rain. We hadn't packed umbrellas.

On the way to the Airbnb we were sharing with Shine, one of Tony's good university friends, we made several stops so I could throw up along the side of the road (I was getting good at it). Outside that house, our feet sank into the waterlogged lawn, getting mud up to our ankles. Our suitcases were wet and dirty. It was a beautiful villa with a porch, a pool (which we would not get to use), and a trampoline. We were the first to arrive. A small lake of rainwater had formed on top of the trampoline. I knew it wouldn't have been the best idea, even in fairer weather, to jump on a trampoline while pregnant, but it looked fun.

Instead, we decided to make a trip to town to have some lunch—I was starving—and to get some provisions for the weekend. The walk to town would take us about twenty minutes, but the rain was not letting up and the wind howled and whined out the window. There was no Uber or Lyft in Xàbia. We called every taxi company listed in the binder our Airbnb hosts had left for us. One man answered and then promptly hung up on me after I asked, *"¿Habla usted inglés?"* Tony called back and got the same response. The other line just rang and rang. My empty stomach rumbled in protest. I finished the emergency Pringles we had bought at the airport.

Finally, we got someone to drive us to town. We ended up in a cute little restaurant with a pan of paella, full of peas and mussels, as large as the whole table. It was the perfect thing for my carb-loving palate, and we scraped up the last crispy bits from the edges before heading back into the soggy day.

There was a grocery store nearby, and just as we were plotting how we were possibly going to schlep provisions back to our villa without a ride, Tony got a call from Shine. He had arrived from Valencia and would meet us at the market. He wasn't sure if the three of us plus groceries would fit in his tiny rental car, but we decided to find out.

And what a store it was! A sprawling grocery mecca with mountains of oranges, rows and rows of brick-red legs of jamón, and jugs of wine for just a few euros. We loaded a basket with tiny crimson tomatoes, a loaf of bread, two kinds of jamón, and a wedge of sheep's milk cheese. There was a machine that turned those oranges into fresh, pulpy juice, so we got some of that, too.

Shine was wet from the rain and all smiles, and we hugged in the cheese aisle. I surveyed our groceries. We were missing eggs—I ran to get a carton as Tony and Shine went to pay.

Back at the villa the next day, Tony decided to crack some eggs for breakfast, but they wouldn't cooperate. It turns out our carton was full of hard-boiled eggs. Who knew! We peeled off the shells for breakfast, eating them with toast and jamón and meaty cheese, listening to the rain patter above our heads and laughing so hard I had to focus to keep my orange juice down.

At the un-wedding, Tony gave a speech that made everyone laugh. The rain stopped long enough for us to gather outside, right on the ocean. Sam looked beautiful in her white dress and with a crown of flowers in her hair. I met another woman who was also pregnant, and people kept bringing us elderflower cordials and glasses of sparkling water. The waves lapped along to the music. Twinkly lights glowed, and so did we. I nearly cried with relief when we made it back to the villa, way after midnight, without anything terrible happening, and then back to New York a few days later.

Back home, I told our friends and family about the pregnancy. If I didn't believe in the ayin hara, I didn't need it to dictate my life. If we lost the pregnancy again, I wanted to be able to call them, crying. I knew it was their kindness that would help us get through anything—that had helped us get through our first loss. But for now, it was happy news to share. They gave me hugs and pink roses. They texted to check in on me. I thought about how they'd cuddle the baby, how we'd walk around Prospect Park together come April, watching Brooklyn blossom and my little one's heavy eyes flutter and fall into sleep.

◆ ◆ ◆

Having an eating disorder meant waging a brutal and constant war against my own body for years. It was enemy number one. As far as I was concerned, my body had failed me—first at puberty, by making me the first girl in my class to need a bra and the second to get my period, and then by continuing to grow in all the wrong places, to be too big, too tall, too much. I envied my classmates their little-girl bodies. Why had mine rebelled?

I willed and prayed it into submission. I ran on the middle school cross-country team, not because of any inclination toward running but because it seemed like the virtuous sort of activity that would result in long, thin limbs and a tummy that would slither inward when I lifted my T-shirt over the slippery checkered gym shorts favored by the Baltimore private girls' school set circa 1998. I worked really, really hard, giving my all at our team's practice runs and sometimes doing my own on the weekends, but I always finished dangerously close to last, and my thighs chafed painfully together under those ugly shorts. In the mirror they looked the same, which is to say many times the size of in my fantasy. I was a very long way from any sort of thigh gap.

I'd read my mom's Weight Watchers literature scattered around the house, and tried to count points. I wasn't great at math, but I understood the equation: less food = less points = less weight. I managed to skip breakfast, no problem, but by lunchtime, the cafeteria fryer smells were dangerously good. I didn't know what to do with my hands as I watched my friends eat their tater tots and chicken nuggets. I couldn't remember the point values for anything I wanted for lunch, or anything I didn't want.

"Hannah, aren't you going to eat something?" someone asked, and I, embarrassed by the attention and feeling my stomach grumble, toasted a bagel in one of those industrial toasters that require four cycles to get properly toasty. Thinking I would save points, I ate it dry. Afterward, I was still hungry but felt full of self-righteousness and definitely thinner. After cross-country practice, where we ran sprints around the soggy lacrosse field, I felt so light-headed I reached for a granola bar someone's mom had brought after we stretched as a team in the fluorescent gym. It tasted so entirely satisfying that I ate another, and then another, and then another.

At home that evening, I added everything up on the cardboard points calculator that sat in a napkin ring on the kitchen counter. Somehow, I had consumed all the points I was supposed to eat that day, mostly in granola bars. Surely that couldn't be right. I did the math again. Actually, I had managed to go over. I went to bed without dinner, telling my parents I had already eaten, but in the morning, I looked the same. My scratchy blue uniform skirt did not feel even a little bit looser around my waist. In the cafeteria that morning, I bought a chocolate muffin with chocolate chips and savored the warm, sugary relief of my defeat as I scrambled to finish that day's math homework. At thirteen, I was a Weight Watchers failure.

My many attempts at dieting were all similarly short-lived until my senior year of high school. When I got into Columbia in New York City, I felt I had finally cracked some sort of life code. I would start a new, shiny life in the city I had adored since I'd first laid eyes on it. I would be surrounded by smart, weird people who also didn't fit into their small towns and sprawling suburbs, people who loved tiny cafés and used bookstores and experimental theater and Homer.

There was just one problem. In my vision of a new life, I was thin. Thin not like the models, but like the hipster girls in their complicated glasses and flowy clothes that stopped just in the right places to show off their flat stomachs and the jutting weapons of their hip bones. I was hopelessly curvy and soft around the edges. Even after the breast reduction surgery I had begged my mom for and finally gone through the summer between my junior and senior years of high school, my breasts were still unfashionably, stubbornly large. This was pre–*Mad Men* and the gorgeously non-stick-ish Christina Hendricks, and pre-Instagram body positivity and hit-or-miss Dove beauty campaigns. Every single image of every kind of desirable girl—thin, thinner, thinnest—was a body type that stood in stark contrast to everything about my own body.

I had a new confidence: if I had managed to get accepted to Columbia, I could do anything. I could shrink myself, become someone new, be reborn. Weight Watchers had recently launched an online-only program, where I wouldn't have to show my face at the meetings. I had brought my homework and hidden in the back as a kid while my mom stood in line to weigh herself. I couldn't get behind the humiliation of standing in a line and stepping on a scale in public. *The horror!* But from the privacy of my own desktop, I signed up. I told no one.

I dieted with a zeal that bordered on religious. I experimented with first eating foods with lower and lower point values (Pickles! Veggie soup! Weird fake meat!) and then just eating less and less food. I'd obsessively save up my point values for whatever I felt was "worth it," scouring grocery stores for the perfect single-portioned treat—I couldn't trust myself with a larger package. My middle school granola bar experience had repeated itself more times than I could count. Best to just bring home one smallish bar of dark chocolate with walnuts, or one sadly diminutive peanut butter cookie and savor that like it was the last yummy thing on earth, which it sort of was, since I had relegated my diet to such a pathetic handful of safe foods. I ate a lot of apples, and fat-free yogurt with no flavor, and cottage cheese with packets of Splenda mixed in, and hundred-calorie packs of popcorn. It makes me sad just thinking about it.

But it worked. I weighed myself every week, and every week I saw a lower number on the scale—first the one at the gym in New Jersey near my parents' house, and then at the Columbia gym, which I would faithfully trek to every Thursday morning, even if it was snowing or I had been up studying all night—and felt a buoyant pang of pride at getting a bit thinner. When the scale went the opposite way, when I ate an actual meal or had a full-blown binge in a moment of "weakness" that could also be defined as hunger, I felt full of such a virulent self-loathing that my brain turned, for the only time in my life, to self-harm. I thought of cutting myself, or burning myself, but instead, I just renewed my vows and dieted harder. I was a ball of ferocious energy and annoying hunger pains and stubborn resolve. No more popcorn! No more apples! I had been eating too many carbs. That must be it.

That number on the scale was so much bigger than me. To me, it represented my worth as a human being.

This was an unsustainable way to live on every level: emotional, physical, spiritual. I must have known this, even in the thick of it, and my eating-disordered brain twisted this into more panic, into the more-more-more of more extreme restriction and more violent binge-ing, more self-loathing, more secrecy and hiding and fear that bubbled away inside me, even when I was writing an essay on Lacan or working my restaurant hostessing job, which I was convinced I had landed only because I was thin.

The war against my body meant constant vigilance. I must always be planning and plotting my next trip to the gym or to the scale, what I was going to eat or not going to eat; the next binge and then the next renewed my resolve never to binge again. Food was always on my mind.

I was always losing this war. When I was very thin, at my thinnest, for a whisper of time, it was never thin enough. I was always so hungry, and then I'd make myself sick eating until my insides ached in protest.

In eating disorder recovery, I had heard many times to think not about how my body looks but instead about what it does for me. How my legs carry me and my arms haul unreasonably large bags of grocer-ies. How my hands pet Ace and feed him his dinner and yank him, on his leash, away from running headfirst into oncoming traffic. How this body of mine takes me through my days and through my life.

It's a nice thought, and it's true, but it didn't fully resonate until my pregnancy. I've always felt, intuitively and positively (and falsely), that my body was fundamentally flawed. Yet here it was doing the most common yet magical thing: creating another human. It was growing a tiny nose and a heart with all four chambers and eyelids protecting tiny eyes. As I wrote this book, it was busy doing all those things. As I walked Ace, answered emails, and curled up next to Tony to watch a silly rom-com, my body was busy making another body. It was wild. I knew every single one of us was born. Still, it was hard to wrap my head around.

So many things in my life have required such focused effort, from getting into college to finding an amazing life partner to recovering from my eating disorder. But pregnancy took almost no effort whatsoever.

Sure, I read a lot of books and researched and spent more time at the doctor than I ever had in my life. I watched videos on hypnobirthing and signed up for prenatal yoga. But mostly my body just did its thing, and I let it. I rested more than usual. Most nights, Tony had to (gingerly) scrape me half-asleep from the couch and take me to bed. I worked and wrote and cooked, and meanwhile, an embryo was becoming a fetus was becoming a baby. Before every doctor's appointment and sonogram, I had trouble sleeping. I was prepared for the worst. But after eight weeks, then twelve, then sixteen, good news kept coming. Everything was progressing as expected. The baby was growing. My body was making somebody. My body was magic.

"Pregnancy is all about waiting," my mom said. Waiting was by far the hardest part. I am a horrible waiter. I figured I'd get some practice. I did a meditation class online with the theme "patience." Tony smiled knowingly—cultivating any real patience was going to take much more than a few consecutive days cross-legged on my couch, watching my thoughts come and go like clouds in the sky. But I figured it was a start.

On a Friday morning, I got a text alert from the company that conducted the DNA test that my doctor had ordered. The "advanced carrier screening" checked to see if I had any genetic variants that could affect my children.

My OB had explained that the test was super comprehensive—it looked for 283 possible inherited abnormalities, so I shouldn't be alarmed if it turned out I was a carrier for one thing or another. Of the 283 diseases, 100-ish of them are associated with Ashkenazi Jews (that's me!), so my chances were extra high. I clicked on the link in my text alert to set up an appointment to talk with a genetic counselor. The next availability wasn't until Thursday. I'd have to wait almost a week to see my results. Immediately, I felt my heart rate quicken. Not knowing was the worst part. Would they bother making me wait for a genetic counselor if nothing was wrong? Surely the news was bad.

I cried to Tony. I did my patience meditations. I took Ace for extra-long walks. I let work distract me completely. When Thursday came, the counselor emailed over the report: I had tested positive for three obscure genetic disorders with incredibly long scientific names that I could not pronounce. (Congenital adrenal hyperplasia due to 21-hydroxylase deficiency, AR fumarase deficiency, and medium chain acyl-CoA dehydrogenase deficiency.) The report was in dense scientific speak that I could not decipher, but I figured the counselor's job was to translate it into laywoman's terms for me. Instead, she just read from the report. It said things like, "A heterozygous (one copy) pathogenic missense variant, c.841G>T, p.V281L, was detected in the CYP21A2 gene (NM_000500.6). Please note that this variant is typically caus-ative for the non-classic form of congenital adrenal hyperplasia (PMID: 29450859)." I was lost and terrified.

I sent Tony the report. He's incredibly smart in a more scientific way than me; surely, he could make some sense of it. But he was stumped, too. Next I forwarded it along to my friend Ursula, who is an actual scientist. Certainly, she could understand.

She wrote back almost right away: Wow, that is super confusing! and offered to pass it to her dad, who is a geneticist. I thought back to AP Biology, but my memory was hazy. If Tony was also a carrier, there was a 25 percent chance that we would pass along the defect to our baby. If he was not, that number was zero.

Meanwhile, I *had* managed to get one question answered by the genetic counselor—"What do we do?" She suggested Tony take the test, too. They sent us a little vial with instructions for him to spit *a lot*; they would need a seemingly ridiculous amount of saliva to run the test on his DNA. Then we'd get the results in four to six weeks, which was surely way too long. How could I be asked to wait for more than a month? What if I was passing some kind of awful, scary disease on to my future child? What if my genes were messed up and I had no business having babies after all?

They had also mailed us a box and shipping label to send the saliva to the lab. Tony said he'd bring it with him to work, but he had a ridiculously early meeting and headed out before dawn. When I set out to walk Ace, I saw the box sitting on the kitchen counter, where we had left it the night before. Tony is responsible and on top of things. He is excellent at showing, in ways big and small, that he cares. He had recently brought home three flavors of Popsicles, remembering a craving I had mentioned offhandedly. But, in that moment, I had my first irrational but persuasive rush of pregnancy despair. I was convinced, just for a dark moment, that he had forgotten to mail the DNA test because he didn't actually care about the pregnancy. Luckily, I had therapy that afternoon. I dropped off the box in the mail on the way there. As soon as the words left my mouth, I knew they didn't add up. I knew Tony cared deeply. I knew he loved me and our proto-baby with the same big, fierce love I felt for him. We were all ridiculously loved.

Ursula's dad wrote back, You are correct: there is no problem if Tony is not a carrier of any of the above. Hannah's prior probability to be a carrier of at least one recessive on this panel was about 50 percent, so it should not come as a surprise. I thought of what the OB had said—lots of people test positive for one thing or another. I don't know her ethnic background, but the V281L variant in the 21-hydroxylase gene is said to be present in up to 20 percent of Ashkenazi Jewish people. It's a mild variant and unlikely to cause much trouble, no matter what Tony carries. I anticipate that this story will have a happy ending.

A happy ending! I held on to that prediction as the days and weeks unfolded.

Almost a month later, as fall started to turn the leaves outside all sorts of burnished oranges and brilliant reds, Tony got the same text message about setting up a meeting with a counselor that I had received. There was another week's wait for the results, and I had another bout of fear. His phone call with the genetic specialist was scheduled for 10 AM on a Wednesday morning. I had made sure to be extra busy that day. Ace and I were in Riverside Park when my phone buzzed with the news: Tony was not a carrier at all. That meant a zero (or just about zero) percent risk for our kid. I exhaled a gigantic sigh of relief.

The biggest news that Tony had come back with was that the counselor didn't know what box to tick off when it came to Tony's ethnicity—Caucasian or African? He's not African American, as Tony is not American. His dad is African. I was grateful for our genetic diversity, and so relieved by the news that I let out a little squeal right there in the middle of the park. Ace looked up at me to see what was going on. I fished a treat for him out of my pocket. I smiled at the breeze in my hair and those glorious first autumnal leaves, fires on trees.

When I went back to look at my genetics report—to find the names of those obscure things I was a carrier for in order to write about it here—I saw a tab called "my health" on the website. And there in plain font, clear and center on my screen, was a three-digit number: my weight. Not just for the past month, or the month before that, but for every doctor's visit I'd had since fall of 2013, more than six years ago. Up, down, up again, the same, down a bit, up again.

I stared at it for a second, not quite processing. I hadn't looked at these numbers all those times I'd stepped on the scale backward, but of course someone did. And now here they were, plain as could be in front of me.

The old me felt slapped. The old me felt disgusted at how big those numbers were, how ungainly and undainty and out of control. The old me wanted to kick and scream in a toddler-esque tantrum, and the old hurt felt deep and, at its core, true. All those weekly treks to the scale in the early morning to try to measure something unmeasurable: me. For what? The old me wanted to pick up the ratty blanket of my eating disorder and cocoon myself in its familiar comfort, anything and everything to shrink myself, to make that number smaller.

But the new me, well, that me clicked away, out of the screen, and got up and poured myself a glass of water. That me squeezed some lemon into the water and took a long drink and went back to my laptop and looked again, willing myself to take a deep breath.

My eating disorder said that everything that had unfolded in the last years, falling in love and getting married, graduating grad school and starting to teach writing, publishing a book and traveling, making friends and laughing so hard it hurt, being pregnant, losing Sweet Pea, and getting pregnant again, didn't really count. But the recovery part of me knew that these things meant everything.

Something about creating a human being in my uterus was reorganizing my brain. It felt powerful and extraordinary. Think about it! As I sit and write this, little eyelashes are growing, cheeks are chubbifying, baby organs are coming into being inside the very body I spent so many years fighting and fixing and loathing. The number on the scale had nothing on that.

Tamy

Fall 2019

On most days, I don't miss working in restaurants—my first career that I began during college. I still love restaurants—great restaurants—the buzz, the precise rhythm within the chaos, the feeling of something happening there that isn't happening anywhere else. But I don't miss how, when I worked in the restaurant industry, my friends stopped inviting me out on weekends, or evenings, or pretty much ever. They assumed, correctly, that I'd be working. I don't miss aching from my feet up to my hip bones. I don't miss the tyrannical boredom of a slow shift.

When I worked in restaurants, I had a side hustle as a freelance writer. One of my jobs was writing a series of profiles on food entrepreneurs for a business website. I interviewed Steven Jenkins, one of the partners of Fairway Market, and left our conversation inspired. On a whim, I emailed to ask Steve if he was hiring. I started behind the cheese counter at the newly opened Upper East Side Fairway the very next month, but they knew that I was a writer. Soon, I was scribbling descriptions for the cheeses I cut and wrapped behind the counter, the little jars of raw acacia honeys, the new Korean hot sauces. This revelation has stayed with me for the last decade or so—I can actually get paid to write about food. Food writing/copywriting/teaching has been a job with a much more reasonable schedule than managing restaurants, and it comes with the added perks of countless yummy experiences and wonderful fellow travelers who become friends.

Attending the pre-shift meeting one Thursday at Colonia Verde in Fort Greene, Brooklyn, did make me remember, despite all that, precisely what I miss about being part of a restaurant. At pre-shift meetings in restaurants around the world, staff huddle up before service starts to talk about special dishes on the menu, new bottles of wine, and plans for the night ahead. Colonia Verde is on a brownstone-lined street, pretty close to the neighborhoods where we had been apartment searching. It's dimly lit and cozy, with a long bar stretching to a dining room and a walled-off back garden. Tamy, the restaurant's owner, had invited me for the weekly wine tasting she conducts for her staff, who gathered at the bar as she poured tastes of low-intervention wines from a list she carefully curates. She has a soft spot for female winemakers and "renegade" winemakers, rebels in the industry who aren't afraid to do things differently. "Wine has a way of bringing down barriers, and that's even more true with natural wine," said Tamy.

Natural wines are made organically, with minimal intervention, and usually by small-scale, independent producers. The wines are fun, funky, relatively affordable, and fans say the winemaking methods even help ease hangovers (I'm not convinced, based on my own experience). Without filtration or refinement, natural wine is *alive*, like cheese or kombucha, full of beneficial microbes in each glass.

We were sipping a Grüner Veltliner blend made by Milan Nestarec in the Czech Republic.

"What do you taste?" Tamy asked her dozen or so waiters and bartenders, their noses tucked into their glasses as they inhaled. They were an eclectic group, dressed in jeans and checkered shirts and ironic vintage tees.

"Fresh-squeezed orange juice!"

"Totally," she encouraged. "Don't be shy."

"Honeysuckle," someone chimed in.

"A gas station."

"Oysters. The ocean."

"Yes!" Everyone was on the edge of their seats as Tamy explained that vitality captured in the glass, the way Milan believed gentle methods of growing grapes and fermenting them spontaneously made for the best wine—wine that captures a sense of a place and its spirit. It's a philosophy shared by many natural winemakers.

Tamy has a knack for creating a sense of family and community with her staff, that familiar sense of "We're all in this together." It's the quality that has always made a restaurant feel like home to me. It's what made me, for a long time, aspire to start my own restaurant. It's the same thing that lit up my mom's dark days at Ciral's House of Tiki.

Tamy didn't start out as a sommelier, nor with aspirations of owning her own restaurant. She worked in marketing as a strategic planner, first at the advertising and public relations giant Ogilvy in their Mexico City office, the city where she was born and raised. That's also where she met Felipe Donnelly, her husband and business partner. He was an ad guy, and the two of them would often take cigarette breaks together. They were each dating other people when they met, but they became fast friends.

Tamy's job took her from Mexico City to Miami and then to New York and away from her friendship with Felipe. Years later, though, they reconnected in NYC, where Felipe had also settled. They started dating. They got married.

Ten years later, they had amassed two kids, two restaurants, and one catering company together. But before all that, Felipe and Tamy slowly had become more and more dissatisfied with their advertising work. Felipe loved to cook, Tamy loved throwing parties, and the two began hosting epic dinners at their first shared apartment in Tribeca. "We had some rules," Tamy explained. "We had to invite different people, and cook different recipes, every time."

Some people retreat into their lives after they get married, closing in their couple ranks. Tamy and Felipe didn't want that at all; they wanted to keep meeting new people and creating a vibrant social life. Their dinner parties were a conscious effort to keep that excitement alive. "We were capturing the magic of New York City—we invited all kinds of people and misfits." They started with friends, and then friends of friends, and then, when their own circles started to feel exhausted, they began finding potential guests online during the early days of Twitter. "We discovered we're really good at bringing people together." They had a talent for finding strangers who would feel more like—and often become—friends, and for creating spaces where all sorts of very different people felt at home.

I discovered that about them, too. All of Tamy and Felipe's ventures attract interesting, fun people. As guests at Colonia Verde, people feel as privileged to be there as they do at Tamy and Felipe's intimate gatherings. Most Sundays, they host what they call a Sunday Asado, where guest chefs from Mexico or California or London take over the grill on their restaurant patio to create a meal while a featured winemaker pours their bottles.

Over brunch at Colonia Verde, I knew it was this mix of kindred spirits communing and connecting over food and drink that made me feel at home; it was Tamy's warmth that made me feel like I was somehow a part of the restaurant she created. Tony and I sat at the bar one Sunday after visiting a long string of open houses and dug into duck confit chilaquiles and whitefish arepas. The place buzzed around us with hungry, happy people. Tamy brought over mezcal spritzes and sat down with us, just for a minute, to tell us about her own move to Bed-Stuy a few years ago. Tony and I had fallen in love in Brooklyn and we couldn't wait to be back.

◆ ◆ ◆

We eventually found an apartment. After spending all of our evenings scrolling through StreetEasy and our weekends riding the subway and walking along big avenues and small alleys, we found seven apartments and made seven corresponding offers. After looking at what felt like hundreds that ranged from new condos with sweeping views to floors of old brownstones with fireplaces that had been closed up with bricks, we'd narrowed our search to Prospect Heights, Crown Heights, and Fort Greene, three neighborhoods in Brooklyn. The commute wouldn't be too cumbersome for Tony, who worked in Midtown, and we could still (sort of) afford a home there. More than anything, we wanted to like our neighborhood. I thought if we didn't love where we lived, if we didn't enjoy taking long walks with Ace on the weekend, if there weren't plenty of coffee shops for writing and restaurants for date nights, we might as well live in the suburbs.

At the time, I would never have thought I could say this, but I am so grateful our first six offers didn't work out. It turned out, in each instance, a different buyer could afford to pay all in cash or someone had offered more and more money. Some sellers wouldn't even entertain whatever we had proposed. Tony and I still walk by the apartments we lost on our way to the gym or the grocery store, and we scrutinize the block and the light in the morning and decide we love our home the best.

Number seven was unequivocally my favorite. I sit in that apartment as I write this, typing away on my laptop, settled into my couch. Out the window, snow is pattering into the building's garden. I am wrapped in a gigantic pregnancy pillow that Tony got for me that looks sort of like a snake, and Ace's little head rests on the pillow, too. Tony is away for work today, and when I walked Ace this morning, the Velcro on his little raincoat kept coming undone, exposing him to the wintry weather. He almost tripped over it. I was getting frustrated and wet, so

I took a lot of intentional, deep breaths. It was a weirdly quiet morning, and the snow stuck to both our noses.

Our apartment is perfect, really. It has a newly renovated kitchen, two proper bedrooms—so many of the "two bedrooms" we saw had bedrooms so small I doubted any type of bed would fit inside. It has high ceilings and closets (not a lot, but we saw apartments without any closets at all) and there is a garden outside. Finding an apartment in New York City for most people is all about compromise—no storage but lots of light, room to live but you have to trek up five flights of stairs and put up with windows that look out into a brick wall—but the one we landed was so close to what I had envisioned for our family. Most astoundingly, we could afford it, almost. We had to ask my mom and dad for help on the down payment, a fact that both Tony and I felt uncomfortable with. We would pay them back, we reassured ourselves more than anyone else. Slowly but surely, we would.

The whole process made my head swim. We needed to hire an attorney, who then drew up a contract that took hours on the phone to parse through. Then there was a back-and-forth with the seller's attorney, who wanted to include seemingly strange stipulations that our lawyer wanted to nix. There were riders and addendums to the riders. Suddenly, we needed to refinance Tony's loan from business school. Everything took ten times longer than I would have guessed it should.

There were endless documents needed for the bank's mortgage approval—I became a regular at my local branch. "Hannah, what can we help you with?" The nice man with the shiny head greeted me what felt like every few days. That was in addition to constant phone calls and emails—"What about your tax return for 2016? What about this business expense?"—that would pop up all day long and into the small hours of the night. My job as a freelancer made the paperwork more complicated and abundant.

And then there was the fifty-eight-page application from the apartment building's board—who needed to approve us as tenants. We needed to solicit letters of recommendation from friends, employers, banks, and landlords. We needed to obtain documents I didn't even know existed. We needed to tell them all about Ace. (I was sure if Ace had to have an interview, he'd pass with flying colors, but it turns out that was the one thing that wasn't required). Tony and I needed to show up in person for an interview. And we did all this knowing that, in New York City, the board is allowed to deny you without giving any reason at all.

I was afraid we'd go through everything and have nothing to show for it. I was afraid I would change my mind after we had started the process of buying our apartment. There was this looming dread that once we signed the contract, there was no going back. We hadn't seen the apartment for months—what if I didn't love it anymore? I kept looking at the pictures online. They looked great, but they were professionally lit and designed to look amazing. I didn't want to repeat this crazy process for a long, long time.

I'm usually pretty good at interviews. Since I was a kid, I've had a talent for talking with grown-ups (maybe because I'm an only child), for intuiting what people want to hear. And Tony is a star. He's very friendly and well spoken, but the British accent really seals the deal. But I had serious nerves before we met with the board. Our real estate agent had sent over a long list of what to do and what not to do under any circumstances. For example: no asking any questions. Even something innocuous like, "Are there any plans to update the lobby?" might offend someone—maybe the board president was fervently opposed to lobby renovations, and then our chance would be blown and we'd be back at square one, soon to be homeless, all because I'd felt like I had to fill a quiet moment with chatter.

I had studied the sheet. I felt as prepared as ever, staring down my closet in search of the perfect responsible, professional dress. We met in the basement of the apartment building, in a tiny unfinished room.

One of the board members produced a roll of paper towels and wiped down two foldout chairs before we sat in them. Everyone was polite.

There was an awkward silence while we waited for more board people to arrive, so I broke the rules and asked a nice lady, "How long have you lived here?" which led to a discussion of the changing neighborhood. She had moved to her apartment in 1992. The second night in her new home, there had been a murder upstairs.

It was a harrowing story, but she laughed it off. "When the sushi place opened down the street, that's when we knew things were changing."

The last person arrived by the time her story ended, and we got down to business. The six board members asked us some questions about finances, which I let Tony answer. That had been another piece of advice from our real estate agent—decide who will answer what. Then a member started telling us about recycling and parking. Fifteen minutes later, we were heading back to the subway. I had prepared for an inquisition and what we got was a super-brief conversation. We thought it went well, but who could know for sure?

The whole monthslong process was completely opaque and mysterious. The board said they'd let us know soon, but what did *soon* mean? One day? One week? Every time my phone buzzed with a new email, I tried in vain not to panic. My patience meditations had nothing on my nerves. I hated all this waiting.

And then it came, a PDF of a photocopy that had been printed on letterhead. We had been approved. We would be homeowners.

We moved on a Friday. On Saturday it started to rain, and it hadn't let up by Sunday. My parents had come to the city and swooped up Ace on Friday morning. When they dropped him off on Saturday, he sniffed around the boxes and every inch of the new floor. "That's your floor," I told him, "this is your new home," but he just looked at me with those big puppy-dog eyes, so I decided to take him out to get acquainted with our neighborhood. He didn't want to walk in the rain. He put out all four paws in protest and braced his legs against it. We barely made it around our new block. My shoes were soaked, and who knew where I had packed my boots?

At least I was able to find dry socks for the Sunday Asado. It was cozy in Colonia Verde, alive with a very Brooklyn crowd of women in modernist earrings and boots that I instantly envied, men with stubble and jaunty hats. Tamy wore a long red dress and seemed to magically appear to welcome us with some warm cocktail for Tony, a sparkling water for me. I wanted that warm cocktail, but I settled for a small sip of Tony's. Later, Tamy would confess that she'd drunk some wine while she was pregnant. "You have to take care of yourself, too," she told me in her pretty Mexico City accent. Tamy smiled at my stomach even though nothing much was visible there.

After the warm cocktails were finished, the guests switched to glasses of Macari wine from a steep, sandy slope on the North Fork of Long Island. Tamy introduced me to Gabriella—the winery was her family business—and she poured us tastes of a blend that tasted of black cherries and olives, followed by a Syrah like cedar and campfire. We took the wine outside, where the rain tapped on the roof of a tent and the grill puffed with rib smoke. The chefs fed us beef tacos and mounds of mushrooms and greens. It felt like we'd finally made it home.

"This has been the best welcome to Brooklyn," I told Tamy as the night came to a close and it was time for us to head back through the rain to our new apartment, crowded with boxes and stacks of chairs. How did we have so many chairs?

That's what the best hospitality people make you feel—tingly with joy and certain you are exactly where you are supposed to be.

◆ ◆ ◆

During those early years, Tamy and Felipe continued throwing their invitation-only dinner parties that grew and grew, until it was time to make them more official. They named their supper club Worth Kitchen—for Worth Street, where their apartment was. Tamy started blogging about those Thursday gatherings, where they'd sometimes host as many as fifty people at once. One night, a guest was a writer for *New York* magazine. Shortly after, a glowing story about Worth Kitchen ran in the popular magazine, and the city health department promptly came and shut the whole operation down with a cease-and-desist letter.

The setback became motivation for Tamy and Felipe—the dinners had started out as a hobby, but they had already started to turn it into something bigger. Now was the moment to take things further.

They found a small space on MacDougal Street, not too far from their apartment, and fell in love with it. They asked everyone they knew to chip in for opening costs—the rest they raised on Kickstarter. They quit their jobs. In July of 2012 they opened Cómodo. *Cómodo* means "comfortable" in Spanish.

Tamy told *Vogue*, who wrote about Cómodo in 2013, "In Latin America, your parents are always very big about dinner parties. I grew up with all the noise. Cómodo gets noisy, and, it's weird, when I hear that noise, it's comforting, it feels good. It reminds me of being about to go to sleep, and my parents, and laughter, and music, and glasses clinking."

The *New York Times* called Cómodo "almost a cliché of a romantic restaurant." Felipe is of Colombian descent and has lived in Spain, Brazil, and Mexico. From the time he began cooking, his food has represented a sort of hodgepodge of flavors and techniques that are inspired by the places he has lived and eaten. The food was in no way an afterthought—it was delicious, but it didn't stand alone, either—it was part of the experience Tamy and Felipe created every night. As was Tamy's wine.

When the couple had some rare downtime, they began exploring neighborhoods in Brooklyn. Tamy fell in love with Fort Greene almost immediately. "I loved seeing so many different people come together," said Tamy of Fort Greene's diversity. "As an immigrant, I felt at home."

With Cómodo demanding their full time and energy, "We really had no business opening up a new restaurant." But the opportunity felt too good to pass up. They found a shuttered building that was remarkably affordable to rent, especially compared to the increasingly astronomical prices in the West Village. Colonia Verde was born, a dimly lit, cozy-cool neighborhood restaurant with a garden out back and a forty-ounce bone-in rib eye with the perfect amount of char from the grill in that garden.

I met Tamy when she emailed me in response to an article I wrote about where to drink natural wine in NYC. I had left Colonia Verde out (I wish I could go back and fix that), but she didn't even mention the omission. She just invited me to come by and drink some natural wine in Fort Greene, and I said yes.

Tamy had become a certified sommelier when it became clear that they were onto something lasting with this new endeavor as restaurateurs. Felipe had the interest and focus for the chef life; Tamy was much more attracted to the front of the house, and also to wine, which she felt like often had an unnecessarily stuffy vibe that she could help dismantle. It took her a year and a half of studying to become a somm, and when she started the program, she had a brand-new daughter at home. She and Felipe hired a part-time nanny.

"When you have a kid, you have to reinvent yourself," Tamy told me. "You'll see what I mean. Your baby is born, but you're also reborn in a way because all of a sudden, you're split into two. You have to find your place within yourself and your work, as a business owner. I wanted to attach myself more to wine, and I just went for it, all in."

Tamy was becoming a mom and a restaurateur at the same time, and these two big steps meant stepping into a totally new identity. She was still herself, but the challenges every day were new. Being a parent made Tamy better at handling the messiness that was an inevitable part of owning and running restaurants. She had always been a perfectionist, thrived on everything being just so, but having kids meant coming to peace with a certain amount of chaos.

"There is always something that falls through the cracks, messes up, or gets lost in translation," she said, which is true of both being a mom to a kid and to a restaurant. She developed not so much a thicker skin, but a more symbiotic relationship with the mess. She started to see the beauty in it, and the creative advantages of not having every little thing under her control.

Tamy is constantly tweaking and changing up her list, which often features women winemakers she has befriended. "The regulars come in and they want to know what's new." The exciting and frustrating thing about natural wine is you may just fall in love with some weird orange bottle from Croatia, but then that's it. There's no more being made. The search is, in that way, never-ending, and it's about the exploration as much as it's about the discovery.

But as much as they are passionate and their restaurants reflect that devotion in their warmth, Tamy's journey hasn't been all rainbows and sunshine. In 2015 the couple's second restaurant, Colonia Verde (the one in Fort Greene), which had just been nominated for a James Beard Award, caught fire. They were about to celebrate the restaurant's one-year anniversary. At first, Tamy and Felipe thought it would be closed for a few days for repairs and inspection. But it ended up taking five months to undo the damage.

They had a great team of chefs and servers and hostesses, all of whom still needed work, so Tamy and Felipe started a catering business. After all, they knew how to throw a great party. Comparti catering grew to run hundreds of events each year, from weddings to one of New York's premier art fairs, the Armory Show.

◆ ◆ ◆

A few months after our first glass of wine together, Tamy invited me to the staff training for their newest project, the natural wine bar Cosmico, right next to a very trendy Williamsburg music venue, National Sawdust. Their team planned to also run National Sawdust's concession stand for shows. We had just moved, our new home was still strewn with boxes, and the new crib we hadn't yet removed from its packaging.

When I got there, Tamy and her team were checking out the new staff uniforms, unisex black jumpsuits. They had a few samples from some different vendors; they seemed to fit most of the women perfectly fine but none of the male servers. One ducked into a bathroom to change but refused to come out in the jumpsuit. "Nobody needs to see this," he bellowed from behind the closed door. Tamy laughed. They would figure out something else.

It was generous of Tamy to include me, as if I were a part of the family. It was in keeping with all I'd come to love and admire about her. She greeted me with a big hug, wearing a mesmerizing geometric-print sweater and great earrings. We started at the concession stand, where we tasted cocktails straight from little bottles from a Brooklyn company called Wandering Barman, served in stainless-steel cups in the name of sustainability. I was still first-trimester nauseous, but I tried the smallest taste of their marigold and kaffir lime margarita and instantly wanted more.

Felipe was experimenting with flavors of popcorn: the habanero ash and cheddar was no joke, just a bit spicy and superlatively cheesy, but everyone's favorite was his duck fat and rosemary popcorn, which was both light and rich, rich, rich. Freshly baked cookies and *alfajores* would come later. For now, there were packaged goodies like Zapp's potato chips and Pocky sticks.

Next door, the wine-bar-to-be, Cosmico, smelled of sawdust; a construction crew was building tables and finishing the bar. They had just moved their catering company kitchen downstairs, since rent was so much more affordable in Williamsburg than in the West Village.

The whole building vibrated with energy. Besides her natural wines, Tamy was working on her mezcal list, which would also feature small producers. I joined the staff in the kitchen as we tasted a lineup of dishes that would make the debut on next week's soft-opening menu. There was an eggplant that had been roasted until melty, topped with stringy *stracciatella* cheese and lemon zest. I loved the sardine toast, piled with garlic confit and fennel, and the fluffy, oniony tortilla Española. It was exciting, listening to everyone talk about the details of service—how much time each dish would need, how they would pair the eggplant, how they would handle the pre- and post-show rushes. Part of me wanted to ask Tamy if she was hiring.

It was a crazy time, opening a new spot and moving their catering business. I met Tamy at her favorite coffee shop in Bed-Stuy near her kids' day care. Usually, she spent two nights in the restaurant each week and the rest at home with her kids. Because of the opening, her two-year-old son and five-year-old daughter were spending a lot more time with their nanny. "It's a balancing act, and that doesn't mean I'm always balanced," she told me. It was an unseasonably warm day, and we sat at a table outside and shared a fudgy brownie. Her daughter spent a lot of time with her coloring books in the garden of Colonia Verde. "Maybe she'll take over the family business one day," Tamy told me. She apologized when she had to go, wrapping up a leftover piece of brownie in a napkin and stashing it in her purse for her son. "He's going to love this."

Tony and I received an invitation to the friends and family night at Cosmico, where they'd test out a service before opening to the public. By then, they'd found black jumpsuits that fit everyone, and the tables had been sanded down to a sleek finish. It was another warm Friday night in Williamsburg; the sidewalks were full. Candles glittered in the long windows. We sat at the bar and dug into vegan chicharrones and a raw-salmon tostada with a smoky smear of habanero-and-onion mayo. Tony tried a red wine from the Rhône Valley, which I envied. I sipped my sparkling water. Tamy was making the rounds and talking to everyone; Felipe had on his chef's coat and handed out plates of tortilla Española. The place resounded with excited energy—the start of something new.

"This is perfect," I told them.

"Not perfect," Tamy said. "But it's really fun." Which was just as good. Maybe even better.

Moving to Brooklyn felt like moving closer to this energy, moving into the heart of it. It was only a short cab ride back to our new apartment. In the back seat, I felt something shift inside me, like a little fish swimming and swiveling. I put Tony's hand to my stomach, but the fish had already stilled.

Manal

The first time I visited the Eat Offbeat headquarters in a commercial kitchen in Long Island City, tensions were understandably high. The whole staff was on edge about rumored ICE raids. Manal Kahi, the company's founder, had developed a warning system with her staff. They shared a commercial kitchen with a soup startup. If anyone got word of Immigration and Customs Enforcement officers arriving, they'd flick the lights twice. Manal's office was right above the commercial kitchen, so she'd hear any commotion, but she spent plenty of time in the kitchen itself, too.

Finally, I felt like I looked pregnant. I hadn't bought or borrowed any pregnancy clothes yet, but my jeans were uncomfortable, and so I wore an all-leggings wardrobe. There was no good way to get from my home near Prospect Park to Long Island City, and so my route included switching trains twice. After all that, I had gotten off at the wrong subway stop and then rushed to find the Eat Offbeat kitchen without being too late, half jogging down busy Queens roads lined with warehouses and car repair shops. I showed up sweaty and disheveled.

I'd arrived on a busy day, and Manal's catering company was deep into preparing thousands of samosas for an evening event. The space was shiny clean and frenetic, with chefs washing crates of lettuce, whirring herbs in food processors, and frying the flaky samosas. Downstairs was a standard commercial kitchen, with sinks, stove tops, and big ovens stocked with towering piles of sheet trays. Upstairs was a suite of offices. The smell of frying dough was enveloping. Chef Nasrin Rejali, an Iranian woman who'd settled in Jamaica, Queens, was still able to take a few minutes to chat and share her signature baklava cupcakes with me. She led me up the flight of stairs to a conference room. Nasrin's hair was pulled back tight for cooking, but her big brown eyes were perfectly lined and her red-lipsticked lips curled into a warm smile. Immediately, my nerves and general pregnancy malaise disappeared. I felt part of the life of this kitchen, brightened by the busy productivity and the delicious smells. The cupcakes were scented with saffron and cardamom and topped with a crunchy layer of slivered nuts.

"People hear all kinds of things about Iran, and they're mostly pretty bad," she said. "But I can share my food, which is good, which is love."

Nasrin once ran a restaurant next to a gym in Tehran, where she made traditional dishes like eggplant dips and saucy meatballs filled with hard-boiled egg and apricot. She can't remember a time she didn't gravitate toward the kitchen. She's been cooking since she was a little girl, and all these years later—Nasrin has been living in the US since 2014, along with her four children—she loves "all of it, from chopping the onions to frying the onions to most of all, sharing the food." Her signature dish is Chicken Fesenjan, slow-stewed chicken with walnut, pomegranate molasses, and saffron. It's one of Eat Offbeat's most requested items.

When Eat Offbeat founder Manal Kahi arrived in New York City from Lebanon to study environmental and international affairs at Columbia, she was confounded by a city with so many dining options but apparently without a single source of good hummus, anywhere. The grocery store offerings were deeply disappointing.

"I called my grandmother for her recipe," Manal remembers. Manal has curly dark hair and a big, bright smile. She wore an Eat Offbeat T-shirt and dangly earrings. "I would bring it to parties, and it always got rave reviews." Her grandmother is from Aleppo, and that hummus became a symbol of what Manal missed. Manal's grandma was the family cook and matriarch. "It was natural to make a connection to Syrian refugees. I thought: there are a lot of Syrian refugees resettled here; they likely make good hummus for their families, and they would probably enjoy sharing that recipe with New Yorkers."

Eat Offbeat was born. Today, the company's mission goes way beyond providing quality hummus to New York. Eat Offbeat employs resettled refugees from Syria, Iraq, Senegal, Afghanistan, Eritrea, and beyond to cook the food they grew up with, from Iraqi sumac salad to Nepali momos. "I speak five languages, but it's not enough," says Manal. The kitchen is full of a lot of languages (at last count, twelve) and a lot of flavors—they serve authentic meals that are entirely conceived of, prepared, and delivered by refugees who have resettled in New York City.

The dishes include Chef Mariama's Senegalese Chicken Yassa, slow cooked with mustard, caramelized onions, and green olives. There are those veggie samosas, stuffed with potato, masala, and cilantro, the brainchild of Afghan chef Bashir. Chef Dhuha, who is from Iraq, makes rich spiced date truffles dipped in coconut flakes. And then there are Nasrin's addictive baklava.

In Manal's words: "We hire talented home cooks who happen to be refugees by status, we train them to become professional chefs, then we deliver their food to groups of people all over the city." Corporate lunches and private parties in New York make up the bulk of the company's business, but they are primed to grow. Earlier this summer, four of their chefs paired with the restaurants abcV, Porsena, Il Buco, and Lalito in New York to host pop-up tasting dinners as part of New York's Refugee Food Festival. They published a cookbook featuring their signature recipes.

Early on, Manal partnered with the IRC (International Rescue Committee), which supports refugees and displaced people around the world. The IRC introduced her to people who had recently resettled and were looking for work. They had to love food and cooking, but professional cooking experience was not a requirement. She rented a commissary kitchen by the hour so her team would have a place to cook.

Manal asks potential employees to bring her a dish they like to prepare. A cook once brought in food from a street vendor, misunderstanding the assignment, but she had excellent taste. She was hired.

Later, Manal brought on Juan Suarez de Lezo, a Spanish chef who cooked at El Bulli and Per Se, to oversee the kitchen. He helps with training, menu design, and executing dishes to feed intimate dinner parties as well as giant corporate bashes.

Eat Offbeat makes a huge impact on a small group of people. It offers more than a well-paid job, training, and opportunities. A job with Eat Offbeat entails pride and a real sense of agency, an especially powerful thing for people who have been forced to leave their countries.

For some cooks, it's a place to find their feet in a new country before moving on to their own projects. Syrian chef Diaa Alhanoune owned restaurants in Syria, Sudan, and Jordan before coming to New York. He cooked at Eat Offbeat before opening his own spot in south Williamsburg called Sakib in 2019. The Eat Offbeat crew was there to cheer him on (and help wash windows) on opening night.

As for Manal, she didn't come to New York with food dreams. "I had never even been in a walk-in fridge before," she says. But she's not looking back. The world of food has become her home.

That's what food is for—to bring us together. It's a cliché, but it's never been more important than in a time of ICE raids and anti-immigrant fearmongering. A meal from Eat Offbeat is totally high-quality, crave-able food, first. Second, it's cooked with a lot of love by refugees. The city is way more delicious, rich, and strong because of them.

To me, Manal's story is a success, but even just a few months before we met, she told me, she was waking up in the middle of the night panicking about payroll. Just like my freelance writing business, which has busy times and uncomfortably slow times, Eat Offbeat operates in a constant seasonal flux. When we later met at a bakery near Union Square on a bright October day, it was in the middle of busy season—mid-September until about December twentieth. But Manal knew the quiet—"just dead"—months would follow.

"There will be no money coming in, but we still have expenses." This year marks the fourth holiday season the company has weathered, but each time when the uptick of orders comes to an abrupt end, it's newly unnerving.

"There's so much pressure," Manal says. She's gone months without collecting a paycheck, and she knows she can survive that. But her people are incredibly important. There are so many cooks who rely on that regular payment to make sure their family's rent and food are covered. Manal's mood pretty much depends on the financial state of Eat Offbeat.

In the early days, her stress was off the charts. Everyone chipped in, as they still do today, answering the phone and packing up containers of *mafe*—Senegalese chicken and peanut stew. But, in addition to running the company's daily operations, Manal would travel around the city delivering Eat Offbeat's orders. Sometimes she had an important event—a speech to give, or a meeting with an investor—and she would show up sweaty from carrying her body weight in bags of sumac salad and eggplant curry to a corporate lunch.

"Every tiny mistake—maybe we sent someone chicken samosas, instead of veggie, or an order was late—I would almost cry," Manal remembers. But with more time and experience, she's learned to brush the small things off and move on. "We always strive for perfection, but mistakes happen. There will always be traffic. We will always be human." She also has the help of a bigger team and better processes in place to handle everything from taking orders to chopping onions. Things just run more smoothly with extra hands and years of knowledge to draw from.

Manal's husband is a web designer—he built their website—and he also works for himself. Being a family without a real safety net has shaped the decisions they have made. They live frugally, in a one-bedroom apartment in downtown Brooklyn, and pour well over forty hours a week into their work. They haven't had kids—they don't have great health insurance, but more importantly, Manal's business feels like her child: it demands constant time, energy, and love. For now, that's how it is. Maybe one day it will change. Manal is still young, but like all women, she knows she doesn't have forever to make that decision.

◆ ◆ ◆

My parents live in Frenchtown, New Jersey, by the Delaware River, where Tony and I got married. After her stint at Whole Foods, my mom went on to have a pretty amazing career running nonprofits; now, she's a coach and consultant for nonprofit leaders. Their house reminds me of Noah's Ark—all wooden beams and big windows looking out onto the water. Tony and I were visiting them one weekend. I was really starting to show and had conceded to borrowing a pile of pregnancy clothes from my cousin, whose baby was already a toddler, and buying some of my own. I loved the soft, stretchy waistbands and wondered why all clothes didn't have such forgiving and comfortable fits. My mom, Ace, and I went for a walk on the path into town for iced coffee. We met a couple with a tiny baby in a stroller and started chatting. They had just moved to Frenchtown from Brooklyn.

"We've just moved to Brooklyn!" I said, excited about our new home.

"Oh, we had the best midwife ever," the woman said, and the couple proceeded to rave about her, how thorough she was, how well she got to know them, and I wrote down this midwife's name in my phone.

It turns out her office was only a twenty-minute walk from our apartment, she delivered at Mount Sinai West in Manhattan, and she was taking new patients. I loved the idea of seeing a midwife instead of the doctors at my practice, which had felt a little bit cold and machinelike.

The doctors only seemed to have about five minutes for me. It was a medium-sized practice, which meant I'd see a new OB every time during my pregnancy. I never got to know anyone particularly well. I thought back to the conversation with my mom during my first appointment, how the doctor had brushed off the question about the birthing center. I knew I was in perfectly good hands, but I also knew I couldn't expect any warmth or personal connection.

"You'll have a chat with my billing person, Katie," the midwife told me when I called her. Oh, how I chatted with Katie. Over the next few weeks, I filled out forms and more forms. I called the insurance we had through Tony's work to ask for an in-network exception, which required a lot more paperwork and was ultimately denied. Katie talked me through another mountain of documents to appeal the denial, which I dutifully completed. Again, we were denied.

I did a lot of pregnancy reading. We watched the documentary *The Business of Being Born*, which talks about the medicalization of the birthing world. I wanted the best of both worlds—access to quality medical care (I definitely believe in science!) but with a human, caring touch that I hoped would be a part of such an intimate and life-altering event. I wanted to deliver at a birth center that was attached to a hospital, but that doesn't exist in New York City. I researched options, I talked to friends, I talked to friends of friends. Here we were, a couple where one of us worked for a major corporation with great insurance, and I felt lost and without options.

I was disappointed that the midwife wasn't going to work out—we couldn't afford all that out of pocket—but I had formed a plan B. I'd stick with my doctors on the Upper West Side who took our insurance, and hire a doula, a person who was trained to provide physical, emotional, and informational support around childbirth. A doula is not a medical professional, but they are well qualified to deliver that touchy-feely aspect I was hoping for, a more personal connection during a process that seemed to cry out for it. A doula wasn't going to be covered by our insurance, either, but their fees were more reasonable, and it seemed like the type of support we needed to feel comfortable and informed. We reached out to our network and got a lot of recommendations. It turned out that a friend of a friend had just finished her doula training. We'd met at parties before and I had always liked her, but she wasn't available after all. That woman suggested someone else, who was booked all season. It seemed like every decision Tony and I made led us straight into a lot of dead ends. Eventually, I found a sort of doula matchmaking service called boober (that's really the name!) and I interviewed two doulas, a doula team. They answered my questions and described their philosophy—that birthing people's bodies instinctively know how to birth. One of them came over to my apartment so we could get to know each other. She let Ace jump up on her lap. She told me all about growing up in Brooklyn and how having her one-year-old baby felt both like a rupture in her identity and an epiphany. She told me how she planned to support me and also be there for Tony. Having a team of two doulas meant I wouldn't have to worry about a backup if one was attending another birth. I really liked them both. They were hired!

The doulas suggested questions to ask my care provider, which I brought with me to my next doctor's appointment. They included: "What is your induction policy post due date?" and "What are your thoughts about physiological birth?" This was a concept they had to explain to me. Essentially there are two schools of thought when it comes to birth: "physiological," an approach that sees birth as natural and safe, or "pathological," an approach that sees birth as unsafe by nature. That philosophy influences how each doctor will manage your care—including use of interventions and cesarean rates before they are medically necessary. My OB had never heard of physiological birth. I took that as a bad sign.

"Trying to do something that goes against their philosophy is not impossible, but it's pretty hard," one of the doulas advised. "It's like going to a bakery when you don't eat carbs."

I felt like I was back at square one. By that time, I was at twenty-two weeks, more than halfway through the pregnancy. I took a deep breath.

"Do you know if there are any doctors or midwives with a physiological model that take our insurance?" I asked my doula team. I needed an assist.

And sure enough, they had a recommendation for a midwife practice in Brooklyn. I called. Their office was also close to our apartment, walking distance right through Prospect Park. They were in-network. They delivered at a hospital in Park Slope, which we could walk to if the weather was nice, although I doubted we'd be walking there when I was in labor. They had an open appointment the very next week. The crisp walk to their office was pretty, lined with brownstones and the glow of a low winter afternoon sun. The place was not fancy inside; the ceilings hung low and a bit of a cigarette-smoke smell lingered (I was also overly sensitive to any sort of smell). I waited there for only a minute. The midwife talked to me for almost an hour, which had never happened at any doctor I had ever been to. She wore clogs and a drapey cardigan. Her office was crowded with papers and paneled in wood.

"It's not the most glam environment," she remarked, "but we give pretty excellent care, I think." She exuded the warmth that was missing in the Manhattan OB-GYN's office.

We talked about my birth preferences and genetic testing, but also about eating issues, and the neighborhood, and our favorite restaurants. I felt like a human rather than a cog in a machine. I felt grateful to have a reassuring plan for the birth of our baby, one that our insurance supported, but it had been tough to get there.

◆ ◆ ◆

A few weeks later, I spent another day in the Eat Offbeat kitchen. I was frazzled by the time I arrived. I had remembered there was a sign over the door to the kitchen: EVEN TINIER DRUMSTICKS, which I'd typed into Google Maps when I set out to meet Manal. I made the same circuitous subway journey, following the directions to another street lined with squat grey warehouses and loading docks that were definitely not a commercial kitchen. By the time I realized I was wrong, I *really* had to pee. I was more than six months pregnant; this was a common occurrence. Just before I was at the point where a public indecency charge started to look like a valid option, I made it. Manal reminded me where the bathroom was and handed me a hairnet.

It was a typical Monday in the kitchen, busy but not insanely so. Chef Bashir was finishing up the fragrant, autumnal orange *karahi* sauce that would blanket his chicken. Another chef was juggling four separate pots of bubbling mushrooms and chickpeas. A third was on onion duty, chopping whole boxes into what would become the translucent base of countless stocks and sauces.

The kitchen manager had to take the day off at the last minute—
there had been a death in the family—and the chefs were struggling a
bit to figure out their responsibilities for that day without someone del-
egating tasks. They used to employ a massive whiteboard to keep track
of what needed to be cooked and by whom. Now they label the empty
aluminum containers that will be filled with red rice, chicken karahi,
and Shirazi salad with the details, the order number, and the name of
the chef responsible for the dish, who will then fill up those containers
with the finished product. The empty containers act as to-do lists.

Although tasks like chopping onions are shared—each week, a different chef is responsible for dicing the mountain of onions that will
fuel that day's orders—each chef is ultimately in charge of their own
creations.

This collaborative approach is practically radical in kitchens; usually they function as an autocracy, with the singular head chef in charge
of everything from soup to dessert. The old-school French kitchen is
structured like a military brigade, with a strict sense of hierarchy. Orders
come from the top down, and cooks do precisely what they are told. In
kitchens from Modena to Memphis, this sensibility prevails. It's how
every kitchen I've worked in was run.

At Eat Offbeat, the structure and entire vibe is different. There,
each dish includes the name and photo of the chef who created it. It
helps instill a sense of both responsibility and pride in everyone who
works in the kitchen. Nobody wants their picture next to a plate of
something mediocre.

No "*oui*, chef" culture means there might be a monthslong dis-
agreement about the best way to dice carrots or whether or not a food
processor is required to chop several pounds of cilantro. It took weeks of
conversation to come to the consensus that for very large orders, they'd
use the food processor instead of chopping herbs by hand. Everyone
agreed by hand was better, but when it came down to the wire, there
just wasn't enough time. Manal has figured out that the best way to

bring everyone on board is to involve them in the conversation. Nobody wants to be told what to do.

Still, running a kitchen this way is a process. The company is growing and growing, and they continuously find themselves at a place where they don't really have the tools to keep up with their increased workload. On the upcoming Thursday, Eat Offbeat was preparing to feed more than four hundred people. The delivery team, led by Sarujen, uses a checklist to make sure they have all the right food, plates, condiments, and utensils. It's a simple system, but one that took months to perfect. "They had the checklist, but they were completely ignoring it," said Manal, who fielded constant calls about missing baba ghanoush or forks. For months, she had to ask her delivery staff to photograph the list, all checked off, and text it to her before every single delivery. Finally, the process stuck.

Sarujen, the delivery maestro, is the son of one of Eat Offbeat's chefs. He's in college, so he comes to the kitchen sometime around two or three, as soon as his last class is finished, to get to work expediting orders. The dry storage nook with all the bags, plates, and cups has a sign outside that says SARUJEN'S CAGE!! in cheerful, curly script. There he's the captain of a ship, directing the flow of orders and organizing them into bags before the delivery people whisk them away to far corners of New York City.

When I visited, the team was experimenting with variations on Chef Bashir's pakoras for a latke festival. There are millions of pakora variations, but they usually involve fried onions and other veggies. Bashir has made his pakoras before, seasoned with cilantro, mint, and chilies, and they were a serious hit. Everyone agreed they were latke-like, and cool labneh—*maast o moosir*—on top would contrast with the fried richness, just like sour cream on a traditional latke. They thought he could try them with potatoes and sweet potatoes to see how they compared to his original creation.

The vision had been shredded potato, quickly blanched since it wouldn't fry long enough to cook through. But Bashir was boiling the potatoes whole, then mashing them. "He didn't understand," said one Eat Offbeat staffer observing the boiling operation.

"He totally understood, he just didn't want to do it that way," said another onlooker.

Eat Offbeat had been picking up coffee from local shops to serve with their breakfast orders, and they had finally ordered their own coffee machine. After running the numbers they'd realized that making their own coffee came out to about a tenth of the price of buying it premade. But the electricity the coffee machine required was not the same voltage as what the kitchen was equipped with, so the electrician was on the way. They also had to figure out the cups and lids and the milk. Sarujen, who everyone calls Saru, had a plan.

It turned out Saru had a plan for taking care of the daily tasks, too, while the kitchen manager was out. He'd fill out the labels and match them with the proper empty containers for the chefs to fill. Each order would be assigned to a chef, too, who would be responsible for passing them along to Saru.

Meanwhile, the mashed-potato latkes were ready. They were crisp and still hot from the fryer, and everyone took a break to gather around and taste them. The group was split—the sweet potato latkes were the prettiest, but not as satisfyingly crispy. The potato ones were more like a traditional latke, but the traditional patties with just onion, carrot, and cabbage had the punchiest flavor. We chewed and slathered on more maast o moosir and watched the plate empty.

I decided to splurge for a cab ride home. Pregnancy had made me tired, and slow, in a way that felt strange. I was used to going full speed ahead all day, every day. I opened the window and watched my beautiful city fly by out the window. I thought of how much better, stronger, smarter, and more delicious our city was because of Manal and the refugee chefs she worked with.

Manal had imagined a kitchen and a food company in a totally different way. It gave me a huge sense of hope: change was possible, from the culture in our kitchens to the world outside the kitchen. I wondered what a food world with women at the helm would look like, and I knew it looked bright. I'd brought back a little container of Chef Nasrin's flaky baklava, and Tony and I ate them on the couch, my feet up, sticky honey on my fingers, Ace at our feet, eager to see if we'd drop any crumbs.

Allison

In the summer of 2015, when Tony and I had just started dating, I accepted a job offer to manage the content at Murray's Cheese, a beloved cheese shop in Greenwich Village that had turned into a cheese institution. By the time they hired me, they had a thriving wholesale and online business, a cheese bar and restaurant, and 250 mini shops around the country inside Kroger supermarkets. A few years after my tenure there, Kroger, which is the United States' largest grocer, bought Murray's Cheese, which was a surprise to nobody.

The job was a bust. On my first day, my new boss gave me a big PR project—I was to help us celebrate our seventy-fifth anniversary of Murray Greenberg opening the original dairy shop on Bleecker Street. We were supposed to throw some sort of big event and lure a lot of press to cover the anniversary. I didn't know much about PR, but I was game to learn.

"Great," I said. "Who is in charge of PR and marketing?"

"Oh!" My boss sounded surprised. "You are."

I had been through a whole bunch of interviews with everyone from my soon-to-be colleagues to the owner of the company, and nobody had mentioned that part of the job. I knew very little about either. It would have been a fun challenge to learn on the job, maybe, if my plate hadn't been plenty full with the responsibility of writing every piece of copy the franchise needed—internal memos and updates, descriptions of new products for the labels, grilled cheese menus, our blog and the signs in the store, and the massive holiday catalog, which received no fewer than twenty-seven rounds of edits from everyone, from my colleagues to the owner of the company.

The big seventy-fifth-anniversary party kept getting smaller and smaller, until we decided to just install a spin-the-wheel in the Bleecker Street store so customers could try for a free Murray's branded apron or grilled cheese sandwich and call it a day.

I was underpaid and overworked, but the job was not without its perks. At various times, quarter wheels of Alpine cheeses flecked in purple wildflowers would show up in our office and we'd all gather around with a big knife and a few baguettes. Sometimes I would have to spend my afternoon giving a tour of our cheese caves to a journalist, and we'd both suit up in the floppy boots, white coats, and hairnets required for entrance. We'd leave our jewelry in a little plastic bowl outside. As I'd push open the door to the bloomy rind room, full of the delicate blossoms of snow-white cheeses and the mushroomy smell of their ripening, I'd have that fluttery feeling and the clearest, truest thought: *I am immensely lucky.*

I felt the same way on a Wednesday at 6 AM outside Murray's warehouse in Long Island City when we loaded up in my coworker Lisa's car to head on a road trip to Vermont. On our agenda, a visit to three cheesemakers and suppliers: Consider Bardwell, Jasper Hill, and Vermont Creamery. We'd also attend the Vermont Cheesemakers Festival at Shelburne Farms.

"Bring a bathing suit," Lisa told me. Lisa was in charge of Murray's wholesale business, and she had an enviable head of curls and that takes-no-shit attitude of someone who spent the first part of her career in a restaurant kitchen. She had been a pastry chef at a fine-dining restaurant where she'd been assigned to cheese service. She didn't look back, but the chefs trusted her when they called in their orders, and she'd show up to their restaurants with the new shipment from Portugal or something that had just emerged, ash-coated and pure, from our cheese caves.

"A bathing suit?" I didn't associate cheesemaker visits with swimming. Usually we'd traipse through caves in sweatshirts and still emerge freezing, the tips of our fingers and toes threatening to numb.

"The festival is at Shelburne Farms, right near Lake Champlain. You'll have to follow me, we found the best secret entrance to the lake last year—the perfect cove for swimming. We'll sneak away at the end of the festival. It's beautiful."

We packed Lisa's trunk with jams and honeys and vinegars to gift to our cheesemaker hosts (there was no point bringing them cheese, they had plenty). Driving through Vermont in summertime was like hanging out in a postcard. Everything was green fields gently rolling past, red barns, mountains in the distance, everything sun-dappled and luminous. We played the radio and gossiped about our terrible boss and laughed until we had to gasp for air. We stopped for gas station junk food and burnt coffee.

At Consider Bardwell, there were veggies and burgers on the grill and cold beers waiting for us when we arrived. Stiff from all that time in the car, we walked, beers in hand, next door to the goat farm that supplied some of Consider Bardwell's milk. Behind us, the sun dipped behind the hills. The goats rushed over to greet us, bleating and humming their hellos. One of them licked the cold condensation from my glass beer bottle before turning back to a pile of grass.

We were up by 6 AM to watch Leslie the cheesemaker start her day's work—she had already been there for an hour washing the cheeses in their caves. Now that the fresh milk had arrived, she'd begin the process of transforming it into cheese.

A good cheesemaker must carefully examine the smallest details in the weather conditions, the animals, their feed, and the milk and take them into account. They have to stay present and focused. On that morning, it was a cool day when we spoke, after a long stretch of warm weather. That meant the cows would be less stressed and happier, the milk yield would be higher, and its protein and fat content would be up for the day. The smallest variables impact the final product.

We tasted through their cheeses: Dorset, Pawlet, Sylboro. We were working on a new collaboration, Barden Blue, a floral, peppery cheese that started at Consider Bardwell before aging in Murray's caves in Queens for a few months. We had brought a few different versions from the caves, and we lined them up on a table and started slicing slivers. Everyone liked the younger version better, which tasted a bit like milk chocolate.

We drove a lot. From Consider Bardwell to Jasper Hill in Greensboro, which was another three hours. We rolled down the windows and breathed in the green Vermont air. I remember tasting through dozens of wheels of Bayley Hazen Blue, long after the workers in the Cellars, Jasper Hill's beautiful, dungeon-esque cheese caves, had gone home.

The cheese was named for an old military road commissioned by George Washington during the Revolutionary War. No major battle ever took place, but the road brought Greensboro its first settlers, and we drove by it on our way to Jasper Hill. Its namesake is a dense, creamy blue cheese that reminds me of savory fudge. We were trying to pick out which batch we liked best. The thing is, the differences were subtle. Some wheels were more peppery and some had a crumblier texture, but after about number eight it became increasingly hard to keep track. Our buyer was scribbling down notes furiously. We finally narrowed it down to two batches, made a week apart, but then we were hopeless at choosing between the two. We started to get them mixed up. One tasted muskier, but then they both tasted increasingly musky. I closed my eyes and tried to focus on the cheese on my tongue, but my palate was getting tired and so was the rest of me.

Eventually, we decided to revisit the conundrum the next morning. It was already dark when we left the humid, cheesy air of the Cellars for the crisp Vermont night. We drove to a potluck that one of the Jasper Hill founders and owners, Mateo, was hosting at his house with local friends and neighbors and cheese people. Outside in the backyard, there were raw oysters atop mountains of ice and crisp beer from Hill Farmstead, which everyone agreed was the perfect way to wash down the oysters. A few hours before, I thought I'd never want more Bayley Hazen Blue, but there I was spreading a slab of the good stuff onto a crusty baguette, gathered around a blazing fire, feeling buoyant. The sky was dirty with stars.

Still giddy the next morning, we drove to Shelburne Farms, a sprawling 1400-acre working farm and educational nonprofit. The cheese festival was instantly fun—so many cheeses, and cheesemakers, and people I knew or my coworkers said I should know—but Lisa was right. The best part was afterward, when I shimmied into my bathing suit in the back seat of her car and then climbed down the ladder where the trees opened up into the wide lake, dipping my feet, my torso, my head into the biting, smooth water of Lake Champlain, which I let hold me entirely. The sun shimmered on its still surface.

This was another kind of victory for me: in the throes of my eating disorder, I wouldn't have even considered wearing a bathing suit in front of my coworkers. I thought of skinny-dipping with Jenise, Justin, and Sophie all those years ago in the cover of darkness. Today, I didn't much care. Sure, I had a moment of wishing my body took up less space, that my thighs didn't rub together when I slipped off my shorts and left them on the rocky bank, but mostly, I felt at home in my body. After all, it had taken me there, to that road trip full of work that felt nothing at all like work—the sky dizzyingly blue. My body had tasted the Bayley

Hazen Blue, and tasted it again, and taken in the cold, sweet oysters and there it was, being held by the lake and that day and that sky.

◆ ◆ ◆

The next day, we set off for Vermont Creamery. Everyone in our group already knew Allison, the founder and owner—along with her business partner, Bob Reese, who handled the money and organizational side of things. As for Allison, she was a cheese goddess, one of my cheese heroes, and it was the first time I was going to meet her in real life. All the nerves I felt were quickly eased when I was welcomed by her warm, genuine presence, a small woman wearing shorts, with cropped blonde hair and a knowing smile.

Allison grew up in Morristown, New Jersey, and went to Connecticut College. "I wasn't a particularly good student, but I trudged through college because that's what people do," Allison told me. Her junior year, she headed for a spring semester abroad in Paris. At first, she found it an "exceedingly lonely place. Parisians were just brutal, the worst, and I would take it very personally." As the months wore on, as Allison spent long afternoons trudging through different neighborhoods and visiting museums, she started to find her bearings and make some friends. The second language felt like less of a barrier and more comfortable coming out of her mouth.

She was scheduled to return to the States after finishing the semester, but she wasn't ready. She was just starting to feel at home in Paris, and she was in no hurry to head back to Connecticut. The college let her switch her major from history to French, which would allow her to spend the first half of her senior year abroad.

Allison was looking forward to more time in France—she'd have the summer and the fall. But she needed to make a living. "One of my professors suggested I consider working on a farm in exchange for room and board," and Allison thought that sounded like an adventure.

She wrote to the association of organic farmers in France, and a couple who owned a family farm in Brittany wrote her back with a job offer. Allison packed her bags.

"They had goats, sheep, some kids. We made charcuterie and sausages; we churned butter. It was an incredible experience." Allison learned about the concept of *terroir*, or sense of place. Terroir refers to how everything in the environment affects, say, a bottle of wine or a wheel of cheese, from the soil to the terrain to the climate.

On the farm in Brittany, food and land and culture were intrinsically connected. Allison fell for this promise. She loved milking goats, the alchemy of milk becoming butter. Something lit up inside of her.

After her fall semester in Paris, Allison came home, graduated from college, and went to Taipei, thinking she was going to learn Mandarin. But Mandarin seemed impossible, and she felt herself drawn back to Brittany and to the farm life. So she left Taipei behind and headed to a small farm in the Ardèche, in southeastern rural France, halfway from Grenoble to Provence, where she learned to raise bees for honey and make cheese from the farm's own herd. "It was like *Heidi*—the cows would graze during the day in the mountains."

This was the early 1980s, and most Americans didn't even know goat cheese was a thing. Greenmarkets were just getting started in New York City. But Allison had a conviction that goat cheese was special, delicious, and even essential. If people would try it, they might understand.

For a few months, Allison worked on a goat farm in western New Jersey called the Goat Works, but it wasn't a particularly impressive operation. They made cheese that was "mostly bland, and mostly inedible."

Allison's grandmother lived in Barnard, Vermont. "I didn't know what I was doing, I didn't have any plan," she said, but Allison knew Vermont had some fantastic farmland. She paid a visit to Shelburne Farms—the same Shelburne Farms where I went swimming at the

Vermont Cheesemakers Festival—thinking perhaps they would be interested in making goat cheese. They gave her a look like, "How did this person get a meeting with us," Allison remembers. "They said they were not going to be milking any goats there."

Some acquaintance knew of a place in Brookfield, Vermont, where Don and his then-wife Alice Hooper were breeding and milking goats—most of the milk went to a health food store, which is now a Whole Foods. Don sold the rest out of the back of his pickup truck from the farmers' market he'd helped start in Montpelier, along with rabbit meat and live rabbits. In those days, he remembers there being a surplus of people selling crafts and potholders, but only a small handful of farmers. It was hard, thankless work.

The Brookfield farm was a sort of hippie-ish commune. "We all lived cooperatively," Don Hooper, now Allison's husband of more than three decades, told me. "We would take people in who seemed interested. We all had day jobs to make money, but we'd share the work on the farm. We milked the goats at 4 AM and 4 PM every day. Allison came by in 1984, when my marriage was breaking up." It turned out that she never left. She transformed the place into a thriving business.

During that trip with Murray's, we cooked a big dinner with Allison and Don in their spacious kitchen, helping to slice veggies for a salad on their island while the sun set outside the windows, talking until I felt dazed from the wine and exhaustion, but too excited to go to sleep. I didn't want to miss a thing. Allison was a big deal in the cheese world, but she was welcoming and unpretentious and made me feel like I belonged there.

◆ ◆ ◆

Five years after my first trip to Brookfield with Murray's, I returned to spend the weekend with Don and Allison. Their white clapboard farmhouse was surrounded by acres of hayfields. We were sitting by the fire.

Outside the windows, everything was blanketed in boundless white. The afternoon sun ricocheted off the snow, already low in the February sky. Besides feeling empty without all my boisterous coworkers, the beautiful house looked the same, as did Allison and Don. We were all older, of course, but they remained full of youthful energy, fit and bursting with conversation. I felt like I had grown up. In the time that had passed I had fallen in love, gotten married, moved several times, gone to graduate school, written a book, and in a few months my life was about to change in an even more profound way.

It was a seven-and-a-half-hour journey from NYC to Randolph, the closest town to Allison and Don, on Amtrak's Vermonter line. A sleepy, beautiful ride, where the industrial landscape of Connecticut morphed into charm-filled towns of western Massachusetts, and then the dense forests, frozen lakes, and deep quiet of rural Vermont. I shared a train with a group of boarding school boys who were heading for a field trip—a week on a Vermont farm. I went to the bathroom about a million times and read my book. I hoped to get some writing done, but I felt woozy staring at my laptop as the train careened over the tracks.

At their house, Don and I chatted while Allison was playing Saturday tennis. She was in her sixties and exceedingly athletic. Don and Allison had just returned from a biking trip around Cambodia, and she was busy planning her next trip trekking through Nepal.

In 1984, Don's first marriage had been on its last legs. When Alice, his ex, accepted a job teaching agriculture at Cornell without first consulting Don, he knew their relationship was over. Don was becoming disenchanted with his work on the farm. What had started as a passion project no longer felt like his passion—instead, it mostly felt like thankless, never-ending work. That same year, Don ran for a spot on the Vermont House of Representatives and won. Newly energized by political life, he left the farm more and more in the hands of the fellow commune members, like Allison. Alice moved to Ithaca to start her new job, and she and Don separated officially.

Meanwhile, Vermont's Department of Agriculture organized a dinner featuring all Vermont-made products. Bob Reese, who worked for the department and had just gotten an MBA, was tasked with putting on the event. A French chef asked him where he could find local goat cheese. Bob scrambled to find a nearby producer—he was coming up empty-handed. Someone thought of Allison, who was milking goats in Brookfield. At the co-op, there were plenty of goats but no cheesemaking facilities, so Allison whipped up a batch of fresh goat's milk cheese in the sink just for the occasion, using the skills she had mastered in France. The cheese came out gorgeously.

The chef loved that sink-made cheese, and so did all of the other chefs at the event. "How can we get some?" they asked Allison.

It was Bob's wife who suggested Allison and Bob go into business together. Bob had the business chops and Allison knew how to make excellent cheese. This was the moment Allison had been waiting for.

Allison asked Don if they could use some of their goats' milk to make cheese, and he said sure. Allison and Bob both invested $1000 in their new business—they didn't have much more to spare. The United Church of Christ gave the pair a $4000 loan, which they used to renovate the ramshackle barn on the Brookfield property and buy some basic cheesemaking equipment, an upgrade from the sink.

They started with fresh chèvre, a mild, easy-to-love cheese that they thought might delight the American palate. But they did not find instant success. At first, no one really knew what to make of the product. "Nobody made goat cheese and Vermonters didn't eat goat cheese," said Allison. They spent a lot of time trying to sell at farmers' markets, but the reception was lukewarm at best. Goat cheese wasn't on anyone's shopping list, or even on their radar.

"When I reflect, I marvel at the naïve nerve we had in 1984," Allison says. "It wasn't like the market was asking for goat cheese." She used the goat milk to make quark, crème fraîche, mascarpone—delicacies that were pretty much unknown in the US, even to food lovers. The cow farmers, Allison's neighbors in Vermont's White River valley, thought she and Bob had lost their minds, tilting at windmills.

So Allison drove to New York City with a big cooler packed with cheese. In the 1980s, many or most of the New York restaurants that were considered the best were French. French chefs knew about goat cheese. They told Allison, "If you can make something locally that is as good as what we can import, we will buy from you." They had confidence in the product, which was made with high-quality milk and careful expertise. "Chef by chef, we got things going."

Those chefs got Vermont Creamery on its feet. They served their crème fraîche and goat logs in salads, soufflés, and on cheese boards. They helped show diners that goat cheese was a unique and wonderful thing.

"There were no Whole Foods, no Murray's Cheese kiosks in Kroger. We evolved as the market evolved."

Terroir is more than just land. It is resources, money, politics, distribution, and trends. In France, small cheesemakers like the ones Allison once worked with in Brittany often brought their products just a few miles away to market, where they sold in a few days. Consumers didn't mind a bit of blue or green mold on their aged goat cheeses. But as Allison grew her business, she would have to figure out how to ship across the country and have the cheese hang out in a warehouse for a few weeks, without any detriment. And she knew Americans would be squeamish about her wheels being any color but pure snowy white.

It's hard to imagine a time in our food world where *local* and *sustainable* were not buzzwords. But they were just not part of the zeitgeist in 1984. There weren't any meetings about branding or identity. Those things were "just intrinsically part of our DNA," Allison told me. They worked hard. They were not only making a product, they were trying to create a market for it.

There were scares along the way—a big one in 1987, when Allison worried they weren't going to make payroll. They had to rally sixteen people—friends and family—to invest in the company. Each person loaned a few thousand dollars. Among the investors were Allison's and Don's parents, and Ben Cohen from Ben & Jerry's, who was becoming a trusted friend.

Another big challenge was finding goat milk. It soon became clear that Don's tiny herd was not going to support the operation. Allison drove around, looking for backyard hobbyists and cow farmers who might be willing to raise some goats. They were also outgrowing their cobbled-together cheesemaking facility in Brookfield. In 1988, they opened a new, bigger facility in Websterville, Vermont, about fifteen miles away. Even the people who installed the equipment were naysayers. "They had only made cheddar cheese," Allison remembers. "They told me we were doing everything wrong."

In 1989, Allison and Don got married. In August of 1991, the couple's first son, Miles, was born.

I had just started my third trimester when I arrived at Allison and Don's house. When we were planning the visit, Allison asked if I skied. Hitting the slopes on the Green Mountains was one of the big attractions of the area, and Allison and Don also cross-country skied. I had taken a beginner's class on the bunny slope once, in middle school, when I tagged along with a friend's family. That was my first and last time skiing. I wanted to learn, but I didn't think the last stretch of pregnancy was a particularly good time to begin. The only skiing I did during that trip was gracelessly making my way from the driveway to Allison's home. The driveway was icy, and Allison carried my bag as I inched my way forward, telling myself not to slip and trying to reassure myself that it was better to look stupid and slow than to fall and hurt myself and Avocado.

Allison and Don asked about the book I was working on, this book. I told them it was in progress. My manuscript was due two weeks before the baby, so I had an extra built-in deadline.

It was then that Allison told me the story of her being pregnant with Miles. She had just ordered an industrial sausage maker. She and her staff had been rolling logs of goat cheese by hand, which took up an enormous amount of time and energy. "The machine was supposed to replace me—it was my plan for maternity leave," Allison remembers. She found an excellent deal. "It was a ten-thousand-dollar used machine that would have been a hundred thousand had I bought it new." But the discount came at a steep price—no matter what they did, they couldn't get the machine to work. There was no owner's manual, no internet to google instructions. It was a mess, spitting out hydraulic fluid all over the floor. The crank wasn't working, either.

Allison tried her best to troubleshoot the problem, but her efforts were to no avail. "I'm definitely not an industrial mechanic." Meanwhile, Miles's due date came and went. Frustrated and incredibly pregnant, Allison decided to fly in a specialist from Chicago to remedy the situation.

"I had spent weeks trying to figure it out," Allison told me. "This guy took one look at it and fixed it in ten minutes. That night, I went home and lay down on the couch. I started having contractions. The next morning, Miles was born."

"So, do you think he was waiting?"

"Absolutely. He knew I had to get that one big thing done. Which is to say, don't wait too long on your book."

◆　◆　◆

Miles spent a lot of his babyhood in a bouncer on the cheese production table. Once, he bounced so forcefully that he flipped over and landed on the floor. Allison decided it was time for a nanny.

While Allison was building her goat cheese empire, Don was launching his political career. Vermont Butter and Cheese Company (the first name for what would become Vermont Creamery) was growing, and

Don ran for Vermont Secretary of State. When Miles was three, Allison and Don had twins, Jay and Sam. "If the kids spend every weekend loading up into the car and heading to a political rally, well, it just is normal for them," Allison told me. Don won that race. He went on to work for the National Wildlife Federation, until he retired in 2016.

As Americans came to love artisanal cheese, Vermont Creamery was at the heart of the whole movement. Their butter and cheese have won more than one hundred awards nationally and internationally. Chefs like Éric Ripert of Le Bernardin, Molly Hanson of Grill 23, and Dan Barber of Blue Hill cooked with and celebrated their cheeses.

Vermont Creamery gained B Corp status in 2014—which means the business was deeply committed to solving social and environmental problems. "We chose to become B Corp certified not because it's groovy or good for marketing. We pursued this rigorous assessment because it's what we've always done: treat our employees fairly, take care of our animals and those who tend them, and assure that we keep focused on a vision beyond the bottom line. It's simply the right thing to do."

In the morning, Don, Allison, and I turned on the radio to hear an interview with Jay, one of their twins, who had been elected to the Vermont House of Representatives in 2016. Their son Sam owns Vermont Glove, formerly the Green Mountain Glove Company, in Randolph, Vermont, a century-old manufacturer that makes soft and durable gloves from goat skins. Allison slipped me a pair to borrow. They were like butter; I didn't want to take them off.

In the afternoon, the sun tilted into the house, where Allison had started making goat cheese before I was born. Allison slipped me another pair of gloves—I had lost my own inferior pair on the train— and took me to visit her other son Miles at Ayers Brook Goat Dairy, also in Randolph, near the train station. By 2016, Vermont Creamery had a hundred employees. When she and Bob sold their business— really, her first child—to Land O'Lakes in 2017, Miles took over the 150-acre goat farm, which was once a part of Vermont Creamery. They had about seven hundred goats, but it was about to be spring, and the babies would raise the numbers to twelve hundred.

Allison's employees were her extended family. Adeline Druart, who grew up in a small village in eastern France called La Villeneuve, came to Vermont in 2002 to intern for Allison—she was getting a degree in biotechnology in Lyon. Now she's the president of Vermont Creamery and a VP at Land O'Lakes.

Allison stayed on for a few months after the sale to consult, and then she retired. But she's still busy as a trustee at Sterling College, and she's active judging cheeses, consulting, and mentoring for the American Cheese Society. She's on the board at Shelburne Farms Inc. Allison also acts as a sort of unofficial advisor for Ayers Brook Goat Dairy and Vermont Glove. For example, as I slept in her guest room in my pregnant haze, she was up all night brainstorming with Miles about goat genetics, and how they could create another revenue stream by artificially inseminating goats from other farms with a species that produces the most casein-rich milk, ideal for dairy.

Soon, when the baby goats come, Allison will spend long days at Ayers Brook helping to nurse them. Miles proudly showed us his new formula mixers, which had just arrived from Wisconsin. The goats looked up as we came in, pressing their noses up to sniff my hands. We watched them line up to be milked in single file, so neat. "They love it," Miles said.

There are so many buzzwords that are second nature to Miles, just as they are to Allison: they never use hormones or antibiotics; there's the highest standard of animal husbandry and care for the land. "They are our other children," said Miles, who just had his first baby with his wife. It's not easy work, but it's rewarding. He stuffed my pockets with goat salami to take home with me.

"I didn't get to spend a ton of time with my kids when they were little," said Allison, "but I get to make up for it now."

In 2018, Allison won the James Beard Foundation's "Who's Who of Food & Beverage in America" award. In my own career, I had learned her name as soon as I had tasted Cremont, a delicate, crinkly-rinded cheese made from goat's milk with Jersey cow's milk and cream. It tasted like melting ice cream and happiness.

"I don't know why you want to write about me," she said as we waited for the train, hiding from the Vermont cold in her car. "I'm not that interesting."

It sounded silly, but I told her, sincerely, she was one of my heroes.

For my journey home, Allison had packed me some of Vermont Creamery's new quark—she had always wanted to make the tangy spreadable quark, but the moment hadn't been right—along with some leftover sesame noodles and the seared beef we'd had the night before, from her own steers. I bet I had the best meal of anyone on that train. I had packed light, but my suitcase was full of goat sausage from Miles and cheese from Allison's fridge.

The farmhouses and streams of Vermont turned into little factory towns in Connecticut, and, finally, I could see New York City's skyline out the window, home.

Haylee

We were loving our new Brooklyn home. It felt like an urban enclave that was tapped in to places like Eat Offbeat, and all the exciting things Tamy's restaurants were doing. There was even a great cheese shop that sold wheels and slices of cheeses from Vermont Creamery and Crown Finish, a cheese cave just a few blocks away from our apartment. I loved our neighborhood walks around Crown Heights and Park Slope, through Prospect Park, where Ace could run around and make new dog and people friends. Right from the beginning I had the sense that we were becoming part of a vibrant community.

Before we'd closed on our new place, I'd taken the subway on a rainy day to Brooklyn for the apartment inspection. Tony was running out of vacation days—he was taking one the next day for our closing—and my dad had agreed to come along. I got there early but couldn't get into the building. My dad wasn't due to arrive for another twenty minutes. I had worn sneakers, a very poor choice, and they had graduated from soggy to sopping as I made my way up Washington Avenue from the subway exit at Brooklyn Museum. My umbrella buckled and broke in the wind.

Immediately next door to our apartment building is a parking lot, and next to that is Cafe Eloise. It's identifiable by two flags outside: a rainbow flag, and a Black Lives Matter flag. There's a white bench painted with pineapples and a window ledge full of plants. A hot coffee seemed a small miracle on that sort of day. I tossed my useless umbrella in the trash can on the corner and went inside.

The barista, who I soon learned was also the owner, Haylee, wore a beanie and a pink sweatshirt. Even from behind the counter, I could tell she was short. She had tousled brown hair and gave me a smile with her beaming green eyes that crinkled around the edges. I must have looked like a mess. We started chatting, and I told her we'd be moving to the block in a few weeks.

"Fabulous," she said. "I've lived in so many neighborhoods and this is the best one."

"You're absolutely validating our choice," I said. I already loved the area. I kept walking around and peering in restaurants and thinking, *I want to eat there,* and *We need to try this place.* I had scoped out a handful of coffee shops that were definitely going to double as my second and third and fourth offices. Starting with Cafe Eloise, of course.

"I'll be your neighborhood concierge," Haylee volunteered, and I immediately wanted to take her up on it. A man walked in with a giant fluffy dog—like Ace had been scaled up—and a baby in a carrier on his chest. Two women ate muffins at a table in the corner. This place felt right.

I took my latte with the signature Cafe Eloise pink lid to the inspection. I was afraid to see the apartment after so many months, afraid I would somehow not love it anymore. How could it be as nice as I had remembered? But even on this stormy day, the sky outside the window heavy and leaden, even totally empty of furniture and signs of life, the apartment felt warm. Our new home! It was everything I hoped I'd remembered accurately.

We ran the dishwasher and turned on each burner on our new stove. We flicked the lights on and off and tested the buzzer. I was glad my dad was there. He noticed one of the outlets was wonky. Nobody— our Realtor, the seller's Realtor, my dad, nor I—could get the air conditioner in the second bedroom to work. I couldn't manage to feel too upset.

The next day, we were homeowners. Our Realtors had agreed to a small sum to cover fixing the outlets and buying a new air conditioner. Tony and I met at the management office in Long Island City, Queens, for the closing. The bland conference room with greyish, windowless walls was full of people we had exchanged dozens of emails with but never met in real life (our mortgage guy, the seller's lawyer), plus plenty of people we didn't know at all (the seller's bank representative, the management company's representative). Everyone shook hands and gathered around in oversized roller chairs at a giant table. The seller's lawyer explained she had been running around all day and asked if we'd mind if she had a snack. They set a pile of pens in front of us.

We took a picture with the official certificate, then our mortgage guy placed it carefully in his suitcase and said he had to run to another appointment. An absurdly large number of checks were passed back and forth across the table. The hungry lawyer munched loudly on little carrots from a ziplock bag. We signed and signed papers until I needed to roll my wrist around in figure eights; it was cramping up.

"Congratulations!" everyone finally declared, in a great chorus. Our broker gave us a hug and a very heavy gift bag (it contained two Tiffany's champagne flutes and a bottle of bubbly). We took a selfie with our new set of keys on the 7 train. I felt a little bit like a kid playing grown-up.

It was unseasonably warm enough to sit outside at our favorite tapas place on 95th Street, back on the Upper West Side, which we were already referring to as the old neighborhood. We ordered *pan con tomate* with jamón, hot piquillo peppers sprinkled with flaky salt, and paella with rings of squid and fat shrimp. The owners, who we had come to know, brought us glasses of cava and we toasted to all the new adventures that sat right on our horizon, close enough to touch, and resplendent. The sun was still gleaming. We held hands across the table.

◆ ◆ ◆

Every time we walk Ace, he wants to go to Cafe Eloise. It doesn't matter if it's early in the morning or late at night and the place is closed, lights off. He runs up to the green door and peers in expectantly. He'll put his nose right up to the glass, and sometimes a paw against the door.

When we do bring Ace inside, he says hi to everyone in the café one at a time. First the people—he nuzzles into their calves, the height he comes up to—and then the dogs. His little tail shimmies in delight.

One night, Haylee was closing up when Ace darted to the door. She waved Tony and me in, and Ace jumped onto her legs.

"Hi, cotton ball!" she greeted him. "Hi, fluff ball!" She turned to me. "Can I touch your belly?"

Haylee put her hands on my middle, and it tickled a little.

"There are literally thousands of sperm inside of me right now," Haylee said to Tony and me. "I'm thirty-one years old and this is the first time sperm have been in my body."

"Is it weird?"

"Yes, and exciting." Haylee and her wife, Jean-Michele, had gotten married in Seattle a few months before Tony and I were doing the same in New Jersey. A year and a half later, they wanted to have a baby, too.

They had a donor all picked out. They didn't want to choose someone from a catalog; that felt cold and wrong to them. Instead, an old friend of Haylee's was excited to be the biological dad. Haylee and Jean-Michele agreed their friend was cute and smart and pretty much perfect. He was a little hairy, which Haylee felt indifferent about but Jean-Michele took as a good sign of his virility.

But the last two months when Haylee was ovulating, the donor couldn't make it from California to New York.

Haylee was talking about the situation with Talia, who ran the café with her, and Talia's husband, Matt. "I'll do it," Matt said to Haylee, just on a whim. Matt was a carpenter and a little hairy, too (and cute and smart!).

"Is that cool with you?" Haylee asked Talia. Talia didn't even hesitate before she gave her enthusiastic consent for her husband to give her business partner his sperm.

They did it the old-fashioned way, with a turkey baster. Five days later, Haylee was already convinced she felt symptoms—some nausea ("I never feel nauseous, I've puked maybe once in my life"), and lots of trips to the bathroom to pee.

"I know it's too early to feel pregnant," she said. "But I do!"

I didn't know that it was actually too early. Our bodies are crazy, powerful, and mysterious.

"Are you stressed?" I remembered the trepidation of waiting for what it would say on that little stick. The weird discomfort of not knowing what was going on in my body.

"Not yet," she said. "I'm happy to do this for six months or maybe nine months. We're not going to do IVF, I don't think. It's so expensive and brutal on your body. If this doesn't work, we'll talk about adoption. But we have two uteruses!"

I thought about how Haylee and Jean-Michele worked for themselves, how getting good and affordable health care would be an obstacle no matter what. Insurance providers do not usually cover IVF services anyway, where one partner carries a pregnancy and the other provides eggs. IVF costs many thousands of dollars. Having a baby is such an elemental life thing, and it can be profoundly hard for so many.

I crossed my fingers for Haylee and Jean-Michele. Selfishly, I hoped Haylee was pregnant, or would be pregnant soon. It would be fun to be new-mom neighbors together. I also wanted her to get what she wanted. I wanted her to feel as exceedingly lucky as I felt then. Inside my stomach, the baby tumbled in what felt like a perfect arc. Ace started enthusiastically licking Haylee's outstretched hand.

◆ ◆ ◆

Haylee grew up in Indio, California, in the Coachella Valley, which she called the "Arizona part of California" because it's basically desert. Just twenty-three miles from Palm Springs, it's an entirely different world. "There were insurance-funded conversion centers as of 2004," Haylee told me, by way of explanation. Growing up in that environment as a young lesbian was tough.

It took Haylee years to reconcile with her family after she came out. In her apartment a few blocks away from me, we sat on the couch and ate dates she'd brought home from her most recent trip to see them for the holidays. Haylee and Jean-Michele's place was cozy, full of pretty rugs, bookshelves lined with books, and bowls of pears and clementines. She had invited me and Ace over for wine and cheese. The dates were glossy and tasted of caramel. She'd also laid out a purplish blue cheese and Marcona almonds. We had to stop Ace and Diego, Haylee and Jean-Michele's dog, from jumping up onto the low coffee table to snag our treats.

When she was a teenager, she left home. Her parents asked her to return a few months later, but she didn't feel safe there. Haylee was openly queer in the middle of a homophobic community. She dropped out of high school her junior year and slept on friends' couches for months. It was a hard time of just "trying to survive."

Food jobs were a way to do just that. There is a sort of amazing democracy to food service. Workers don't need any sort of degree or pedigree. Her story reminded me of my mom as a teen at the Copper Kettle in Framingham, where she had just shown up and worked hard, just like Haylee. Haylee took her first job when she was fifteen—she lied about her age, claiming she was sixteen—at a Jack in the Box franchise. Then she worked the graveyard shift as a waitress at the Denny's in Palm Springs.

The jobs gave her the money she needed to survive, and eventually move off her friends' couches and into an apartment. She wasn't a foodie—she ate fast food and quick food, affordable meals to keep her satisfied. But restaurant work gave her the sense of community she longed for. She met kindred spirits; she wasn't any sort of outcast at work.

When Haylee started a new gig as a prep cook at Native Foods, a vegan fast-casual restaurant, she found herself actually pulled toward food and service. Her other jobs had been a means to keeping herself clothed and fed. This was different. Haylee worked for Chef Tanya, a woman who cared deeply about the ingredients they sourced and the food they concocted. Haylee remembers washing her way through cases of organic kale, "the bugs falling from them into the sink," and thinking, *This is pretty great.*

Chef Tanya taught Haylee that food could be more than just sustenance; it could be a form of "real artistic expression." Even more, working with food could be fun, passionate. Working at Native Foods gave her a rush that felt simple but profound. "I didn't know at the time that I would chase that feeling over and over again, and that I wouldn't stop," Haylee explained.

Haylee had other jobs, too, administrative gigs and she worked in a library, but none of those experiences felt as satisfying, as fun, as the restaurant biz. In her teens and early twenties, Haylee moved from town to town in California, eventually taking community college classes and earning her high school diploma. She taught at an after-school program with AmeriCorps and became a canvasser to raise money for a high-speed rail that never got built. Haylee "bounced around a lot" in what felt like "a series of figure eights." Wherever she went, she knew "I could always find work in a restaurant." It was the only constant in her life.

She moved to Berkeley in her midtwenties without a job or a big network. She immediately took a job at Elmwood Café, a boutique coffee spot on a bustling corner of College Avenue, Berkeley's oldest commercial district. The quaint, busy spot served poached-egg breakfast sandwiches and smoked salmon toast. Haylee had worked at a Starbucks, but she'd mostly spent her time there "pressing a button" or "pouring stuff into a blender." Elmwood Café was totally different. Haylee was a natural barista. She had a knack for making great drinks from the fancy espresso machine, a shiny beast that demanded serious skill to pull shots and froth milk with consistent quality. It was a whole lot more complicated than the completely automated process at Starbucks, but the skill came quickly to Haylee. It took her just one day to start making latte art—decorating her creations with steamed milk poured into gorgeous designs. Her patterns became increasingly intricate and the clientele—mostly Berkeley graduate students and local hipsters—came to look forward to her work.

When we stopped into Cafe Eloise during Hanukkah, Haylee made Tony and me lattes topped with menorahs and Jewish stars. Then for Christmas, a tree topped with a legitimate angel. They were almost too pretty to drink. We didn't want to cover them with the pink lids she handed us.

At Elmwood, the rule was the employees had to rotate between working the espresso machine and making food—sandwiches and such—but the management made an exception for Haylee, who was always stationed at the coffee bar. "I was a rock star," she remembers. Her secret was simple: she really cared. It may sound trite, but she put love into every cup of milk she steamed.

Elmwood Café was always packed. The money was great—about thirty dollars an hour, including tips. Haylee found that she was "good at people," but that was easy to see as I sat for a few hours at Cafe Eloise, trying to write but enjoying eavesdropping on her banter more. She knows when to ask someone how their day is, when to break into an impromptu dance. She remembers that one of her regulars had a big meeting last week—and asks *How did it go?* She shares funny stories about tattoos.

I wondered if it drained her—so much time being so social. I'm somewhere in the middle on the introvert-extrovert spectrum. I love people and feed off their energy, but sometimes I crave alone time. After a busy restaurant shift, ten or twelve hours being almost aggressively social, I always wanted to shut the door, bury myself in a book, and speak to exactly no one. But after a day all alone writing, just me and my laptop, human connection becomes a sort of hunger. Which is why I love writing in Cafe Eloise, where Haylee introduces me to a steady trickle of friends and new friends. It's become a bit like the coffee shop version of *Cheers*.

All that time with people is not draining for Haylee. She loves it. As a barista, she's "held space for people." She's been there with a pretty cappuccino and a few minutes of the sort of kindness that can't be faked for countless people who have lost a loved one, who had a health scare, who just had the typical bad day at work. Even when people bring her their pain, or their grumpiness, Haylee doesn't mind. "It's genuine human connection. It's better than being alone." When the café is empty, which doesn't happen all that often, Haylee feels empty. Her energy takes a dive. Where have all her people gone?

She's pretty optimistic about people, considering she's with them all day, every day. The one thing that doesn't sit well with her is when people treat her "like a servant." When that happens, she just "takes forever" getting whatever they ordered. They probably won't be back. What Haylee gives—good coffee, food, connection—is a gift. Most of her customers seem to understand this. It's different than going to a franchise, where a latte emerges at the push of a button.

Anything could be happening at Cafe Eloise. It's more than a café, it's like a community center. A regular could be getting a tattoo at the table in the corner. Haylee and Talia could be practicing a partner yoga pose, with Haylee lying down on the counter, her legs stretched up to the sky, balancing Talia's torso, the two women interlocking their hands and wobbling just a little. A friend could be dancing on the new cheerful orange banquettes while Haylee sings.

In December, Haylee dressed up as "your friendly Jewish lesbian Santa." Ace joined a parade of neighborhood dogs to sit on her lap and get treats. She tried to put a little Santa hat over his floppy ears, but he wasn't having that. He squirmed and wiggled, way too excited to sit still. Still, the picture of Santa Haylee, me, Ace, and Tony is maybe my favorite family picture. Our smiles are so big. In my uterus, our proto-baby is the size of a red bell pepper.

◆ ◆ ◆

Haylee's stint at Native Foods brought a new fascination with quality ingredients, so she applied for the Waldorf Astoria scholarship to attend the Culinary Institute of America (CIA) in Hyde Park, widely considered the best culinary school in the country. It was a bit of a whim, but it was the sort of challenge she felt drawn to. After leaving high school early, she wanted a more "official" education. She got the scholarship. After homelessness and taking odd jobs and working her ass off to make ends meet, the two years in culinary school felt like a sort of "dream vacation." The scholarship covered both her tuition and her expenses, which meant for the first time since she was fifteen, there was no housing to worry about, and she didn't have to work, never mind juggle multiple jobs.

Haylee remembers her classmates, most of them several years younger than her, feeling overwhelmed with the pressure of school. "Are you kidding me?" she wanted to tell them. The courses were challenging, led by screaming chef instructors with exacting standards. She spent hours preparing complicated hot and cold hors d'oeuvres, pâtés and galantines, and carving game birds. But it was just school. The stakes felt blissfully low.

Which is not to say that school was easy. The culture was "cartoonishly abusive" and sexist. There were no female certified master chefs, and in two years, Haylee had only one female chef instructor. She was one of two women students in her year. The macho culture permeated every aspect of CIA life. In that environment, Haylee started to notice some ways that women approached cooking differently: "Women have been feeding people forever, way before restaurants," which have been, since their very beginning, the domain of men. The military structure of the traditional French kitchen felt like a far cry from anything Haylee really valued. The women at CIA had to learn to thrive in that culture; they often presented a tough exterior to best protect themselves. I thought of Paola cooking on the line at L'Erba del Re, powering through the sexual and verbal assaults because she wanted to make amazing food.

But Haylee learned a lot, and she worked her way up at a lot of well-respected New York City restaurants after graduation, eventually landing a union job as a sous chef at a hotel restaurant in Midtown. She was not yet thirty, and she spent all day and night in a basement chiffonading vegetables, breaking down racks of lamb, and making sure everything in the walk-in was labeled, dated, and meticulously clean. The food was serviceable but uninspired, and Haylee was responsible for cooking the same things the place had made since the 1990s. Her staff were union workers, too, which gave them protection and benefits, but also made asking anything of them outside their ordinary routine fruitless. They could not be fired, except in the most extreme circumstances. She left for work with the city's morning commuters and didn't get home until midnight. She barely saw daylight.

"I was making so much money," Haylee told me. "But I knew if I stayed there, my soul would wither and die."

Haylee met Jean-Michele in 2010 at Elmwood Café, where Jean-Michele popped in after directing a show at the Berkeley Repertory Theater. The theater had put her up in a house around the corner from the coffee shop. It was love at first sight.

She and Jean-Michele were living in a studio right on Prospect Park when they had the opportunity to fix up a rent-stabilized apartment near my new apartment in Prospect Heights, north of Prospect Park. Rent being as insane as it is in New York City, the opportunity of a rent-controlled apartment in close proximity to a massive park felt like the rarest exception to the madness. Usually, any reasonable rate is hiked up when a tenant leaves or dies. They jumped at the chance.

It's a lovely, spacious apartment, full of soft rugs and green plants. As we chatted, Diego jumped up onto the couch and rested his head on Haylee's leg. Ace barked, jealous. He's bigger than Diego but inept at jumping. He looked up at the three of us on the couch. I knew he could make the short leap; it was all in his head. Instead, he let out a sad little whimper, so I picked him up while Haylee continued to fill me in on her path to Eloise.

After she left the union job, Haylee realized she missed being a barista. The long commute from Brooklyn to Midtown and restaurant hours were wearing on her. She began looking for a job in her new neighborhood and had no trouble finding plenty. She took a position at Lincoln Station, a buzzy coffee shop that also serves wine and a solid rotisserie chicken. Her boss was the manager, Michael. Then she worked at Little Zelda, a tiny neighborhood café with pictures of all the congresswomen taped up on the wall. Her boss there was also someone (else) named Michael—the owner.

Haylee worked those jobs until she opened Cafe Eloise with less than $13,000, a combination of her savings and loans from a few friends. She had been wanting to open a coffee shop for a few years, she just didn't think it was possible. A study from Fundera, a loan company, found that women business owners requested less funding, got approved less often, received smaller loan amounts, and paid more for financing than men. New York City is expensive. But Haylee found an ideal location with reasonable rent. It had belonged to a "hoarder who ran numbers" and then became a very short-lived BBQ business. It was for sale. It was perfect.

"Basically, I was really tired of working for some guy named Michael." In her career, Haylee counted no fewer than eleven bosses and owners named Michael. At Cafe Eloise, there's no Michael—there's Haylee.

She runs things differently than at the CIA or at her union job, or even at Little Zelda. Haylee's in charge, but there's a dynamic, cooperative vibe and her small staff contributes their ideas—some books for the front shelves, a little pineapple figurine, a menu item, their famous cookies. She's not trying to get rich or build a coffee empire; she just wants to create a fun, positive, woman-owned oasis in her neighbors' days, a bright spot of cheerful lattes and good music and genuine conversation, which is exactly what she has done.

As things were coming together, she took a vacation to Montreal and Jean-Michele proposed. They made plans to get married in Seattle. One month later, they opened Cafe Eloise. It was a crazy, exciting time of new beginnings and stress levels dialed all the way up.

In her shop, Haylee pointed out the big mirror hanging on the wall, the canvas of a woman's half-obscured face, the metal trash can by the milk and to-go lids: "I got those all from the trash."

Nobody believed her coffee shop would survive, including Haylee. At first, coffee wholesalers wouldn't even sell beans to her, because she didn't have a business line of credit. But Haylee had worked in coffee shops and restaurants for a dozen years, and she was clever. She had watched businesses thrive and plenty of others go under. She had developed a razor-sharp sense for which would be which.

◆ ◆ ◆

Two weeks after the day that Haylee had been thrilled at the prospect she might be pregnant, Ace and I stopped by Cafe Eloise on our late-afternoon walk. Haylee was wiping down the counters, starting preparation to close the café for the night. The sun was low in the sky, and the street felt unusually empty.

I couldn't wait to hear if she had any news.

Poor Ace was no longer a cotton ball. The nice guy at doggy day care had offhandedly mentioned, "You should get him groomed soon, he's starting to look a little matted."

I made an appointment for the very next day. Ace wagged his tail all the way there, but the groomer ran his hand through Ace's curlicue fur and frowned. He was very matted, apparently, and we would have to shave all his lovely, warm, fluffy hair off. I took the news relatively well until the groomer handed me a waiver to sign. A waiver felt so official. People didn't sign waivers unless the possibility of something bad happening was real.

"Sometimes they get nicked, but not often. Of course, we'll take every precaution we can. But puppy skin can be very tender." I nodded. I asked too many questions, hoping for some nonexistent better alternative, and then I signed the form. On my way out, I cried, thinking of Ace's tender puppy skin.

I worried about him. I'd begun dreaming that something terrible had happened to Ace—he'd run away in a crazy snowstorm, or I'd come home to find him dead. The dreams always felt freakishly real. I'd wake up sweating, my heart pounding, and reach for Ace's warm body. He'd be fast asleep, he'd yawn and blink his tired eyes. I'd have to hold him for a long time before I could fall back asleep, Tony stretched along my front, Ace along my back. I'd count my breaths until ten, in and out, the way I'd learned in meditation class. I'd count the baby's twists and turns somewhere beneath my belly button. My whole little family. Curled up together, safe and sound.

On my way to work from the groomer, I called my mom and left a message for my sponsor. If I was this upset about Ace—and it was just a haircut!—how was I possibly going to handle my human baby?

All afternoon while Ace was at the groomer, I checked my phone. I figured that if something awful happened, they would call me. I rushed to pick him up, antsy the whole subway ride back to Brooklyn from my work meeting on the Upper East Side.

"You're not going to recognize him," the groomer said, half joking.

I took a gigantic exhale: he was completely fine. Ace ran up to me with the same happy wiggle, only there was so much less of him. They had shaved his body close to his skin, which had a pinkish hue that made him look alarmingly vulnerable, but left a puffy shock of hair on his face and ears so that he looked less like a dog and more like a lion. His neck, I noticed, was weirdly long, like a giraffe. Without the fluff, it looked like it belonged to another animal. I had worried that Ace might be getting a little chubby, but it turned out that underneath all that fur, he was tiny and solid. Still, he was handsome. His round black eyes looked even bigger. He jumped onto my legs and I broke into an unbound smile.

At Cafe Eloise, Haylee scooped the naked-looking Ace into her arms.

"What happened?" she asked. I told her about the haircut. But it was her news I wanted to hear.

"I took the pregnancy test," Haylee said.

"Yeah?"

"I peed on a stick."

"And?" Was she going to tell me?

"Negative."

That made sense. The chance of her getting pregnant the very first time sperm had entered her body seemed slim, although of course that chance existed, and of course it was the same as any other time sperm and egg met.

We talked more. Her period wasn't even late yet, and so the test could be wrong. It was early days. There was no way to tell but to wait and see. Still, Haylee's mood had gone from optimistic to sour.

"This whole thing is garbage. And Jean-Michele is over it. If we're not going to make a baby from love, we may as well just adopt."

Adoption was their first choice, although it wasn't a simple one. Adopting requires a serous investment of time, money, and energy. It can cost $50,000 in New York, which is not to mention the paperwork, or the waiting, or the unknowns. In some cases, prospective parents are required to have an entire dedicated bedroom for the child before even being considered, no small feat for a New Yorker.

"Or you might be pregnant." It felt a little soon to lose all hope, but I knew from experience sometimes the crash of hope into sorrow felt way worse than no hope to begin with. Haylee sighed. Ace sniffed the ground intently.

Broccoli

By week twenty-five, my belly was starting to feel hard and globular. I exclusively wore stretchy pants, which to be honest, was something I was also happy to do pre-pregnancy. My baby was the size of a head of broccoli according to one app, and an eggplant per another.

One of my writing mentees and I used to have a regular coffee shop on the Upper West Side where we'd meet to check in and catch up every few weeks. The place was right by Tony's and my old apartment and was one of my favorites—it had excellent lattes, fast Wi-Fi, and comfy chairs. My mentee lived in Harlem and worked near Lincoln Center, so the spot was on her route to work.

After I moved, she and I tried out new coffee shops in the West Village and Chelsea, which seemed like good halfway points. One wintery morning we had made a date for a busy café off 7th Avenue South at nine thirty. I dropped Ace off at doggy day care and jumped on the 2 train. One of the perks of working for myself is that I mostly get to avoid the crush of NYC's rush-hour commute, but that morning I stepped onto a packed train, bodies pressing together to squeeze in before the doors slid closed, thermoses in hand, earbuds in, game faces on.

Nobody had offered me a subway seat yet during the pregnancy. One of my friends suggested I should rub my belly and groan, but I was a little too self-conscious to attempt such a move. Plus, I was perfectly fine standing. I had really needed the seat more a few months before, when I was constantly nauseous but not identifiably pregnant. Those later days I felt tired but basically myself. And I made sure to be wearing the comfiest shoes possible at pretty much all times.

But that morning, I wasn't feeling too hot. I felt relieved to squeeze into the only open seat. I unzipped my winter coat and unknotted the scarf from around my neck. More people squeezed in, the train hurtled along on NYC's ancient infrastructure. I didn't have too far to go.

But as the train moved on, I only felt worse: I was sweaty, I tried to wiggle out of my coat without bumping the people wedged beside me without much success. I closed my eyes and tried to focus on my breath. When I opened them, everything was fuzzy and spinning, zooming in and out of focus. I closed my eyes again. It was like being incredibly drunk. We were almost in Manhattan and the café wasn't far from there.

But between Clark Street and Wall Street—Brooklyn and Manhattan—I realized I would not make it to 14th Street. My body started to shake. I prayed I could make it to Wall Street. I put my elbows on my knees and my head in my hands. Around me, people wore parkas and beanies pushed all the way over their ears. It was January. I felt sweat drip down my back, from my bra to my stretchy maternity jeans. My face was on fire.

At Wall Street I pushed out of the train and searched the platform. I thought if only I could find a bench, sit for a second, inhale some cool air, I could regroup. Wall Street is a busy station at 9 AM, with a narrow platform and an ocean of New Yorkers heading to work in wave after wave of bodies. I tried to locate a bench, but all I saw was more platform and stairs. Everything was pixelated.

A tall woman gave me a shove. "Watch where you're going," she growled at me.

"I'm so sorry, I'm sick and pregnant." I appealed to her sympathy, but she had already disappeared up the stairs.

I was going to fall; everything went wobbly and black. Even undone, my scarf felt like it was strangling me. I sat on the first step, near the edge of a long staircase. It was as out of the way as I could manage but I was definitely still in the way. The wave of commuters surged around and past me, uninterrupted.

"Are you okay?" some angel lady leaned over to inquire. Her features were blurred and her coat was purple.

"I'm not sure," I said. "I just got suddenly very dizzy, and I'm pregnant."

"Stay here, I'll be right back."

The angel lady went to get the angel MTA worker from behind the booth upstairs. "Do you think you can make it to the bench?"

I looped my arms around the two strangers' arms and we walked up the stairs very, very slowly, the sea of purposeful people parting to let us pass. They deposited me on the bench; I had it to myself, which was an anomaly in NYC. The angel lady fished a plastic bottle of water out of her bag and handed it to me. I thanked her over and over again and said I hoped she had an amazing day.

"Feel better," she said by way of goodbye as she left through the turnstile and out into the cold, grey FiDi morning. I took long, slow gulps of the water.

"Let me know if you want me to call for medical," the MTA worker told me from back behind her booth.

I nodded. "I'm already starting to feel much better." It was true. I felt like a tiny bubble, undisturbed by the vast crowd. I was still sweating, but I started to shiver. I wiggled my toes in my boots—they had fallen asleep. Everything began to look a little sharper around the edges. I finished the water bottle.

I had been feeling so strong and confident, a new reality for me. On the subway, my body seemed to be reminding me that it was no longer my own. I shared it with the baby growing inside of me, but also with forces bigger than both of us. I thought back to the miscarriage. With every day that passed, I knew the chance of miscarriage decreased. But I also felt more attached, the stakes seemed higher, unbearably higher, and I felt afraid.

"Do you need me to call anyone?" the MTA worker asked. By then I could make out the crisp edges of her uniform, her little tie knotted in a perfect, neat square.

"Thank you," I said, grateful. "I think I'm okay to get back on the train. I only have a few more stops."

She smiled at me, and I tried to keep her smile with me all the way to 14th Street. I got a seat on this train, too, and by the time the doors opened up at my stop, I felt almost back to normal. I texted my mentee I was running a few minutes late.

Bad train karma, I lied. The wind whistled and I didn't zip my coat. I didn't want my own fear to take away from time that was supposed to be focused on her.

"Wow," she said, when she looked at the new balloon of my belly. We exchanged smiles, and I felt my worry begin to soften.

After our coffee, I called the midwife and my mom. The midwife suggested traveling with water and snacks. My mom asked a lot of questions, and I answered them. I made it back home on the subway without incident.

"Please don't scare me like that," I told Broccoli, curled up on the couch, before falling fast asleep.

◆ ◆ ◆

I couldn't wait for Haylee's pregnancy/non-pregnancy news, but the next time I stopped by for a latte, her co-owner, Talia, was behind the counter.

The next night we went for a walk after Cafe Eloise's closing hour, but the lights were on and Haylee was there, sitting on a new lowboy refrigerator. I waved and she opened the door to let us in.

"We got all this hand-me-down equipment"—Haylee motioned to two new fridges—"but now we have to figure out where to put it."

I related—Tony and I had just driven home from my cousin's suburban house in Baltimore with a trunk full of baby gear. My cousin had an exceedingly cute two-year-old, and her kid's baby stuff was meticulously organized in boxes in her basement. (She had about ten times more space than we did in our Brooklyn apartment, but I still knew I could never be quite that organized, even if given infinite space.)

I thought she may want all those boxes if and when she and her husband had another kid, but she said our baby would be finished with it by then. It was a generous offer, and I was grateful. But as she assembled the second Pack 'n Play with all its various attachments—bassinet conversions and changing tables—showing us how everything snapped and buckled into place, I started to feel overwhelmed. There was just so much damn stuff. If I felt intimidated by baby gear, how could I handle an actual baby? And where was all this stuff going to go?

Back in Brooklyn, the nursery was still home to the random, copious stuff we had never managed to unpack—from a meat smoker Tony had somehow acquired to a whole pile of suitcases to all those chairs. We still were the owners of an epic number of chairs. I had the urge to take them all out to the sidewalk and give them back to the NYC trash economy, but Tony felt more attached to our stuff. We still had a few months to find everything a place in our home.

"So how did it go with the pregnancy test?" I blurted out. It was probably uncouth to ask like that, but Haylee had always been refreshingly open with me. When it had been me obsessing about what it said on that stick, I had desperately wanted someone to talk through everything with.

"Well," she said, "I'm having an ectopic pregnancy."

"Oh no!"

"Or a chemical pregnancy." She was describing scary things, yet she had a calm, matter-of-fact presence.

I'd heard about ectopic pregnancies when Tony and I had been trying. It occurs when a fertilized egg implants and grows outside the uterus, and it can be a major medical emergency. The pregnancy isn't viable. A chemical pregnancy is a very early pregnancy loss.

Haylee had taken another test a few days after the initial negative one, and this time it was positive. But then almost immediately after the test confirmed her hopes, she started to bleed, and then she kept bleeding. I felt my heart drop for Haylee.

"I'm so, so sorry. Are you okay?"

"I'm okay. I'm talking about it."

I was so happy she was talking about it, which often proved to be both the hardest part and the most helpful.

"I'm here if you ever want to talk more about it."

Maybe she would, but a few days later there was something else to talk about. The ice machine at the café had flooded, and with it came sudden and serious water damage.

"We need to rip up all of the tile all the way down to the subfloor, let it dry, and install new flooring," Haylee explained. "Oh, and we can only afford to close for one weekday (which will have to be the day we install the new tile to let it set) and it's just so, so stressful."

When Haylee had opened, she didn't have much experience working with contractors. The electrician she hired had claimed he could also take care of plumbing, woodwork, drywall, and a bunch more work around the shop. But over time—just over a year—Haylee began having to replace almost every single job the electrician had taken on. It had cost her thousands of dollars and plenty of stress.

The contractor had neglected to seal the tile he had installed, so when the water from the broken ice machine accumulated on the floor, it seeped into the plywood and stayed trapped. Luckily, she caught it before it rotted out the subfloor. The bill looked like it would come to about $5000, making it the biggest unexpected cost the café had taken on to date. She worried it might end up costing even more. "Thankfully, we had a good year, but I'm still going to have to take out a loan to pay for this one."

A few days later, Haylee met me a little bit lighter. The floor news was much better. Haylee had raised $3500 for the project on GoFundMe, and found a quote for $2700, which meant she could afford to have the work done and close for the two days it would take to do it.

As I chatted with Haylee over the next few days and weeks, the swings of my own loss and joy felt fresh. At first, Haylee and Jean-Michele were decidedly over the idea of Haylee being a gestational mother. They were worried about the stress that infertility might put on their marriage. But they did want to be parents, and found the resolve to keep trying. Matt was happy to help, and so was the California friend. In the meantime, they hosted story hour at Cafe Eloise. They went upstate and took mushrooms. They lived their lives, a couple of pretty excellent lives.

◆ ◆ ◆

People say the third trimester is tough, but I was feeling good when week twenty-eight, its official start, rolled around. Sure, I was having freakishly real dreams and waking up sweating, trying to reorient myself back to my reality, my bed, my home, my husband and dog. And my body seemed to ask for no fewer than nine hours of sleep. But on good days, I worked all day, and maybe even went to a sculpt class at the gym and dinner with friends. I was pregnant and living my life!

But as week thirty and thirty-one came around, things felt more and more difficult. An acid burn—reflux!—erupted in my chest. My lower back started to ache, first with a dull discomfort, and then in alarming spasms that stopped me midsentence or midwalk. I had to get up in the middle of a movie and walk around until the jabbing sensation in my rib cage died down. My mornings began, once again, over the toilet, throwing up nothing but water and bile. The smallest hurdle in my day, a delayed train, a work annoyance, Ace barking for no apparent reason, felt impossible. My head would begin a relentless pounding at any random moment, as if trying to escape my brain.

Broccoli grew into a spaghetti squash and then a pineapple. I started to feel more like myself. But when I looked in the mirror, I did a double take. Who was this lady with the round face and the round belly? I felt like someone else entirely.

And then another shift into sickness. Followed by another day, and then a series of days, where I felt absolutely fine. Sure, I'd fall asleep on the couch by 9 PM, my head on Tony's lap and Ace's head on my calf, and I'd have to pee about a million times during the night, but I was content. I walked through Prospect Park to visit the midwives. I wrote at Cafe Eloise and at my dining room table and, sometimes, in bed. I went to the fancy bakery to pick up their pliable sea-salt chocolate-chip cookies.

"I feel so pregnant," I told Haylee on one busy day. The sun was streaming into the windows of the café.

"You don't really look pregnant," she said. "You just look chubby."

"Ouch," I said, and meant it.

◆ ◆ ◆

Tony assembled the crib while Ace barked and scratched at it. My dad came over and helped us hang wallpaper we'd found on Etsy, a map of the world with hot-air balloons. Things were starting to come together. My parents agreed to keep some of our extra stuff in their shed. The rest, we stashed or donated or left on the sidewalk, where it quickly disappeared into the Brooklyn abyss.

My mom and aunt were planning a baby shower for us. Eat Offbeat would cater. One day Talia brought in the most gorgeous cake I had ever seen to Cafe Eloise, a vanilla sponge with orange curd and honey rosemary buttercream. I'd grown out of the days when I waited for my grandfather to show up with his weekly cake, and was not a cake-loving adult, but that beauty was too spectacular to refuse a slice. The cake was light, smooth, sweet but not too sweet. It was decorated with dried orange slices and sprigs of rosemary. Talia clearly had a talent.

"I'm having a baby shower," I told Talia. "Would you bake a cake for us?"

She said yes. What she showed up with was even prettier than the first one, somehow.

Our timing for the party was perfect and perfectly weird. On March 7, friends and family came to celebrate—my cousins came to my aunt's apartment on the Upper West Side from Baltimore, Washington, DC, and Long Island. Eat Offbeat delivered a fantastic spread perfectly on time. Friends came from the pub after the rugby match, which Tony watched the first half of before joining us. There would be no silly games, just good food and drink and gaiety. There was a llama balloon, which made me irrationally happy.

But a few friends didn't join. One had a cough and was being extra careful. The other was on some pretty serious immunosuppressant drugs, and her doctor had told her it was best to avoid group gatherings. The first novel coronavirus cases, which we had all read about in China, Iran, and Italy, were now being diagnosed in Seattle. Everyone was on edge. On the pregnancy app, people talked about canceling their baby showers. Some thought it was the responsible thing to do, others thought that as long as guests were healthy, there was no real reason not to celebrate.

My aunt got her apartment deep cleaned, just in case. She put a bottle of hand sanitizer by the door. Some people were giving hugs, but other people were giving elbow bumps, or just keeping their distance.

And then everything changed. The virus was officially a global pandemic. The next week, New York City shut down. Schools, movie theaters, and gyms closed. Broadway went dark. Tony's office, which was a very traditional place where everyone was expected to show up every single day, all day, was having everybody work from home. The grocery store was out of toilet paper and cleaning supplies and weirdly, onions. Wipes and diapers were also suddenly gone, and suddenly an issue for me, as I was now thirty-six weeks pregnant.

Danny Meyer announced he was closing all of his restaurants, and then David Chang followed suit, and then, a few days later, the mayor ordered that restaurants could only open for delivery and takeout. Thousands lost their jobs; thousands more were in limbo. My people. I was lucky: I had work, I had Tony, I had my parents. We were healthy and safe. Still, I felt the blow straight to my heart. I loved this industry and everything it meant to me, my community, my city. I kept seesawing back and forth between genuine gratitude and existential dread.

The baby was shifting under my ribs. I asked if the hard ball I felt rolling around was the baby's butt. The midwife smiled and said yes.

What a disconnect—on Twitter and the news, it felt like the world was burning. Outside, spring was starting to bloom. Cherry blossoms exploded in Prospect Park, and the sky looked Insta-filter blue. We went for walks with Ace and without Ace. People kept their distance, which was all of a sudden the only responsible thing to do.

Haylee was selling coffee through the window at Cafe Eloise. She wore her gloves and her mask. I said I was scared when she asked how I was doing. What a weird time to have a baby.

"Do you want to do a little stretch with me?"

"Sure!"

Haylee emerged from the café and stood on the other side of the sidewalk. Together, we lifted our arms up and back, opening our hearts, then folded forward, "Or as much as you can with your big, pregnant belly." I stood wide and let my head fall. She sprayed me with some eucalyptus oil. She made me an iced latte, the first of the season. I felt a little bit better.

"I'm so glad you guys are here," I told her. It made my day feel just a little more normal.

"We're going to be like the violin players on the *Titanic*," she said. "We'll be here until the bitter end."

I felt heartbroken, but the food women I spoke with were resilient and creative and strong. We were in this together, even from our own apartments. They were donating the entirety of the ingredients in their restaurants to hospitality workers. They were setting up Venmo accounts for their cooks and servers. They were sending meals to hospital workers. Eat Offbeat was offering stay-at-home care packages: a week's worth of meals and snacks from around the world. It wasn't the same as having a thriving business, but the options were closing their doors or doing *something*, anything. Tamy was "not thinking too much of the future otherwise I get very stressed and emotional . . . we are speaking to various bankers, accountants, and lawyers tomorrow about how to activate the stimulus package for small business that was offered up by the government. Hopefully we will know more and can take some actions toward that next week."

"We're closing for two weeks to flatten the curve," Haylee told me, just a few days later. I knew it was the right thing to do. All of California had been told to "shelter in place." Danny Meyer had laid off 80 percent of his workers, about two thousand people. Still, my eyes flooded with tears.

I felt selfish, but a few days in I already missed the color of my neighborhood and my life. I missed the flowers at the farmers' market; it was the season for ramps, artichokes, and asparagus. We switched the food writing class I was teaching and my therapy appointments to video, as everyone else did, but people's faces on the screen weren't a substitute for them in real life, perking up with an idea or frustration, the light from the window reflecting off their soft smiles. I missed spending a few found minutes browsing in my local bookstore. I missed writing at Cafe Eloise. I missed going out to dinner. I missed hugging my friends.

Tony worked from the couch and I perched at the dining room table. We made sure to go for a lot of walks, but when my parents offered to have us spend some time in their big house—so much bigger than our apartment—in Frenchtown, New Jersey, by the Delaware River, it seemed like a good idea. We could each have our own room for an office. We could take Ace to the giant dog park at Horseshoe Bend and he could frolic. He kind of looked like a bunny when he ran—half forward motion, half bounce. We could sip our coffee and look out on the river, rushing by out the window, brown after a storm and crystalline blue the very next morning.

I asked my midwife what she thought.

"How old are your parents?" she asked.

They were over sixty, old enough that the outbreak was even scarier for them, but they were healthy and being very careful, meticulous about wiping everything down. Both of their hands were dry from so much washing and hand sanitizer. My dad did his high-intensity workout every day, making the floor shake as he performed his jumping jacks and high knees, and my mom went to the gym. Or before the virus, she went to the gym. In Frenchtown, we would walk together along the path until the rhythm of our steps echoed in our ears, and then we would turn around and walk back home.

"The only other risk, besides them," she told me, "is that you won't be able to get back to the city for your appointments, and to deliver."

There were rumors that everything was going on lockdown. They were only rumors, but things were changing at a dizzying speed. The subways were empty, even during rush hour. For the first time maybe ever, they smelled like bleach. The State Department issued a statement telling Americans abroad to return home, unless they were planning to remain abroad for an "indefinite period." Schools were closed everywhere. The gate to the neighborhood playground was locked. It felt like the apocalypse.

Our doula wrote to say she would no longer be offering in-person labor support, only virtual. I couldn't imagine having a baby with a doula on FaceTime. I had spent so much time picturing and planning having this baby. It hit me: nothing would be how I planned. No stream of visitors to our Brooklyn apartment. No trips to the bar and Cafe Eloise with the baby snuggled up, strapped to my chest. Tony's parents in the UK, which was dealing with its own outbreak, wouldn't be able to visit for some time.

Frenchtown was about an hour and a half from Brooklyn. We decided that the next week, I'd drive back to the midwife for my appointment. But in the meantime, we'd look for a backup option near Frenchtown. There was a hospital nearby with perfectly good reviews, and I called a women's health practice that delivered there.

"I'm sorry," they said. "We don't take new patients after twenty-eight weeks."

"I understand that." Of course I did. "But these are really unusual circumstances. Would you consider making an exception?"

They said they'd call back. Five minutes later, the woman on the phone told me they were taking no new people, period, because of the virus. I called another OB office and got the same answer. We even searched out a home-birth midwife, but she wasn't seeing anyone new, either.

But I was okay, and the baby was safe inside me. At my appointment, the midwife stretched a tape measure over my belly. She explained that the labor and delivery floor was totally separate and sacred. Even in a time of emergency, people still gave birth. She seemed so calm and collected, and I thanked her for making me feel better.

"You do a lot of hibernating with a new baby anyway," she reassured me.

But it felt weird to be excited about the new baby when the world felt so dark. Weddings and bar mitzvahs were canceled. Trips and festivals. Everything else.

Doctors had to decide who to save. There weren't enough masks. There weren't enough respirators. There could be no funerals for those who died. The world was changing—the world had changed.

We had brought Ace's bed with us to Frenchtown, but he preferred to sleep with my parents. I missed his furry face next to me at night.

My mom went to the doctor at a family practice in Milford, just a short drive from the house. They delivered babies at the local hospital. They weren't taking new patients, either, especially from New York, the center of the epidemic. But my mom called back and begged. She explained we had been quarantining in New Jersey, the pregnancy was low risk. I didn't have a fever, or any COVID-19 symptoms.

We were both so relieved when they said they'd see me the very next day that we cried.

That weekend, hospitals in NYC announced no visitors or birth partners would be allowed in with the laboring woman—no husbands, no wives, no doulas, no moms. I had wrapped my head around not having a doula with us to rub my back, around my parents not being able to come visit the baby in the hospital, but I just couldn't picture giving birth alone, without holding Tony's hand, without him placing the new baby on his chest. The sadness that came over me then felt like a flood. I didn't want to have the baby anymore. I wanted to stop time.

Our midwife friend called me, the one who had come to the hospital after my miscarriage. She worked in a hospital in Queens that was ground zero for the virus. The parking lot was now full of emergency tents. The hospital's picture was in the *New York Times*.

"I'm so sorry," she said. "These new rules might come to New Jersey. They may come everywhere. We don't know. Things are changing so fast and nobody can keep up."

The new doctor in New Jersey was immeasurably nice. She spent almost ninety minutes with me. She walked me through binders full of paperwork—I could tell it was dated, there was plenty on Zika virus but nothing about coronavirus. We did an ultrasound, which I had not had since week twenty-two, when the baby was the size of a zucchini. Now, it was a honeydew melon. "It's not too big and not too small," she said. "That's the heart. That's your baby, sucking their thumb." The baby's head was down, just as it was supposed to be. Suddenly, I felt less afraid. I wouldn't be alone no matter what the rules were. I couldn't wait to meet them.

On the way out, she tested me for COVID-19, just to be safe, since I had been in NYC. It felt like she stuck the swab all the way past my nose and into my brain. She had to do it in the parking lot, as per policy. (Which seemed weird to me since I had just spent more than an hour inside the office.) It had started to drizzle, and I pulled my hood up as I thanked her.

That night, I called Jenise. It had been a long time since we'd talked. She lived in Queens, where she had had a job managing the front of the house of a small, lovely restaurant owned by a team of women. She'd been laid off along with everyone else a few weeks before I called, when the restaurant had closed. She was in good spirits, though. She said she had come a long way in the last few years, choosing better friends and lovers, and she'd discovered that she liked her own company. She was cooking a lot in quarantine and sharing food with some older neighbors.

I Skyped with Paola in Italy. Her country had been in quarantine longer than mine, and she admitted that at first, she'd been despondent. It seemed too overwhelming. But she was making peace with a slower way of life, for now. "I usually have an airplane ticket for every month or six weeks." Paola had just gotten back from Saudi Arabia, where she'd stayed with Abdul. Before that, she had been to London, and Paris, and Dubai. She had been planning a trip to New York, to stay with me, which got canceled.

"These days I travel through food, through recipes." She had just tried a recipe for kibbeh, a Levantine dish made of bulgur, minced onions, and ground beef, but it didn't come out so well. That was part of the process for Paola. Her cooking-class business was booming. Everyone was looking for ways to connect, and new things to cook to keep themselves from the boredom.

I asked her about how she saw the way we cook and eat evolving. "The role of chefs will change forever—we will teach people how to cook for themselves," she said. The sureness in her voice surprised me. "Abdul tells me, 'You think you will change the world through food.' But I don't think that, I absolutely believe it. We will be more human; we will be more connected. Food will revive our souls."

I've never had more home-cooked meals in my life than I did in quarantine. I love to cook but I also love going out to eat. I love to walk with Tony and Ace to pick up everything bagels on Sunday mornings, and build sandwiches with lox and onions and cream cheese back at home, some of which I let Ace lick from my pinky finger. I love seafood towers on date night, sucking the last sweet shrimp from its little shrimp head, negotiating over the dessert menu. I love ordering in pho when we're not feeling too great, mixing in extra sriracha and feeling the steam rise onto my face.

In quarantine, my family made breakfast, lunch, and dinner. I prepared some and my mom cooked often. We had a lot of soup. I baked a banana bread. One night, Tony made steak. We ate it with fingerling potatoes and crunchy salad with blue cheese dressing and wine for my parents, kombucha for me.

The next morning, I made us eggs on English muffins with avocado and chipotle mayo. It reminded me of my favorite egg sandwich from Cafe Eloise, only theirs is served on crusty multigrain bread. Haylee and Jean-Michele had retreated up to Maine. Haylee tested negative for coronavirus, but she wasn't feeling well. In Maine, they had lots of fresh air and went for long walks. They sell coffee beans online. They are still hoping to get pregnant.

Allison stayed in Vermont. She canceled her hiking trip in Nepal and a trip to Scotland that was supposed to happen in May. She knew how lucky she was. She'd been playing the ukulele that her son Jay gifted her. She stopped going to the farm to help with the goats or see her grandkids. "I am a person who is used to moving all of the time and not sitting still long enough to use my mind. It takes effort for me, but I try to embrace this moment to explore," she said.

Wendy had been alarmed in the spring by the abrupt cancelation of what was going to be a busy season on the barge, by the swift and brutal blow to her industry, but she was quick to try to make the most of it. She jumped straight into "loads of work that we never had the time or energy to get around to doing before." She regrouped; she leapt into making the barge even more functional and more beautiful. There was something about the opportunity to pause the rush and reset that was surprisingly cathartic, even in those often frightening and uncertain times.

The virus made the very foundation of the restaurant and travel industry, bringing a lot of people together in intimate spaces, impossible. My people—these women who had been sharing their lives and passions with me—were hurting and they were also growing. Their jobs—so focused on sharing food and experiences with people, nurturing environments—were swept aside. They were making focaccia and throwing birthday parties on Zoom. They were napping a lot, or they were working extra hard, or both. Sometimes they were full of dread and other times, hope. They were taking care of their loved ones. They were finding new ways to connect. It felt like such a lonely time, with everyone holing up in their homes. Reaching out almost obsessively to friends kept me sane.

Here I was, getting ready to have a baby and thinking about all the things these women, my heroes, had birthed. All the immaculate logs of goat cheese and the lattes with the perfect foam on top, the portobello tacos and restaurants and events and barge cruises. The bringing people together, the lifting them up, the introducing them to new flavors and memories and possibilities. We were making new books and babies, new businesses and restaurants and projects, and then the virus came along and interrupted everything. Now we were figuring out how to adapt to our new world. We were falling back in love with our elemental goals and passions, figuring out how we could take these things with us as the ground shifted beneath our feet. What would we give birth to next?

Any day, my baby was due to arrive. He or she was fully cooked. I wondered if she would like egg sandwiches with chipotle mayo. We will have so many stories to tell her one day. For the moment, we were crying a lot, and laughing, and taking walks, and writing, and praying even, for this fragile world where we were all so alone and so together.

Simone

In my childbirth class, they had told us labor very rarely happens like in the movies, your water breaking suddenly in a big, dramatic gush. But for me, that was exactly how it happened.

I was thirty-nine weeks pregnant—the baby was the size of a pumpkin—and the days felt terrifically long. It was eleven at night; I had just fallen asleep around ten and already I had to pee. When I got to the bathroom, the liquid was clear and flooded from me in a great surge. *Did I wet myself?* I thought, groggy. I woke up Tony. We tried not to wake up my parents. We called the doctor from bed.

"Have you felt any contractions yet?"

"I don't think so." I was just excited and a little scared.

"Get some rest," she suggested, which I knew was the general advice in early labor. There would be long hours, or even days, ahead. "Call back in an hour or two, or when things start to change."

I curled myself into the C of Tony's body. But there was no way I could sleep. In just a few minutes, I felt the rise and fall of a wave of pain from the bottom of my back down into my butt. The contraction was a force of its own, which propelled me out of bed and onto my hands and knees. My body wanted to lower itself to the ground, to sink down, which I did until I was all the way against the carpet. It was slightly scratchy.

I yelled up to my parents' bedroom, "I think my water broke."

"I think you would know," my mom said, thrilled but half-asleep.

"I know it broke," I clarified. "We called the doctor. I'm going to labor here as long as I can, then we'll head to the hospital."

Tony drew me a bath. Even though I was immersed, the water—the fluid that filled the membranes of the amniotic sac—kept spewing from me, which felt entirely strange. The warm bath held me, my round stomach sticking out from its surface. I started to shiver. My legs began to shake, which reminded me of the miscarriage. I tried not to think about that.

Tony started to time the contractions. They came every five minutes, then every three, then every five. I made all sorts of noises I had never heard myself make. The contractions were in my back and sides and stomach.

It was hard to put on clothes after the bath. The waves of pain kept stunning me. I had half packed a hospital bag, but I hadn't brought too much stuff to New Jersey and wasn't entirely sure what I would need. I put a few pairs of underwear and my comfiest pants in the gym bag that I had stashed in a closet. Between contractions, I started stuffing more things inside: a toothbrush, ChapStick. Then I ended up with the bag and myself on the floor again. I wanted to be present for this big life event, but everything felt wobbly.

"Why don't you let me do this for you," Tony urged about the hospital bag, but I couldn't think straight.

I told myself if I could make it 'til morning, 5 or 6 AM, before going to the hospital, that would be ideal. But it was at 3:30 AM that the contractions felt suddenly and decisively like too much to ride out. They were so much bigger than me. I had spent the last few hours in a loop—floor, bathtub, bed, toilet, floor, bathtub, bed, toilet. There was no such thing as time. I kept drinking water and puking it back up. I shivered and sweated. My body was no longer mine.

We called the doctor. She said she'd meet us at the hospital.

My dad couldn't hide his excitement. We had the car seat and our bags ready to go. My mom handed Tony a bucket, in case I needed to throw up more on the twenty-minute drive. I sat in the back seat, all hunched over, so I'd have more room to slither and writhe in pain. I was self-conscious about the groans I was making, the wails and cries. I opened the windows and tried to focus on the cool air.

"I'm sorry," I kept saying. I was not a stoic laboring person.

"You don't need to be sorry," Tony kept reminding me.

We called the hospital from the parking lot, outside the locked front door. Everything was shut down because of COVID-19. We stood there in the middle of the night in the dark in our masks, waiting for someone to come let us in. Tony had the car seat, as we wouldn't be allowed to leave to get anything once we went in. My dad hugged us goodbye. There were tears in his eyes.

The nurses were so nice. They already had my paperwork. Tony handed them my birth plan, what we had put together in writing what felt like forever ago with the doulas, before coronavirus. I didn't want an IV unless medically necessary. I didn't want pain medication unless I asked for it. I hoped to have an unmedicated birth.

I knew there would be time to rest between contractions, but they came so fast, every few minutes, and so hard, I couldn't see or think or even breathe. The doctor and the nurses kept saying, "You're doing great." They brought me a birthing ball, and then another one shaped like a peanut to wedge between my legs. They brought a diffuser with lavender essential oil. Tony rubbed my back. I jerked away from him, and then toward him again, wanting his touch and then not wanting anything to touch any part of me.

I was supposed to keep my mask on whenever a care provider was in the room, but I kept needing to puke. The inside of my mouth felt like cotton balls. We had packed snacks, dried mango slices and granola bars and cashews, but I had no thought of eating.

"I'm going to die," I told Tony, not in jest. The pain kept getting more intense when I thought that was no longer possible.

The doctor explained that they needed to place an IV port in my wrist, just in case. That was fine by me, even though I had asked to forgo it in my birth plan. In my mask, with pain pummeling me, that sort of thing felt like an insignificant detail. But the nurse missed my vein on her first try, or her jab was too shallow. A red and then purple bruise started to bloom on my left hand as she tried again on my right, where she had more luck. It hurt, and I thought it was cruel that I should have to experience anything else painful on top of the blinding contractions. The port kept threatening to come out and nurses kept retaping and adding more layers of tape, until my whole right hand was covered in surgical tape.

The pain was brutal, but it was my exhaustion that propelled me to ask for an epidural, which was also not part of my plan. Through the window shade's slats, the sun rose outside. I hadn't slept all night and hadn't slept too well before then. I tried to take it one contraction at a time. I thought I could endure another hour if there was an end in sight, but when I asked the doctor, she said there was no way to know. It could be an hour, or five, or ten. All I wanted was to close my eyes without being startled awake by superlative pain.

Still, I wasn't entirely sure. As soon as I asked about the possibility of the epidural, they were on it. The anesthesiologist seemed to be there the next minute. He looked like an anesthesiologist from a movie, an older white guy with close-cropped grey hair and a no-nonsense stare. They made Tony stand outside while he did the procedure.

"The most important thing is not to move," he instructed, which seemed impossible with the contractions, but the nurse gave me a pillow to squeeze and stood in front of me so I could hold on to her shoulders. I thought she must be pretty beneath her mask, although it was impossible to know for sure. I couldn't quite tell what anyone looked like in their layers of protective equipment. I thought if I was to run into her in the grocery store the next week, I would have no idea it was her.

Almost immediately, the pain subsided. Instead I felt a furious tingling in my feet, like they had fallen asleep during a long car ride. I wiggled my toes, which only made the situation more pronounced. The nurse reassured me that this was totally normal. The prickly numbness spread up my legs. They didn't feel like legs anymore, just weird tree trunks. I asked Tony to rub my feet. That seemed an essential way to assure myself I still had feet.

Tony's eyelids were as heavy as my own. The night had been just as long for him. For a few blissful hours—him on the couch, me in the hospital bed, the diffuser puffing lavender air around us—we both fell into an opaque sleep. Every so often someone would come in to check on me, or check Tony's temperature—a COVID-19 precaution. My mask smelled sour. I was sure I didn't have toes anymore.

When I had arrived before dawn, my cervix was dilated about three centimeters. Now the sun was high in the sky and I was *still* around three centimeters dilated, which meant I was still in the early stage of labor. That seemed crazy to me.

The doctor recommended Pitocin, a synthetic version of oxytocin, which would stimulate contractions. I hadn't wanted Pitocin originally because I thought the Pitocin might lead to an epidural; I'd read it can make the contractions super intense. Having had the epidural already, I told them to bring on the Pitocin. It was starting to feel very far away, the idea of actually birthing this baby.

They explained they would start with the smallest possible amount to see how the baby and I reacted. If all went well, they would slowly up the dose. All was fine, so they kept adding more and more Pitocin into that port that I had reluctantly consented to what felt like forever ago. When I touched the skin on my leg under my gown, it felt like rubber against my fingers.

"Do I still have feet?" I kept asking Tony.

The Pitocin was working. There was good news: I was fully dilated, ten centimeters. It was almost time for me to push.

If only I could rest for a minute first, I thought. Everything was bleary. A few minutes of closing my eyes, and then my new life could begin.

When I opened them, half-asleep, there was a nurse standing over me. She looked concerned. Her hand was on my shoulder, firm.

"I need you to move over onto your right side." She couldn't get a good read on the baby's heart rate. I couldn't flip myself over very well with my tree-trunk legs, so she and Tony both helped me. I felt like a bag of sand.

"Let's try the left." She and Tony turned my lower body while I hoisted my torso.

"Nope." Her voice was louder. "Let's go back to the right. The baby doesn't like that."

She called for the supervising nurse, who called for a doctor, who called for another doctor. Suddenly there were four, five, six people, a collage of face shields and masks around me and over me. My drowsiness was gone. Someone pressed an oxygen mask over my face. "We need you to take long, deep breaths." I tried to focus on *in, out, in, out*. Tony was there, too, next to the bed, his beard peeking out of the blue paper of his mask, his eyes bright. I reached for his hand. I wasn't scared, yet. I couldn't let myself be scared. Someone was pressing hard on my belly, her hands cold and strong.

The baby's heart rate had dropped a lot, suddenly. Moving me around, compressions, the oxygen were their attempts to fix that. They didn't work. The head OB made the call; the baby would have to come out now.

"We can't risk the distress of pushing," she said. "We need to do a cesarean."

Suddenly someone was shaving me, someone else painted my belly with something cool. Many things were happening very quickly. I was scared.

"I'm so sorry," the other doctor, the one I had been seeing, said to me. She said it very meaningfully, slowly, amidst the fast-moving dance all around me, looking into my eyes, and my own heart stopped. Until then, I had felt that things were unfolding as they should, that these very professional and serious nurses and doctors had everything under control, even if things were not going according to my own plan. That was the moment when panic shot through me, from my dumb numb feet to my mouth, foul-tasting under my mask. I thought back to the last time I had been in a hospital, the blood and Sweet Pea, and I started to cry.

"What's happening?" I asked her. "Is the baby okay?"

"We don't know why the heart rate is dropping. Usually it's a complication with the umbilical cord; it's wrapped too tightly around the baby. We are going to do a C-section, and you are going to meet your baby soon. I'm sorry because I know you didn't want to have a C-section."

I thought back to our birth plan, the bullet points so neat and optimistic on their sheet of white paper. The nurses ran with me on the hospital bed to the operating room. They ran so fast and it all really was cinematic—whizzing through the bright lights and wide, empty hallways, the weird point of view of looking up from the bed.

Later, Tony told me he was terrified, too. They gave him a surgical suit and a hairnet to change into and left him alone in the room. Time passed in silence, nobody came, and Tony waited. It felt like the world's most interminable wait.

Finally, an orderly brought Tony to the operating room. The anesthesiologist was back beside me. The lights were blindingly bright. He explained the morphine would make me itchy and the anesthesia might make me nauseous. For the itchiness, he'd give me Benadryl. He had something for the nausea, too. He had something for everything, I should just let him know how I was feeling. The drugs and panic put me into a deep haze.

I was in the OR for five minutes or five hours or five days. The anesthesiologist kept telling me not to move my arm and I kept saying, "I'm not," although part of me was aware I must have been moving it after all. He was on the head side of the blue curtain that fell beneath my chest. Tony was there, too, holding my other hand.

"What's happening?" I kept asking, and the doctors kept very patiently telling me from behind the curtain: "We're preparing the area, we're about to make the incision."

There were physical sensations—an enormous pressure, something very cold and weirdly heavy. But it was my fear that threatened to swallow me.

Then a wail, big and glorious. I've never heard a happier sound than my baby's cry. "It's a girl," they said. Tony's eyes were filled with tears, and my heart leapt way outside my body. The joy and relief were boundless.

They let her cuddle with me for about one minute, her chest on my chest. I looked at this tiny person who had been inside of me and was now outside of me. She was so beautiful it hurt. We cried together. The two of us made all kinds of noises, mother and daughter.

They whisked her away with Tony while I lay there missing both of them. They gave me a cup full of ice chips. They took my blood pressure over and over again. I thought of my daughter's face. I tried to re-create it in my head. I thought of the word *daughter*.

◆ ◆ ◆

Her name is Simone. She was born April 9, 2020, at 1:33 PM, in the middle of a pandemic. She was as healthy as can be. We'll never know why her heart rate dropped so precipitously (there were no complications with the umbilical cord). She had big almond-brown eyes and a fluffy poof of hair. She had ten fingers and ten toes and scrawny arms and legs that kicked and wiggled. She was perfect.

I wonder who she will grow up to be. Will she like stinky cheese, saffron-scented paella, and sticky baklava? Will she feel at home in a kitchen full of the smell of sautéing garlic and the jangle of laughter? I hope she loves her body and carries it, just as I carried her, with pride and joy. I hope she finds her people, and that they are as brave, loving, and generous as the people I am lucky enough to call my friends, my family. I pray that the world is a little less cruel, and that she works to make it even better. That she knows how loved she is.

Lying on the operating table in that moment, I couldn't wait to hold her again.

ACKNOWLEDGMENTS

Thank you to my amazing agent, Andrea Somberg, for believing in me and in *Plenty*. Huge thank-you to my editor Laura Van der Veer, for your brilliance. Thank you to Carmen Johnson, Emma Reh, Merideth Mulroney, Holly Ovenden, Selena James, and the wonderful team at Little A. I am enormously lucky to have the best book people.

Heartfelt thanks to the women in the book for sharing yourselves and your stories with me and all of us: Jenise Addison, Paola Martinenghi, Haylee Welsh, Tamy Rofe, Manal Kahi, Allison Hooper, and Wendy Carrington.

Thank you to my writing friends and early readers, Kate Fridkis Berring, Kelsey Blodget, Simon Morris, and Rena J. Mosteirin, for your generosity in reading and in all things. Thank you to Kaitlin Kabrich for telling me about the redwoods. Big thanks to the amazing writing community at Bennington Writing Seminars.

To my mom and dad, Rachel and Marty Howard, there is no way to thank you for your unending love, kindness, and support (and child care!).

Thanks for your wiggly tail, Ace. Thanks for making me a mama, Simone.

Anthony Mulira, I love you with all of me forever (ever).

ABOUT THE AUTHOR

Photo © 2020 Michelle Chin

Hannah Howard is a writer and food expert who spent her formative years in New York eating, drinking, serving, bartending, cooking on hot lines, and flipping giant wheels of cheese in Manhattan institutions such as Picholine and Fairway Market. She has a BA from Columbia University and an MFA from the Bennington Writing Seminars. The author of *Feast: True Love in and out of the Kitchen*, Hannah has also been published in *New York* magazine, *Salon*, and *SELF*. She mentors women recovering from eating disorders by helping them build happy, healthy relationships with food and themselves. She lives in New York City. For more information, visit www.hannahhoward.nyc.